CHOOSING HANDGUN AMMO

THE FACTS THAT MATTER MOST FOR SELF-DEFENSE

PATRICK SWEENEY

Copyright ©2017 Caribou Media

All rights reserved. No portion of this publication may be reproduced or transmitted in any form or by any means, electronic or mechanical, including photocopy, recording, or any information storage and retrieval system, without permission in writing from the publisher, except by a reviewer who may quote brief passages in a critical article or review to be printed in a magazine or newspaper, or electronically transmitted on radio, television, or the Internet.

Published by

Gun Digest® Books, an imprint of Caribou Media
Gun Digest Media, P.O. Box 12219, Zephyr Cove, NV 89448
www.gundigest.com

To order books or other products call toll-free 1-800-258-0929
or visit us online at **www.gundigeststore.com**

CAUTION: Technical data presented here, particularly technical data on handloading and on firearms adjustment and alteration, inevitably reflects individual experience with particular equipment and components under specific circumstances the reader cannot duplicate exactly. Such data presentations therefore should be used for guidance only and with caution. Caribou Media accepts no responsibility for results obtained using these data.

ISBN-13: 978-1-946267-03-0
ISBN-10: 1-946267-03-1

Cover Design by Dave Hauser
Designed by Sandi Carpenter & Dane Royer
Edited by Corrina Peterson

Printed in the USA

10 9 8 7 6 5 4 3 2 1

RELATED TITLES FROM GUN DIGEST

Big Book of Ballistics by Philip P. Massaro

P.O. Ackley: America's Gunsmith by Fred Zeglin

Cartridges of the World 15th Edition edited by W. Todd Woodard

Understanding Balistics: Complete Guide to Bullet Selection by Philip P. Massaro

Straight Talk on Armed Defense by Massad Ayoob, et. al.

Deadly Force: Understanding Your Right to Self Defense by Massad Ayoob

GunDigestStore.com

DEDICATION

This book is dedicated to all those we wish to protect, who depend on us, and who are secure in the knowledge that we will do all within our abilities to keep them safe.

For some, it is the populace they serve. For others, it is the country. For me, it is family and friends.

In particular, Felicia and the rest of us here.

TABLE OF CONTENTS

ACKNOWLEDGEMENTS	8
INTRODUCTION	9
CHAPTER 1: WHY? AND WHAT DO YOU NEED TO KNOW?	12
CHAPTER 2: HOW AMMO IS MADE, AND WHAT IS +P?	22
CHAPTER 3: WHAT IS "STOPPING POWER"?	50
CHAPTER 4: WHAT MATTERS IN A FIGHT, AND HOW BULLETS WORK	64
CHAPTER 5: HISTORY OF STOPPING POWER FORMULAS	80
CHAPTER 6: IWBA BEGINNINGS AND HISTORY	96
CHAPTER 7: THE FBI ENTERS THE PICTURE	106
CHAPTER 8: THE FBI PROTOCOLS	112
CHAPTER 9: LESS-EXPENSIVE OPTIONS	126
CHAPTER 10: TESTING	136
CHAPTER 11: MICRO GUNS	144
CHAPTER 12: .32 & .380	156
CHAPTER 13: .32 REVOLVERS	166
CHAPTER 14: 9MM PARABELLUM	172
CHAPTER 15: .38 SPECIAL	186
CHAPTER 16: THE .357S	202
CHAPTER 17: THE .40 S&W: ONCE KING, NOW FRIENDLESS	210
CHAPTER 18: 10MM AND CHOICES	218
CHAPTER 19: THE .44S	224
CHAPTER 20: THE .45S	230
CHAPTER 21: HUNTING	244
CHAPTER 22: IN SUMMARY	252
APPENDIX: AMMUNITION PERFORMANCE CHARTS	270
BIBLIOGRAPHY	284

ACKNOWLEDGEMENTS

I'd like to extend thanks to all those who, through the years, have helped me in this endeavor. Starting with Jeff Chudwin, who lured me into law enforcement firearms training with the inducement of loot, glory, fame, easy work and a long and steady future of fun. The fun, yes; the easy, ..?

To Jeff Hoffman, of Black Hills, who was so generous with his images of gelatin shots, who patiently answered my questions, and who sent me any and all ammunition I have asked for through the years, to study, test, shoot and learn from.

To all the guys at Hornady, from the top on down, who have been so patient with me. When you ask a question and the response is, "We don't know, we never thought of that, let us get back to you," and they do, in a real short time period, you know you are dealing with consummate professionals. That's the crew at Hornady; Neal Emery and Neil Davies, Jason Hornady and Steve Hornady, and Steve Johnson.

To Shannon Jackson, the rep for Sig ammunition, who seems entirely too eager to ship me ammo. If I'm not careful, one of these days she's going to bury me in it.

I have had the same response and support from other ammunition manufacturers, but I wanted to make a point of naming these people in particular.

Thanks a ton, all of you.

INTRODUCTION

It may sound glib, but a handgun without ammunition is an awkward club. You must have ammunition, and it must be appropriate ammunition for the handgun you have. In some situations, selecting ammunition is not actually an option. For instance, if you are a law enforcement officer, you will usually be issued the ammunition that you will use. No other is authorized, and unless you are shooting at the range with ammo you paid for yourself, getting caught with the "wrong" ammo can have unfortunate effects on your career. Ditto for ammunition in a military unit. You use what you're issued, and no other.

The reasons vary. In LE, the department wants to ensure that its officers, deputies, agents, whatever the term, are using the most appropriate ammunition for the firearms they are authorized to use. In both LE and military situations, there is also a strong impulse to keep the otherwise uninformed from choosing poorly. That's right, uninformed. You see, and I'm not slamming anyone here, many people in law enforcement and the military are not firearms experts. In fact, in some departments and most military units, being "the gun guy" is not necessarily a good thing.

Generally speaking, users receive the type, amount and thoroughness of training that those in authority have deemed appropriate and budgetarily possible.

How often do you go the range and practice? Once a year? Twice? Once a month? Most police departments deem firearms "training" to be appropriate when done once a year, including both training and qualification. It may consume as much as 100 rounds, and it may not.

In the military, once a year is a high standard. Unless there is a war ongoing and a unit is rotating to the noisy place, military personnel who have small arms issued to them will go to live-fire (real ammunition) once a year. Maybe. If the unit is going overseas, they'll get refresher course, more range time and more ammo. If not, then it is possible for someone in the services (USMC an obvious difference) to shoot a rifle

I've been studying terminal ballistics for a long time, but the early days were the film days. This is the earliest useable photo I have of bullet testing, and the date on the back is from the Clinton Era. We've learned a lot since then.

in basic training, and then for the rest of their career participate only from time to time in an odd social event called "Fam Fire." Fam Fire, or Familiarization Firing, can consist of being handed a small arm – rifle, handgun, shotgun – with a limited number of rounds in the magazine. They point it in a safe direction, pull the trigger until the ammunition is exhausted, and hand it back.

That's it.

I say these things, true they are, not to embarrass anyone, but to make a particular point: your friend the police officer or your distant relative in military service may not be any more familiar with firearms than you are. In fact, should you have any knowledge at all and visit him or her, you might find yourself in the odd position of being the Subject Matter Expert on firearms at that place and time. Not that they would defer to you, there's the matter of status to consider.

You may have an encyclopedic knowledge of the subject, but due to their authorization and certification they will mostly expect you to defer to them. If you ask a question and get a wrong answer, it will be almost useless to argue, even socially an error.

I tell you this not to depress you, but so that you will recognize the landscape you are in, and to prepare you for the upcoming information.

In this book, I have a number of goals. I want to dispel urban myths, Internet fables and "common" knowledge that just ain't so. I want to impart knowledge on anatomy, ballistics, the law, physics and hydrodynamics, mechanical engineering and perception. I also want you to recognize that while I'm telling you all this, doing so to the best of my own knowledge and abilities, I am not a doctor, a ballistician, a lawyer, a physicist or a certified professional engineer. So, if I tell you "two plus two equals four" and you are going to bet your life, freedom and bank balance on it, it behooves you to get a second opinion. Chances will be very good that you will find those who agree with me, and those who do not. That's life, and this is America.

Also, I want to prepare you. While I've been told I'm a funny and entertaining writer, and that I'm an easy read, there will be parts of this book that will not be funny. They won't be easy. And they won't be grist to make you popular at cocktail parties. This is serious business, because we're going to discuss the need to shoot human beings in self-defense. There, I've said it.

As much as I hate to hear anti-gunners say, "Its only purpose is to shoot people," about the "bad" gun they currently hate most, we are specifically embarking on a journey to learn about defense ammunition used to shoot humans. I'll talk about use on game animals, when appropriate, but when it comes to defensive use of a handgun there are a lot more instances where lawful defenders have had to use a handgun to shoot a person than those where they had to shoot a bear. As a matter of probability and statistics, there are more people than bears looking to hurt you. And you have an astronomically larger number of interactions with people than with bears. So, people it is.

In the course of the book I also say some things that some might construe as a bit critical of the FBI. Look, I know FBI agents. But where my knowledge, experience and education brings me to a different conclusion or perspective than that of the FBI, I would be derelict in my duty as an author to not say so. I have worked to dial back the snark.

There is knowledge from "forever" and there is knowledge that is newly learned. Some of what "everybody knows" is correct, and some of it was wrong or has been superseded by new knowledge. I'll try to sort those out and explain why, when and what.

Where appropriate, I will tell you the source of the information I have gathered. Some of it came from confidential sources and, while the knowledge gained is useful, the particular people involved are either not germane or do not wish to be identified. Some things you just aren't going to know and you'll just have to take my word for it. So, if I haven't already scared you off, let's get down to it.

My intention starting out was to offer the best loads in each caliber. What I found was that the world had moved on. Had I written this book 20 years ago, it would have been possible to offer sage advice on the good loads, the marginal loads and the bad ones. Today? Everyone makes good ammo. No one makes bad ammo. Some of it might not perform as well as you'd like, but that is more a function of the limitations of the cartridge or the shooters using it than the ammo company's abilities.

So, I changed plans. Instead, I explain the reasons for what we do, the process of testing the results in calibers, and how to pick a load for yourself.

I'm sure someone will complain, "Sweeney chickened out. He didn't tell us that so-and-so makes a lousy bullet. Or that my favorite, the best one ever made, he slighted and he's stoopid." Really? Every maker makes the best bullets they can, or know how to make. No one makes a bad product, simply because if they do no one will buy it and they'll go out of business.

Learn, choose, live with it and be happy.

1

WHY?
AND WHAT DO YOU NEED TO KNOW?

Why this book? Why defensive ammo? Why does it matter? Simple – because this is America and you have a choice. Since you have a choice, you have the right to the knowledge to make that choice wisely. And that's where I come in. I won't tell you that I have all the answers. No one does. If anyone tells you they know everything and they know exactly what is the best ammo for you, keep a tight grip on your wallet, turn and walk away. Do not stop and do not entertain any entreaties about what you are missing or how you will be stuck with lesser ammo choices.

How then, do so many people have the knack for standing up and saying, "This is best"? Simple, see above – this is America. If you have the right to a choice, then anyone and everyone else has a right to advise you on that choice.

How am I different? I won't try to tell you, "You must use this, or your livelihood, manhood, future and honor are at stake." I'm going to assume that you are an adult, that you have a reasonable set of decisionmaking skills, skills gained from life experience, schooling or just luck, and as a result you can figure things out for yourself. Me, I'm just here to show you the path.

Okay, you've decided you need a handgun for every day carry (or EDC, as it has become known). But, you have to pick

This is really good ammo for use in places where the predators are two-legged. Not so much for a place where they are four-legged. Still, you use what you've got, until you can use something better.

CHOOSING HANDGUN AMMO | **13**

Bullet technology has advanced a great deal, but some things don't change. Yes, a .45 Colt with a proper JHP will expand, but a full-weight lead flat-nose at full velocity is not ever going to be an inconsequential option.

something to carry. This is when the real problem begins, as an empty firearm is a clumsy club. Having chosen something to carry, you must make even more decisions about what ammunition you will put in it, both for practice and for carry, because those two may not be the same.

You need information. Actually, you need decades worth of information. And, you have an afternoon (or a day, a week or a month) to pick something, learn it, and then decide if you need something else instead. You see, it isn't easy and it isn't necessarily permanent. The EDC decision you make today may have to change some time in the future. There may be something better invented, or something you just hadn't known about. Or, as you get older, you find that the big gun that was so comforting is now too uncomfortable. Or, you move from a place where the main predators have changed from four-legged to two-legged.

Asking the local police officer isn't usually much help (if they'll even answer). As previously mentioned, most police officers are not firearms experts.

In the distant past, a lot of departments were pretty casual about what they permitted on the streets. Detroit was perhaps the exemplar there. As long as an officer carried a Colt or S&W, that it was a double-action (pistol or revolver) and they could shoot a passing score, they could carry it. Their ammo choices were limited. They could carry lead bullets in revolvers (no hollowpoints) and FMJ in pistols.

Those days are gone. Pretty much every department across the country issues (or has a very short list to pick from) the sidearms carried by their officers, deputies, agents, etc. And everyone carries the same within a department. (Okay, NYPD doesn't, but they allow four brands and a very short list in each, if any choice at all.) DPD issues Glock 22s and 23s, and the FBI, well, they are in the midst of deciding if they can bear the shame of issuing 9mm pistols again to all their agents, except for the extra-special ones who can use something bigger. When they do, those will all be the same brand and only a few models of that brand, because "we have to have commonality in issue."

Law enforcement officers are almost all issued ammunition. Very few have to buy their duty ammo, and if a department is so cash-strapped they have to have officers buy their own, then there are bigger problems than whether it is on the approved list. Asking what they carry would be more properly phrased as, "What caliber and load does your department issue?"

Departments select ammunition for a number of reasons, and some are not entirely rational. A department might use or avoid a particular brand because an influential member of the selection team has had a good/bad experience with it. They can be so adamant in this that the rest of the team simply refuses to fight them on the issue of ammo choice and just gives in. It could be chosen for political reasons or the command from higher-ups. What the officers of your city's department carry as duty ammunition may have been selected by a process less rational than throwing darts at ammunition company advertisements.

Also, departments will be selecting from a very short list. They will be selecting from 9mm, 40 and or .45 ACP, and most of them only from 9mm and .40. It is a rare department these days that has .45 ACP on the approved list. Plus, it will be a rare department that deviates from the highest-scoring loads on the FBI test list. Again, the FBI has a large amount of cachet in law enforcement circles. If the FBI does it, then it has to be pretty good, right? That leaves a lot of otherwise good choices out in the cold, because the FBI is interested in ammunition for the FBI.

If your selected carry handgun happens to be a .38 Special, you aren't going to find much joy in the FBI list. And if you pack a 10mm pistol, a .44 revolver or other relatively common handgun, you will be out of luck in finding law enforcement support for your choice. There will be no law enforcement choice (no department issues them, or so few you

Given a choice when the time comes to solve a knotty problem, the SEALs, SpecOps, etc., guys would probably rather have a couple of pounds of these toys handy than a pistol on their belt. What works for them does not always work for us, and we have to make our choices based on our problems, our tools and our rules.

CHAPTER 1: WHY? AND WHAT DO YOU NEED TO KNOW? | **15**

Back before smokeless powder, there was no controversy about stopping power. There was simply a need for the biggest hunk of lead you could hurl, with enough powder behind it to get there and through. This Whitneyville Walker was the epitome of "enough gun."

can't find them) and no FBI guidance.

Other sources of "information," "guidance" and "recommendations" are the current popular SpecOps or Navy SEALs. "My friend, who hangs with the Seals, says that...," is a good way to be led astray. First, the military is like police departments on steroids. A police officer might be able to carry a non-authorized load, and if caught get a minor talking to. The military? Sorry, but the problems, depending on what you were caught with and where, could start with a loss of rank and privileges and end with a bad conduct discharge. So, your military buddies use what the supply system sends them, and they use it regardless of how much they complain among themselves.

"But, the Tier One guys get to use what they want!" Do they? Your buddy, who is admitting he has gotten the information third-hand, probably doesn't know how military supply works. The secret guys do get to use ammunition not in the regular supply line. But that doesn't mean they can just pick up a box of whatever they want from their local big-box sorting goods store and go off to sandy, dusty third-world pits to test it.

If they use something non-standard, it is an item that has been discussed, tested and approved by people high enough in authority to approve it. And then, and this is the important part, they keep their mouths shut about it. They are all big boys and know the rules. If it becomes provable that they are using the super-effective "Splatmaster 2000 fragmenting, expanding, eviscerating bullet," then they won't be able to use it any more. And whoever opened their big, fat yaps about it will be doing push-ups until someone in the Pentagon gets tired.

Besides, their needs are not your needs. Their tools are not your tools, and their rules are not your rules.

Don't go by vague advice from someone who wants to inflate his importance; don't fall for the "Seals use it" line of persuasion.

TECHNICAL STUFF: SCIENTIFIC METHOD

If you can't use the advice of the local "I'm buddies with Spec Ops" guy, what

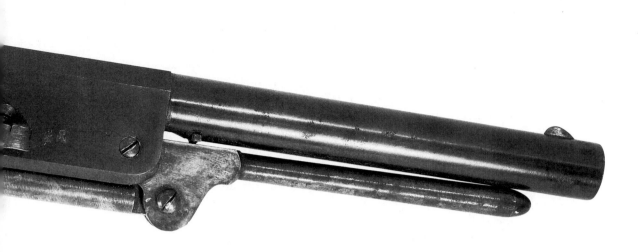

do you do? And what do you need to know? To start, you need a bit of technical education and knowledge. I don't mean to insult you, but a lot of what people "know" about ballistics, physics and things engineering-oriented is either wrong or has been badly explained. If I'm in the middle of explaining a technical detail about ballistics and you don't know what "ballistic coefficient" is, or what a "joule" is, then you will have to stop, go find out, come back, and get back to reading and learning. That can be annoying. So, I'll give you the info you need, here and now. That way you'll both have it up front and can come back here to look it up when you run into it five chapters from now.

First, the nature of the scientific method. Science is a process where you propose an idea. This we'll call a speculation. Something like, "What if the world is not flat?" The next step is a hypothesis. "What if the world were round, like a sphere?" The final step is declaring, "The world is round, and I have provisionally proven it by this method." That is called a theory.

Right away, you can see that a whole lot of people have been mis-using the word "theory." Every hare-brained idea that is proposed is not a theory. Let me repeat that: not everything is a theory. It is most likely a speculation, at best a hypothesis. A theory is something that has been proven correct, as best we know, but has not yet been proven utterly. A theory brings along with it a proposed method of proof. If there is no proposed method of proof, it isn't a theory.

However, regardless of how much it irks me, I'll still keep referring to them as theories, because that's what most shooters will do.

To circle back, what makes the difference between a hypothesis and a theory? The difference, if you are following the scientific method, is this: a theory proposes that if a given hypothesis is true for a given reason, then a predictable outcome can be calculated because of that reason. And a test can be constructed to test that reason and its linkage.

Speculation, hypothesis, theory, test. Result: theory proven or disproven.

It is the test that makes it a theory. A successful test makes it a proven theory.

What does this have to do with stopping power and ammunition selection? The test. We can't just shoot a random selection of people to see what happens. So, strictly speaking, all stopping power speculations are at best hypotheses and none are theories.

Sorry, but them's the rules.

TECHNICAL LINGO

Units of measurement must be in a scale of and in units that describe the system being studied.

A Joule is a unit of energy, the base description of which is two kilograms moving at one meter per second. If I were to tell you that a .45 ACP generates 478 Joules, that doesn't help much. Expressing muzzle velocity as a percentage of light speed doesn't help much, either. That's why, here in America, we express bullets by their caliber, their decimal diameter in inches. We express their mass in grains, at 7,000 of them to the pound. (And yes, strictly speaking, pounds are not mass, but as long as we are living in a one-gravity environment the two are equal – pounds are mass. When we are not, then this will have to be updated, obviously.)

We express the speed of the bullet in feet per second. And a perhaps pedantic note, velocity is a descriptor that includes direction. A bullet you fire has a muzzle velocity, because it is leaving the muzzle, and has a directional component. A bullet passing by has a speed. If you happen to know its direction, then yes, it does have a velocity.

That's the easy part. Do you know the difference between momentum and energy? Momentum is an object's mass multiplied by its speed. That .45 bullet, 230 grains at 850 fps, generates 195,500 grain-feet per second of momentum. In scientific parlance, that would be known as:

195.5x10² gr-ft/sec

Not much use, eh? However, if we put it into the context of the competition end user, and call that a Power Factor of 195, now we're cooking with gas. Power Factor is used in USPSA, IPSC and IDPA competition to measure the felt recoil of, and delivered momentum (despite being called a Power Factor) of, a given cartridge. In those competitive events, your load must exceed a certain threshold or your score will be downgraded or thrown out.

Energy can be measured one of two ways. (Or stored, as well.) We have kinetic energy and potential energy. Potential energy is simple: the books on the shelf over your head are stored (potential) energy. A one-pound weight, one foot over something, has one foot-pound of potential energy. Ten feet up, it has ten foot-pounds of energy. If it falls, that much energy will be delivered to the floor, where it will be dissipated (this is entropy, something you'll need a semester or three in physics to get a good handle on) in the production of heat, noise and the damage done to book or floor, if any.

Kinetic energy is expressed/described with the following formula:

$$E = \frac{1}{2} mv^2$$

That is, the mass times the velocity squared, divided in half. For our .45 ACP, this gives us a pretty messy number:

83,087,500 grain/feet-seconds squared, or 83 million pound-grains. Ouch.

Making it a proper kinetic energy number isn't much help – that translates to 487 Joules. So, we'll put it in the familiar form. We end up with 369 ft-lbs of energy.

Ft-lbs. of energy is used by some Departments of Natural Resources to determine if a given cartridge is powerful enough to be used in hunting a particular game animal. It is also the figure used to determine the recoil effect for a rifle or shotgun.

So, momentum is weight times speed. Energy is weight times speed, times speed, divided in half. Which do we use in describing a bullet in action? Good question, and when someone comes up with a suitable answer, we'll all know. Why is that?

Remember the example of a book on a

shelf? When it falls, the potential energy is converted to kinetic energy, and then that energy is dissipated in the form of heat and sound. And some book-damaging as well.

The scale we use to describe a bullet is not nearly as important as the form of its energy dissipation. Don't believe me? How many Major League players are hit by pitches each year? It is a surprisingly difficult statistic to dig out. However, I discovered that there are a number of players who have been hit many, many times. Seven of them over two hundred times in their careers. 85 of them over 100 times. (You've just got to wonder, why?)

A Major League baseball weighs five ounces. (Actually, the allowed range is 5.00 plus or minus .25 ounces, but five is a nice, round number.) If a fastballer throws a pitch that arrives at home plate at 90 miles an hour, we can calculate the momentum and energy of the ball.

The Power Factor of the baseball in question is 288. By the PF scale, a baseball is as powerful as a .44 Magnum. However, it is going so slowly (tell that to the batter) that it "only" has 85 ft-lbs of energy. 115 Joules, for those keeping track in the metric system.

So, which is it? A .44 Magnum, or a mere 85 ft-lbs., and to give you a sense of the problem this presents, a 200-pound man walking at a steady but not excessive 3 miles per hour generates 60 ft-lbs, or 82 Joules. He'd have to be walking at a brisk 3.5 miles per hour to equal a .44 Magnum or a 90 mph fastball in energy.

To match the PF scale, he'd have to be traveling at 0.0002 feet per second. A good lean, in fact.

That last part makes it clear where the emphasis is for each formula. Momentum favors weight/mass, while kinetic energy favors velocity.

If we took the Power Factor of the baseball as its true measure, we'd expect a dozen dead baseball players a year. Since there are not, as well as the fact that some will be struck hundreds of times in a career, we quickly grasp that the manner in which the energy is delivered has as much or more to do with what happens as how much energy is delivered. This scenario also demonstrates that if you take a measuring scale too far out of its usual use it becomes absurd. Measuring the Power Factor of a walking man generates silly numbers. At 3 mph he generates 60 ft-lbs, but his Power Factor is 6,160. Twenty-one times as powerful as a .44 Magnum? To steal a phrase, "I don't think so, Tim."

So we have to be careful what units and metrics we use when describing bullet effectiveness, and what scale we are attempting to construct. Otherwise we end up with very strange numbers.

Just to throw out one more example of measuring systems that don't always tell you the same thing, how about automobiles, with torque and horsepower? You could have a high horsepower car stuck in a snow bank, and you'll end up with a low horsepower but high torque tractor pulling you out.

Use the measuring system in the appropriate way, and it will tell you what you want to know. If not, you'll end up stuck.

HOW TO SPOT A THEORY

A theory predicts, as discussed. But the way to tell if the theory under discussion is in fact a theory is this: ask for a predictive chart. If someone says, "Sure, here it is," look closely. You want to see if it has a few important characteristics.

First, is it linear? A linear chart is a simple one: there are X and Y axes, the two lines bounding the chart. Then there's a straight line, at an angle, that predicts the outcome. "If you double this, you get more of that." A low angle means you get half-again as much for doubling the input, and a high angle means you get more than twice for your money/velocity/bullet weight.

A linear input would be a thrown pitch. The faster it is thrown, the faster it will be when it arrives at home plate. Yes, it seems obvious, but sometimes the obvious has to be explained. If a "stopping theory" depends on mass, then doubling mass doubles results. Ditto cross-sectional area (read caliber).

If it is not linear, then is it exponential? Forget all the sports and political talk about "exponential." What we mean is simple: does the line in the graph not stay straight, but change in an upwards-bending curve? At a certain point, you add a little more and you get results out of proportion to the input. A theory dependant on kinetic energy is exponential. At a certain point, you have doubled the velocity (Ke is velocity squared, after all) and it becomes absurd.

Last, is it a bell-like curve? This chart starts low, builds to a high point, and then the curve drops off. This would be the explanation for something like an expanding bullet that depends on maintaining weight. Pushed too fast, the bullet breaks up and effectiveness drops off. (This, of course, flatly contradicts the kinetic energy approach, and thus you see the problem.)

No chart means no prediction, and a lack of predictive ability means it isn't a theory.

However, we can be quite happy with a non-theory that simply explains what we see in real life.

That's an approach some took, and got roundly crucified for it.

ONE MORE NOTE

In the course of the book, I use the word "victim" in a specific and narrow way. I use it not to describe the good guy, but the person who has been shot. The victim of a crime is the person who has been subjected to a criminal act. The victim in this book will be the person who got shot. It may well be in a given scenario that the victim of the crime and the victim of the ballistics are two different people. I'll be using it, almost exclusively, to describe the person who got shot.

Do not assign any other meaning to the word, unless instructed otherwise.

2

HOW AMMO IS MADE,
AND WHAT IS +P?

We know the basics, right? Bullets are projectiles, and they go into cases, over powder, with a primer at the rear. So, let's get our terminology straight.

Bullets are not ammunition. Bullets are the flying parts, the ones we direct at targets. Some reloaders (and reloading companies) call them "bullet heads," which is just wrong. Bullets are projectiles, but projectiles is too formal a word, and also eleven letters instead of seven. In the course of an entire book, that adds up.

Bullets have a base, which can be flat or beveled. They have sidewalls, also known as the "bearing surface," which is the surface area of the bullet that actually makes contact with the bore and rifling. They have a point, a hollow point or a flat, known as the meplat. The meplat can be full diameter, which is known as a wadcutter, from the clean hole it makes in a paper or cardboard target. A semi-wadcutter has a full-diameter shoulder and a nose that projects forward, usually for feeding purposes, but also to maintain bullet weight in the normal range.

A jacketed bullet can be fully covered, an FMJ or full metal jacket. If the open end of the copper cup is forward, then the bullet will be a soft-point or a hollow-point.

The bullet sits in the case, also known as brass, over the powder. Cases, a.k.a. brass, empties, are not "shells." A shell is an artillery projectile or loaded round.

Ammo is not just ammo, and just because it fits doesn't mean it is a good idea to use it. You'll want to make sure your handgun is up to the task before you load it with +P+ ammo of any brand.

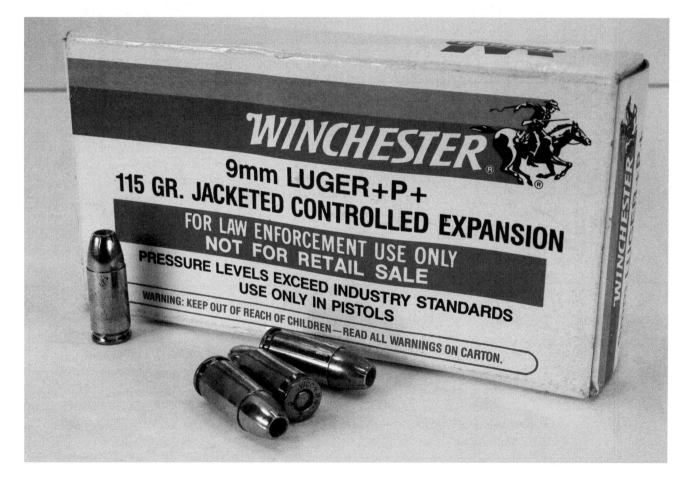

CHOOSING HANDGUN AMMO | 23

Shotguns fire shells. Handguns do not.

Powder is powder, plain and simple. And the primer at the back is also just a primer.

A caliber is a particular diameter of a bullet. You have a 9mm caliber, a .38 caliber, etc. The numeral used to describe the cartridge is not always the actual diameter of the bullet. A 9mm Parabellum is, indeed, a 9mm-diameter bullet. (.355 inch across); but a 9mm Makarov is not, with a bullet diameter of .361 inch, more or less. A .38 Special uses a bullet that is .357 or .358 inch in diameter, but a .38 S&W uses a bullet that is .360. A "32" can use a bullet specific to its case, between .308 and .321 inch in diameter. It depends on which "32" you are talking about. So, for a given cartridge name, there is a specific diameter bullet it uses, but that diameter may not be closely related to the numeral used to describe the cartridge.

A cartridge is a loaded round, of a given caliber. To say "A 9mm cartridge" narrows it down to only a couple of dozen potential cartridges. Ditto a ".38 cartridge," but maybe not two dozen.

And a particular handgun will fire a specific cartridge. A .38 Special revolver fires a .38 Special cartridge, with some of them offering the option of a +P or not a +P. You can't use other .38s in that one, they won't fit.

Why does this matter? Because we're trying to be precise. And we have to discuss bullets, cartridges, performance and the details, and we'd best get on the same page at the start so we can spend less time arguing. Let's take it from the easiest to the most difficult.

PRIMERS

Primers are the impact-sensitive component of ammunition. When we made the transition from flintlocks to percussion caps, the chemical compound used was fulminate of mercury. This had at least three drawbacks (besides excessive sensitivity): the mixture usually included ground glass, the combustion byproducts were hygroscopic (they attracted moisture), and the mercury could "poison" brass cases. The glass was there to provide friction to initiate ignition. The mercury, as the end result of combustion, embrittled the brass case and made it unsuitable for reloading. The hygroscopic residue attracted water, bad for bores.

None of these, however, were a problem before smokeless powder. The liberal powder residue of black powder so diluted the mercury residue and the hygroscopic feature that it didn't matter much. Plus, the common procedure when shooting a black powder rifle was to swab the bore to clean out the powder residue, which also washed out the mercury and hygroscopics.

To later reuse cases, for any reloaders who cared to do so in the last quarter of the 19th century, they went directly out of the rifle and into a bucket or bottle of water to soften the powder residue for later reloading.

Smokeless powder changed all that. There wasn't enough powder residue to protect the cases from mercury. Even going directly into a water bath didn't help much. The greater heat and pressure of smokeless made scrubbing out the mercury more difficult. The hygroscopics meant bores rusted. It took some time and experimental testing to prove it was the primers, not "acids in the powder," that were the agent attacking bores.

The replacement priming compound was lead styphnate. It did not produce hygroscopics, and it contained no mercury. It and fulminate of mercury is/was/are also incredibly stable over time. I have an ammo can of .45 ACP loaded from WWI through WWII, and now and then I pull out a magazine's worth and pop them off. None have yet failed to ignite.

Lead, however, has a problem; it is bad in some situations and in a high enough dose. The lead from the primer escapes on firing and trace amounts are released. For most of us this is not a problem. It can be a "problem" only if you do stupid things, like eating, drinking, or worst of all smoking on the range or while shooting. The major incidence of lead poisoning is institutional. Police officers who have range duty will be on the range eight hours a day, five days a week. They will be around officers who are shooting. While they might not actually shoot much more than a normal amount (however one defines "normal" for ammunition consumption), they will be in the range while hundreds or thousands of rounds are fired, daily or weekly. Their office will likely be located near the range, for convenience, and thus they cannot escape the cloud of lead by retiring to the office for a few hours.

This can be a particular problem for big-city agencies or those in cold climates. At indoor ranges, it can take only a few months for an officer to have sufficient lead uptake to pose a medical problem.

I can offer myself as a counter-example. I am a state-certified law enforcement firearms instructor. The agency I teach for requires an annual lead serum test. The threshold of sensitivity is pretty low, measured in single-digit (down around one or two) micrograms of lead per deciliter of blood. I have, for the decade or so the test has been required, pretty much hammered the scores. (What can I say, I'm a competitive guy.) My highest score has been six. My lowest four or five (I'd have to dig the med sheets out, but I do not remember a three).

Physicians don't even pay attention in adults until the number is over 20, and they don't start looking to remediate until it is near 30. Plus, a person who has never fired a firearm in their life could easily have, even absent other known lead exposure vectors, a lead serum level equal to mine.

Ammo? For two decades as a competitive shooter and gunsmith, I averaged 35,000 rounds a year just in practice and competition. This did not include test firing of customers' guns. Overlapping that was law enforcement teaching. I have probably personally popped a million primers in my life, and have been on the range while officers fired another couple of million. A decade or so of the competition was spent on indoor ranges, for PPC, IPSC and bowling pins.

Why such a low score, then? It could be that my system doesn't take up lead as quickly as others, or that my system scrubs it faster. But, my resolute insistence on not eating or drinking on the range, and certainly not smoking, helped.

All that is to explain why you will see such insistence on lead-free primers in some circles. (And bullets, too, more on that later.) While there are some who need to be protected from lead, most of us do not. So, if most of us don't need protection, and most don't even have firearms as a vector, why the lead agitation?

Lead gets into the public body through two historical vectors: paint and gasoline. Lead-based paint was used for centuries simply because it worked better and lasted longer than paints that did not have lead in them. Lead, in many forms, has a sweet taste to it. (There is literature of lead acetate being used as a sweetener in Rome, during the days of Republic and Empire.) Chips of lead paint taste sweet to a small child. Not knowing any better (in much the same manner as a dog, lapping up sweet-tasting antifreeze) they will be poisoned by it.

Leaded gasoline contained tetra-ethyl lead, a compound that prevents knocking, and acted as a coolant to valve seats. Every gallon of gasoline burned hurled a certain amount of vaporized tetra-ethyl lead into the air. And it then settled onto the ground, and in large cities it settled in large amounts, relatively speaking. It has been decades since leaded gasoline was at all common, but our big cities have dirt, dust and mud that still tests positive for lead.

No amount of lead-free primers will ever solve those situations, but that's another rant, for later.

That leads us to an urban myth: that

Cases are punched as "coins" from strips of gilding metal and then progressively drawn more and more into little cylinders.

the government was trying to develop primers with a "shelf life." That is untrue. There's no way to do it. What was happening was the first few generations of lead-free priming compounds were barely experimental, but law enforcement agencies insisted on having them anyway, even without long-term testing. The problem wasn't just lead, but also barium. Used in priming compound, it is as bad (potentially) as lead. The primer chemists had to get rid of both, and that was a lot more difficult. The initial test lots, and early production of the compounds, did not have a long shelf life, and it was an unpredictable one at that.

They finally found replacements (the real long-term life is still in testing) but the myth got started. Blame police administrators, who could not wait for the full test panel, for that one.

POWDER

Smokeless powder types burn at different rates. They also have a most-efficient burning pressure. That is, they have a powder burn curve where, at pressures below the optimal for a given powder, they burn inefficiently. This leads to a lot of powder residue, and even unburned powder in some instances. At its most efficient pressure, each type burns cleanly.

Above the efficient pressure, the powder can act in what is known as a "non-linear" manner. Think of the gas pedal on your car. Press more, you go faster. Ease up, you go slower. The correlation between pedal pressure and speed is linear, a known and even rate.

Some powders behave nicely and give you more pressure from more powder. At least up to a point. (This is controlled by the amount of powder and the size of the case it is in.) Others are not so polite, and if you increase powder by, say, 20% over the optimal pressure level for burning, you get 100% more pressure.

Others simply do not appreciate certain powder-weight to case-size ratios. An example is an experience I had with the 10mm cartridge. A certain powder that was in the correct band of burn-rate powders for the 10mm was not listed for use by the powder maker. The reason? It was absolutely squirrely in the 10mm cartridge. What seemed like an entirely suitable powder charge gave me an average of 800 fps, with an extreme spread of 400 fps, and finally (in less than a magazine) a blown case.

While it is not exactly alchemy, powders cannot be swapped willy-nilly in cartridges, bullet weights or applications. A given bullet, in a particular case, with a maximum allowed pressure, might only have a few likely candidates for powder choice. I'll go into this in more detail in the +P section, because we need a whole host of details in our grasp before we have that conversation.

Powders also have two variables that manufacturers have to consider, that may not ever be something an end-user even knows or cares about: density and flow. Consider a 9mm Parabellum case. It is a small case and there is only so much room inside. A given powder may have the perfect burn rate for the 9mm, but if it is not dense enough you can't fit enough into the case, seat a bullet and have it work. Sure, the magic of hydraulic machines means you can squeeze it all together, but another variable you may not consider – some powders are not "happy" being compressed when assembled.

If it won't fit, it won't fit. At the other end, a target-power level charge of powder in a .357 magnum case doesn't even come close to filling it. The powder, if the bouncing-around is just wrong, can end up bunched against the base of the bullet an inch away from the primer. On the next shot the powder might be bunched up in the base, pressed closely to the primer. That's not good for consistency.

Flow is the rate and consistency with which a particular powder will pass though the automated powder-dispensing system to load cases. A powder that does not flow in a smooth, consistent manner can't be loaded as quickly as one that is smooth and even. So, a powder choice for a cartridge has to take into account the maximum allowed pressure, the peak-efficiency curve of the powder, the case capacity/powder density, and the rate at which the ammunition can be manufactured.

Happy combinations make for successful ammunition, and unhappy combinations create ammunition that is expensive or unsuitable.

CASES

Brass cases are created by a method known as deep drawing. A "coin" gets punched out of a long spool of sheet brass. (Actually, gilding metal, 95% copper and 5% zinc.) This is repeatedly pressed into or through dies until it is a long tube with a square and solid end.

The ends are then treated to be shaped to the caliber desired. Both handgun and rifle cases have the back end lathe-turned to create the rim. The repeated working causes the brass to harden, so they are routinely annealed between draws, that is, heated and slow-cooled to soften them again. They are also cleaned after each anneal. The last few steps of the process do not involve annealing the case

heads, as the rim and the head with the primer pocket has to be hard to withstand the work.

Necks (and shoulders on rifle cases) are annealed. The neck and shoulder of military rifle cases are not cleaned after the last anneal, to leave visible proof of annealing. The military insists on it.

Handgun ammunition used to be mostly brass cases with a brass exterior. A generation or so ago it became common to use nickel-plated cases in many applications. This reduces friction and makes it easier to extract fired cases. It also slows oxidation. There are now a number of

Bullet and cartridge case manufacturers have interesting problems. What do you do when your bullet-jacket cupping machinery produces cups faster than the lead core cutter can produce cores? Box 'em up and stash them in the hallway, that's what.

Lead: a dense, soft, cheap metal, and one that has been essential to making bullets for a long, long time.

processes that leave cases bright nickel or black, as the nickel or other surface treatments both reduce friction and allow for marketing identification.

Cases are made for a specific caliber, and while some firearms can use more than one cartridge (for example, a revolver can fire both .38 Special and .357 Magnum if it is made as a .357 Magnum), the great majority are made for one specific cartridge.

BULLETS

Bullets are the part of the cartridge that does all the important work. The performance of the "best" cartridge ever made will suffer if it is loaded with less-effective bullets. The best bullet is a matter of speculation and also of need (what you need for one situation may not be what you need for another).

Bullets used to be just bullets. Now we have so many it is hard to tell them apart without a scorecard. Rather than going through the background and descriptors in each caliber breakdown, I'm putting the bullet descriptions here, in one chapter. That way you can see them explained, side by side, and hopefully absorb the details for later analysis. Also, if you want to refresh your memory on a given bullet while reading it in a particular caliber chapter, they are all here rather than scattered throughout the book.

The first projectiles were stones. The first firearms projectiles were stones. Hey, why not use what is cheap and what works, right? The first firearms used, called bombards, had such odd and often generous dimensions that a gun crew would find "close enough" stones and then use hammers and chisels to make them fit better. When artillery became more robust, iron cannonballs came into vogue. Even then it took a while for standardization to settle in.

Even when gonnes (the ones an individual could use) became more common on the battlefield, they would be made on a one-by-one basis. Each firearm came with its own bullet mould, and you'd use that mould for that firearm.

The metal being molded was lead. Lead has a number of virtues for this application; it is dense, soft, common and has a low melting point. Melting at 621 degrees, it could be melted and cast over a hot campfire. Lead has a density of 708 pounds per cubic foot. Other metals with similar or greater densities are gold, hafnium, iridium, mercury, osmium, palladium, platinum, plutonium, tungsten, and uranium. Once we eliminate those with high cost, high industrial values, impossible hardness, unavoidable radioactivity and melting points off the chart, we're left with lead. Good old lead.

It was a big deal for manufacturers and armies to adopt a common bullet size – "This size, no more than this smaller or larger" – so they could be mass-produced and issued to troops. The big step here came with the British. The Land Pattern Musket, or Brown Bess, adopted in the early years of the 18th century, depended on musket balls and powder charges being uniform.

For a long time lead was all anyone needed. There was no need for something else, as the maximum velocity black powder could generate was 1,300 to 1,400 fps. When smokeless came about, lead would not suffice. The initial velocity expected from smokeless rifles was 2,000 fps. Lead can't take that, and even if it could the heat of combustion of smokeless was much greater than that of black powder. The bases of bullets would melt, depositing lead in the bore and quickly ruin accuracy.

Rifles got copper, then gilding metal jackets. Handguns? Not so much. Then, the first high-velocity handgun cartridges came out, and handgun bullets in some applications got jackets as well.

Which leads us to the current situation, where handgun bullets are for the most part made one of six ways: lead, jacketed, plated, coated, all copper and sintered. We'll cover lathe-turned bullets at the end.

LEAD

Casting lead bullets is a time-honored process. However, there are other ways to make bullets. The fastest one in common use is swaging (pronounced: sway-jing). Here, a coil of lead wire gets fed into a machine. The machine chops off specific lengths of the wire, each containing enough lead to make the desired bullet. The wire diameter differs from one caliber to another.

The sections of wire are then fed into the swaging machine, where a hydraulic

Lead can be hydraulically shaped into bullets, a process called called swaging.

press compresses dies together, the dies being the shape of the bullet required. The press (multi-tons, depending on the bullet size and the speed of production desired) squeezes the lead into the bullet shape. After that, it is a relatively simple process to bathe the bullets in a lubricant sufficient for the velocity at which they will be fired. That lubricant protects the bore of the firearm from the metallic lead of the bullet.

The lead has to be pretty much pure, with only a few alloying constituents in very low percentages. If it is too hard, the requirements of press size, die size, and production rate losses become too great. Alloying ingredients interfere with the ductility of lead, its ability to be physically re-shaped through pressure or impact. As a result, swaged bullets are used primarily for two applications: .22LR and target ammunition. The soft lead, even with a good lubricant, will lead the bore if velocities become too great. Target velocities are not so fast as to produce unmanageable leading.

But, they are amazingly uniform, they are inexpensive to produce, and at target velocities they do not lead.

Above: Lead cores go into copper jackets, and that's how babies are born. No, wait, that's how bullets are made. Bullets can be as simple or complicated as the need, or the customer demand.

Right: A jacketed bullet with no opening in front will not expand. It may deform, but usually it looks just like this at the end of its journey.

What they are *not* is durable terminally. A soft lead bullet is easy to swage, which is its downfall terminally. A soft lead bullet won't expand, it sort of smooshes into irregular shapes. Hollow-point bullets will distort, but they rarely deliver the mushroom-like expansion we have come to expect from a properly designed and fired bullet. The distortions cause wound track divergences, not straight paths. They also limit penetration.

Swaged bullets fail miserably in barrier tests, as the ductile lead simply wads into a ball and then continues on (if it does) into the gelatin. Once wadded, it cannot expand in a controlled manner.

Casting allows for other options. One, it permits the introduction of alloying ingredients to create a harder bullet. Tin and antimony are the primary choices, with a resulting bullet hard enough that it does not smoosh or distort except when it strikes bone. Even then, it distorts only minimally.

Tin and antimony each harden bullets, but of the two antimony is less expensive. We read of lead shot used in shotgun competitions as "high antimony" lead pellets. While it makes bullets harder, tin is primarily valued for allowing the molten alloy to completely fill all the spaces of a mold. This is why there was an alloy known as Linotype. A Linotype machine cast lines of type for newspa-

30 | GunDigest.com

pers, back when newspapers were printed with lead type. (The use of Linotype was phased out decades ago, even before the digital era started making newspapers into historical artifacts.)

A harder bullet can also be driven faster; it is less likely to distort as it travels onwards in the case and bore, and the extra hardness resists leading in the bore. But even hard-cast bullets need bullet lube. (Leading is also a matter of proper fit to the bore, and lubricant selection, but that's for another book.)

Finally, casting allows the mould designer to create grooves to hold the lubricant, and to provide a location for the crimped-in case mouth to gain added case mouth and neck tension purchase.

Hard-cast bullets, especially those with large meplats, penetrate deeply and on a straight line. They do not expand, that is their virtue.

JACKETED

A jacketed bullet can be made one of two ways: with a copper sleeve (again, almost always gilding metal) or by plating. A jacket is made in much the same way as the case (deep drawing) but in a smaller scale. The jacket is punched out of sheet gilding metal as a coin-shaped and sized disk, then cupped, and depending on thickness and number of steps, it is usually annealed somewhere in the process. This can be a few or many steps of drawing, annealing, re-drawing, etc.

Once it is a jacket enough, it gets a section of lead wire dropped in as the core (maybe even from the same machine that made lead slugs for the swaging machine), and the lead core is hydraulically swaged into the cup. Just as in the swaging operation, the lead must be relatively pure or it becomes difficult or impossible to get it to completely fill the cup of the jacket.

Then, the bullet receives the final steps of rolling the cannelure into the jacket (to hold the core in) and nosing the bullet, the steps to turn the jacket base edges inward in FMJ bullets, or form the hollow point,

Here is one of the excellent Hornady XTP bullets, cut in half to show the jacket around the core.

and bring the bullet to its final shape.

This is known as a "cup and core" bullet. Only the frictional bond of the lead core swaged into the jacket holds it together, along with the shape of the jacket forward of the center of mass. That is, the taper of the nose.

In an FMJ bullet, this isn't a problem. The open end is at the back, and the bullet won't break apart. But for a soft point or hollow point, it can be. If the bullet does actually expand, the opened-up jacket has less area to hold on to the bullet. The earliest jacketed bullets were known as "full patch" bullets, what we today call a full metal jacket. There was/is no exposed lead at the tip. Since the earlier, big-bore black powder rifles (a .40 or .45 was considered a "medium bore" in the black powder era) had not expanded, no one was looking for expansion with the new ones. But it didn't take long to reverse the jacket and have the open end on the front. The experimenting began.

For a long time this wasn't a problem in rifles. A standard cup-and-core bullet, in say a .30-30, is so long, and the bullet traveling so modestly (1,900 fps, back then, was "high

Here is an expanded Hydra-Shok bullet, showing the post.

CHAPTER 2: HOW AMMO IS MADE, AND WHAT IS +P? | **31**

velocity"), that expansion-causing jacket-core separation was rarely a problem. As rifle velocities moved up, it became a problem. A .30-30 delivers a 170-grain bullet at 1,900 fps, and a 150-grain bullet at 2,100. A .270 Winchester fires 150-grain bullets at 2,850 fps, and a 7mm Remington Magnum fires a 170 at that same velocity. At close range, a big, tough animal can be too much for a cup-and-core bullet at muzzle velocity, so rifle hunters for a long time sought better bullets.

The experimentation didn't proceed quickly enough for a lot of shooters. The lag time between high velocity and better bullets caused a few gun writers and hunters to look backwards. In time, not in results. Elmer Keith was one who advocated rifle calibers .33 and above for serious hunting. He felt the .30-06 was a fine medium-game rifle, but for elk, moose and bear he felt you needed a bigger bullet. This was due in part to the failure of soft-point cup-and-core bullets on the biggest animals.

This was also the reason British hunters in Africa started with the .375 H&H as a suitable rifle caliber and moved up in size from there. They settled on dangerous game rifles in .40 caliber or larger, with heavy and long bullets (400 grains and more) at velocities of 2,200 to 2,400 fps. On game, big, heavy and long bullets could be counted on to penetrate and would not break up. They would not expand, but that was why you used a big and heavy bullet.

These solutions were not available to those using handguns for defense. It was not possible to get any bigger than they already were in bore size, and a heavier bullet would either go slower or add too

Above: Plated bullets are only as tough as they have to be. This plated bullet tipped when it was loaded, and the result was the copper plating was sliced right through. This could still be loaded and shot for practice, but it serves better as a reminder and illustration.

Right: The Gold Dot bullets are lead cores, plated and then punched, shaped and otherwise swaged to become bonded, copper-jacketed bullets.

32 | GunDigest.com

much extra recoil. Handgun users had to wait until the 1970s for truly expanding bullets to be available, and they didn't really start appearing as serious options until the late 1980s.

By the late 1980s we were seeing the first of the improved JHPs. One such was the Hydra-Shok, with its post in the middle of the hollow point. The post was meant to ensure expansion. They worked well, but designers found that the post wasn't needed, so they moved on.

BONDED & PLATED & JACKETED, OH MY

Plated bullets are created for one of two reasons: to erect a barrier between the lead core of the bullet and the bore, or to provide an expansion control structure to the bullet. The bullets designed to prevent leading will have plating as thin as will get the job done (less expense that way.) Those designed to control expansion will generally have thicker platings, but again, only enough to do the job.

A plated bullet is a product of a multi-step process. First, lead cores are cut and then swaged to, or close to, their final shape. The cores are then placed in machines that electroplate copper onto the lead cores. This is not as straightforward as it might seem, as the process has to allow for uniform, complete plating of individual cores, and not end up with a mass of lead and copper all bound together. Think great big washing machines, with agitation, chemicals for electroplating instead of detergents, and a big electrical charge being pumped into a bar of copper suspended in the tank. And all of it proprietary information not subject to the inspection of nosy gun writers and their cameras. It isn't easy, so why let everyone know how to do it?

The final steps in some brands call for the finish-plated bullets to be swaged again, to work-harden the plating and bring the bullets to final shape. Some of these are known as "double-struck," as the core is swaged and then the final, plated bullet is swaged again. You can usually identify these by a telltale circular mark on the base, where the hydraulic bumper

This is a Gold Dot bullet, showing the small "dot" of copper in the center of the expanded petal.

CHAPTER 2: HOW AMMO IS MADE, AND WHAT IS +P? | **33**

Winchester
9MM 127 Gr. Winchester Ranger +P+
4.625" barrel

This is a ballistic gelatin test of the WW Ranger 127 +P+ 9mm load, and the track is quite impressive. The bullet held together, which is essential.

pressed them into the final forming die with great pressure.

In a clever variation, the Speer Gold Dot bullets are plated and then swaged, pierced in the nose and punched into the shape of hollow point bullets. The name Gold Dot comes from an artifact of the process: there is a small dot of plating, down at the bottom of the hollow point.

When the bullet expands, that dot becomes a prominently visible marker in the middle of the expanded face of the bullet.

The plating process offers several advantages. One, it is relatively inexpensive. The plating machinery is less expensive than jacket-forming machines. It depends on bars of copper, not coils of sheet copper that have to be ordered

from mills. The plating can be as thin or thick as you want or need for a given application, something a bit more difficult with regular jacketed bullets. And, the jacket and core are bonded. That is, it is more than a physical attachment between jacket and core. The copper is electroplated to the core, they are inseparable except by melting. That's the big deal for the Gold Dot line.

BONDED BULLETS

Bonded bullets are a recent advance as terminal ballistics go. Here, the process of making jacketed bullets and bonded bullets starts out the same. It changes once there are nearly finished jackets and lead cores. The two are brought together, and the jacket-core combination is heated until the lead melts, bonding to the jacket. Anyone who has done any soldering or welding can see the details that have to be handled here. First, both jacket and core have to be clean and unoxidized. Next, you need some kind of flux on the jacket interior to prevent heat oxidation, which would prevent full bonding. And, the process cannot allow any lead to get on the exterior of the jacket, which would prevent the bullet from working properly or from even being stuffed into a case.

As a last detail, only soft lead alloys can be so-bonded to jackets. You cannot bond a high-antimony or tin-alloyed lead core to a jacket. It won't bond. There's a reason the standard soldering method is known as the "soft-solder" method, it uses nearly pure lead as the solder. And with the silver solder melting point running 1100 degrees or more, that isn't an

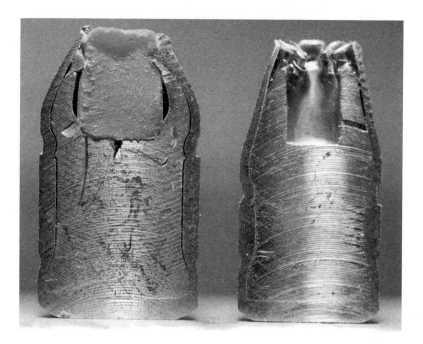

Above: The Hornady Critical duty bullet is mechanically bonded and uses a polymer-filled tip to initiate and control expansion.

Below: In this collection of Hornady Critical Duty bullets, I had to mark the bases according to the test. Otherwise, they performed so equally in all the tests that I could not have told most apart.

The new Federal Syntech is a coated bullet over a lead core, for practice and competition. The bright red makes it easy to tell from regular jacketed bullets.

option for bullets.

So, a bonded bullet, with one brand exception, has a soft lead core, which makes the combination ductile enough to expand when needed, but not separate core from jacket.

The extra steps and care needed make for a more expensive bullet. However, the expansion of the resulting bullet will not permit jacket-core separation, which is a very highly valued detail in the FBI tests. Plated bullets, as mentioned above, are bonded bullets, but the term as used in the firearms industry is meant to describe non-plated, jacketed bullets. So, if someone says their bullet is bonded, they mean it starts as a punched jacket, with the lead core essentially soldered to the jacket. A plated bullet will either be a Gold Dot (if made by Speer) or a plated bullet with a hollow point.

It may be a bit pedantic, but if someone describes a plated bullet as a bonded bullet, they are not using their jargon correctly.

MECHANICAL BONDING

One brand, Hornady, uses a different method of bonding: mechanical locking. They use internal ribs and rings in their jacket so, when the higher-antimony lead core is inserted and swaged in place, the two are locked by the rings. This is their Critical Duty bullet, and Hornady did it this way because they were not happy with the performance of soft lead-cored bullets, even bonded ones.

They wanted a harder-alloy lead core, to hold together better in barrier penetration, and were willing to go to the extra effort. Judging by the results, they were smart to do so. When I tested Critical Duty bullets in the barrier tests, I quickly found that I had to mark the bullets I recovered. Usually, the bare gel and the barrier bullets are each distinctly altered in their tests. The bare gel and heavy cloth looks perfect, and each of the barriers creates a distinct expanded bullet.

Not so the Critical Duty. Extracted from the gel, they looked so much alike that I had to write on the base of each which test it had been recovered in. Otherwise, once they were jumbled together there would be no way to tell them apart.

COATED

This is a new one in large-volume production, but has been used for some years in competition. The idea is simple; swage a bullet, then "paint" or coat it with a substance that keeps the lead away from the bore. The original use was a bullet known as "Nyclad" from the 1970s. It used a nylon-based polymer coating to keep lead off the bore but still provide expansion in some bullet designs. (This was long before the FBI tests were developed.) These were swaged lead semi-wadcutter bullets (for the most part, this was back when revolvers were still the most-common defensive arm carried), and while they worked well, they suffered like all other swaged bullets when the barrier tests were added.

Federal re-introduced Nyclad in 2009, and then in 2015 unveiled Syntech bullets, which used a different coating and were not meant for defensive use, just high-performance competition and training ammunition.

The coating used in competition bullets was meant as a replacement for lubricant and to control costs. The thickness of the Syntech is no greater than needed to protect the bore from the lead of the core. A casual shooter shooting a few hundred to a thousand rounds a year might not care that something costs a bit less. A competition shooter who shoots tens of thousands of rounds per year would find even ten dollars of lower cost per thousand rounds of ammo attractive.

The coated bullets also offer the advantages of less smoke (which can be important in a match) and less bore-scrubbing needed to clean out the leading from even well-lubed and hard-cast bullets, given the volume fired.

Left: The newest bullet design is all copper. Properly designed, they don't care about barriers, they expand (obviously) and they remain intact. There can be no core-jacket separation, because it is homogenous.

Below: All-copper bullets are relatively new. They expand and hold together, but because they are less dense than lead, they are either lighter or longer than lead bullets in a given caliber.

CHAPTER 2: HOW AMMO IS MADE, AND WHAT IS +P? | 37

There are a few companies that make coated bullets for competition shooters. Competition shooters can be a bit particular in their choices. Once they find something that works, they are for the most part loathe to change. Finding a bullet/powder combination that shoots as accurately as their match load, with a cheaper bullet, they'll order a literal truckload and load it for as long as their supply lasts.

As an example, back just before we all transitioned to jacketed bullets in the .38 Super for competition (115 to 124 grains in weight) I ordered a batch of 150-grain hard-cast lead bullets for my own use. I ordered 50,000 of them (I had tested them, they were accurate in my gun, and worked 100%) and met the caster at one of the USPSA Nationals to pick them up.

My truck was a bit put out by this, as they totaled just about 1,100 pounds, with each 500-round cardboard box included. Of course, the caster was driving a Ford F450 Super Duty supercab duallie, with something like four tons of bullets onboard. No sudden stops for him, obviously. And, also obviously, I was not the only competition shooter who was taking advantage of buying as many bullets as they could haul and not have to pay shipping on them. Bullets cost, but the shipping on 50,000 bullets? Ouch.

ALL-COPPER

Copper has limited ductility. But it does have some, and that's what bullet designers have taken advantage of. With a hollow point of sufficient size, and thus thinner sidewalls than a lead-jacket bullet design, you can get an all-copper bullet to expand. The petals basically unfold.

However, that brings with it other problems. First, copper is not as dense as lead. It has 79% the density of lead. That means that, for two bullets of a given size, an all-copper one will have 79% of the weight of the lead bullet. A standard 9mm bullet of 125-grain shape, when made solely of copper, will weigh 99 grains. (Yes, the jacket of the lead-core JHP changes that some, but not a lot.) To bring the all-copper bullet up in

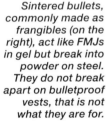

Sintered bullets, commonly made as frangibles (on the right), act like FMJs in gel but break into powder on steel. They do not break apart on bulletproof vests, that is not what they are for.

weight, we have to make it longer. (We can't make it bigger, we're comparing on a caliber-to-caliber basis.)

But some cartridge cases aren't long enough to contain a longer bullet. And the twist of some cartridges also won't permit it. The twist rate needed to stabilize a bullet depends on its length much more so than its mass/density. Make a bullet too long and it won't be stable or accurate.

The exemplar in this instance is found in AR-15s. There, a barrel with a one rotation in 12 inches twist rate (designed for the 55-grain FMJBT bullet) using M855 bullets will not be accurate. The heavier and much longer 62-grain M855 bullets are too long for the twist of the 1/12 barrel, which was optimized for the 55-grain bullets.

As if all that wasn't enough, a much longer all-copper bullet can run into other problems, primarily bearing surface. A markedly longer bullet will have more surface area scrubbing against the bore, adding resistance. That increases pressure and lowers velocity. The solution to lower velocity is to add powder, which increases pressure even more. That then requires a step back in burn rate, to a slower-burning powder. Now, with the added length of the bullet, and the slower-burning powder, do we have enough room in the case for the weight of powder we need?

Changing bullet composition while also seeking the maximum performance is not always an easy task. Also, many all-copper bullets are lathe-turned, as it is not possible to cast or swage copper.

The need to decrease sidewall surface and control pressure is why we see all-copper bullets with grooves in them, like lubricant grooves, but which do not contain any lube. They are there to reduce bearing surface area, and by that, control pressure.

SINTERED

Sintered metal parts manufacture is an old technique, as the industrial age goes. The process is analogous to swaging lead bullets. Instead, you take a powder of the metal you want to use, and sometimes a binding agent. You then pour the correct amount into a hydraulic press and, with

Frangible ammunition is made for specific training and range requirements. It is not meant for use in other places or for other applications.

CHAPTER 2: HOW AMMO IS MADE, AND WHAT IS +P? | **39**

much, much higher pressures than lead bullet swaging, you compress the powder into the shape you need.

Where a lead bullet press might be a few to tens of tons of hydraulic pressure, a sintered metal press working on harder metals like steel could be hundreds of tons.

The pressure generated, along with the grain size of the powder (and the binding agent, if used) determine the structural integrity of the finished product. It is possible to manufacture parts via the sintering process that are as strong as if they were machined from solid pieces of metal. That is not what sintered bullet makers are going for.

Sintered bullets are made primarily for reduced-range, indoor use and for applications where close-range targets are used. There, they are called "frangibles," for use in a "shoot house," a building with steel plates, or steel-plated walls for instance. Here, you are going through the range, which is a bulletproof building, hunting for the bad guys, represented by steel plates. Where a lead (or god forbid, all-copper) bullet, fired on a steel plate at five feet would be quite hazardous (to the shooter, the instructor/range officer, and to viewers), a sintered bullet will break into dust. The solid-metal, lead, copper or jacketed bullet would not shatter, but break into pieces. Some of those pieces may be large enough to cause injury.

It must be emphasized here how sintered bullets work; they need a smooth, hard surface on impact. If they do not have one, they will penetrate, often in much the same manner as an FMJ. A frangible will not "frange" when it hits a bulletproof vest, for instance. It will act much like an FMJ if tested in ballistic gelatin. They are, with one exception, meant as training ammunition only, and even then are dangerous if misused.

Frangibles are usually all-sintered bullets, using copper and sometimes tin or other binding metals, compressed into bullets. Some brands use a copper powder pressed into thin jackets for greater durability in handling and feeding through the firearm.

The exception is Polycase ARX bullets. They are made of powdered metal, but they are molded, not pressed. The molding incorporates a binding resin. The flutes of the ARX cause it to stop in

Here is a set of Polycase ARX bullets recovered from testing. They did not deform or expand, but they stopped in the same distance as a JHP. You literally could load and shoot them again.

ballistic gelatin in distances equal to that of efficient JHP bullets. But, they will break apart on steel like frangibles.

SINTERED WITH A DIFFERENCE

Polycase makes a sintered bullet, but it isn't like your normal sintered bullet. As I just mentioned, they are made of a slurry of powdered metal, mostly copper (they are rightly not telling us all the constituents, but there is no lead or barium) and the copper is mixed into an epoxy mixture. The slurry is then injected into a mold and allowed to cure. (This is part of the proprietary process, a trade secret, and all companies have them.)

The finished bullet is hard enough to withstand being loaded into a case, being loaded into a magazine or revolver, and being fired, all without damage to the bullet. In fact, I have recovered bullets where it was difficult to see, and almost impossible to photograph, the rifling marks of firing.

The flutes cast into the bullets are designed to resist the lateral/rotational thrust created when the bullet enters a medium denser than air. In trying to push aside the water/gel/tissue that enters the flutes, the bullet disperses its energy into that medium. The result is a bullet that stops in ballistic gelatin as quickly as an efficiently expanding bullet of the same caliber would. Does this mean the Polycase ARX (the specific Polycase bullet with the flutes) is as good at stopping as an expanding bullet would be? Until we have a sufficient database of shootings with it, we can't be sure. However, there have been game animals hunted and shot with the ARX, and the results have been impressive.

LATHE-TURNED

This process is older than you might think. It is simple; rods of suitable metal are turned on lathes into the shapes of bullets, which are then loaded and fired. This process was the way the French made rifle and machine gun bullets in WWI, using bronze to make Balle D 8mm rifle-caliber bullets. They even marked on the base which firm made that bullet, for tracking and QC purposes. Even with an auto-indexing turret lathe (that's one with a rotating toolhead at the back end, where you can park 4-5-6 tools, each to be swung around and used in turn), it had to be incredibly boring work. And, if a machinist could produce bullets at the prodigious rate of one per second, you'd need ten lathes to keep up with one machine gun.

Today, with fully automated CNC lathes, you can make them 24/7. You can even pre-load rods into an automated feed rack, so one operator can keep four

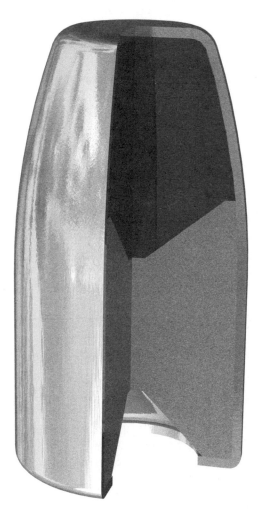

Federal makes a bullet that is an FMJ but expands. The trick is the front of the core, which is a polymer that deforms under impact.

Bullet design keeps getting better. The old FMJ might have worked in come calibers, but JHPs are very, very good now. And the latest, like the ARX and the Honey Badger, promise to change things utterly.

or more machines fed and running. Such a setup, with multiple machines, could make bullets at the rate of one per second.

HONEY BADGER

A new design of all-copper bullet has been making an appearance. Called the "Honey Badger" by Black Hills (from the meme "Honey Badger don't care"), it is a lathe-turned bullet but the nose has been machined into flutes, with the flutes forming an X or cross on the nose. The flutes, combined with the rotation of the bullet, act as brakes on the bullet in a dense medium such as water, gel or tissue. As a result, they disperse their energy into the object but do not expand. They also do not deform in barriers, but punch through and then decelerate in the gel or tissue. As in, Honey Badger don't care there was a barrier in the way.

Being all copper, they are lighter than the usual weights, which aids in increased velocity to improve terminal efficiency. They are quite impressive in gelatin and barrier tests, but until we have a base of reported shooting with them, it is hard to tell if they will perform similarly in real life.

EXPANDING BUT NOT HOLLOW POINTS

There's one place on earth, or at least in the free part of the earth, where you cannot own a hollow-point bullet. Care to guess? Yep, that's right, New Jersey. Using or even owning hollow point handgun ammunition there, unless you are a law enforcement officer, is a crime. That, and the visceral dislike of hollow points in some quarters and in some jurisdictions (even when it isn't against the law), is what led Federal to design the Guard Dog line of bullets.

The manufacturing process is a bit involved. First, they make jackets just like you'd make FMJ jackets. But, during the process they use a forming die on the hydraulic ram that has a set of splines on it. These splines score the inside of the jacket and cut it through, or almost through, to the outside. These jackets are nickel-plated, by the way. The cuts only extend along the length of the bullet ogive, not the meplat or the bearing surface.

Then, in the front end, where the nose and the spline cuts are, they insert a synthetic blob. This is a special synthetic, one that can withstand a cer-

tain amount of force but will compress once the force exerted on it reaches a high-enough level. Then, they insert a lead core behind the blob and crimp the jacket down over the core.

Those who have been paying attention will immediate note that the bullet will be lighter than normal. It has to be, the synthetic blob inside has less density than lead, and so unless they are willing to make the bullet longer (too long to fit) it has to be lighter. And so they are. However, the lighter weight allows Federal to load the ammunition to a higher velocity, and velocity is what causes expansion.

When the Guard Dog strikes a dense medium, the blob collapses under the pressure. The splits in the jacket allow the jacket to expand, like an umbrella opening, and increase frontal area.

Now, as we use the description "expand" in this book, the Guard Dog bullet doesn't really expand. It deforms under load, much as an all-lead swaged bullet would, but in a controlled manner. And yes, it does increase its diam-

Left: Pre-notched or sliced jackets will expand in a controlled and uniform manner.

Below: Ammo makers inspect, test, and inspect and test some more.

eter, and frontal area. It also does this reasonably well with barriers in the test. Which is a lot of work to go through to satisfy the irrational demands of the New Jersey legislature.

CHAPTER 2: HOW AMMO IS MADE, AND WHAT IS +P? | **43**

WHY ARE MODERN BULLETS BETTER?

One reason modern bullets are much more likely to expand is that the institution of a uniform test allows manufacturers to measure their bullets against an accepted standard. Before, each manufacturer was pretty much on its own, trying to determine just what customers wanted and how to deliver it. With a commonly accepted yardstick to use, they could get on the job of making bullets perform. One can argue that the yardstick isn't quite right and should be something else, but that misses the point. Three engineering factors have helped. First, the selection of lead alloys for expansion and weight retention. Before, I'm pretty sure the cost of an alloy (or lack of, in the case of dead-soft lead) was the determining factor. It is hard to get performance, expansion- and penetration-wise, when the over-riding factor of cost trumps all.

Second, manufacturers adjusted the jacket alloy, heat and work-treatment, and thicknesses.

But the third, and greatest factor, was in pre-stressing, or slicing the jacket to initiate and control expansion. When you make a hollow-point jacket simply by punching it into a cup, the open edges of the hollow point are uniform. When expansion begins, the jacket attempts to uniformly expand. It has to tear at the weak points, and if those weak points are not equi-distant around the opening the jacket will peel back in a non-uniform manner.

If, on the other hand, you pre-notch or slice the nose, the edges or the radius of the nose, then you have created ready-opening stress points. With uniform expanding and peeling open, the bullet now will expand in a uniform and controlled manner.

With variable-thickness jackets, pre-made stress points, and bonding of core to jacket, the modern bullet performs amazingly well in the gel tests.

WHAT IS +P?

What is pressure? When you drop the hammer or striker you ignite the primer. That ignites the powder charge. Depending on the caliber and powder, the powder may ignite all at the same time (small

Every round you handle has been gone over by dozens of people before it gets into a box and is shipped off to your local store.

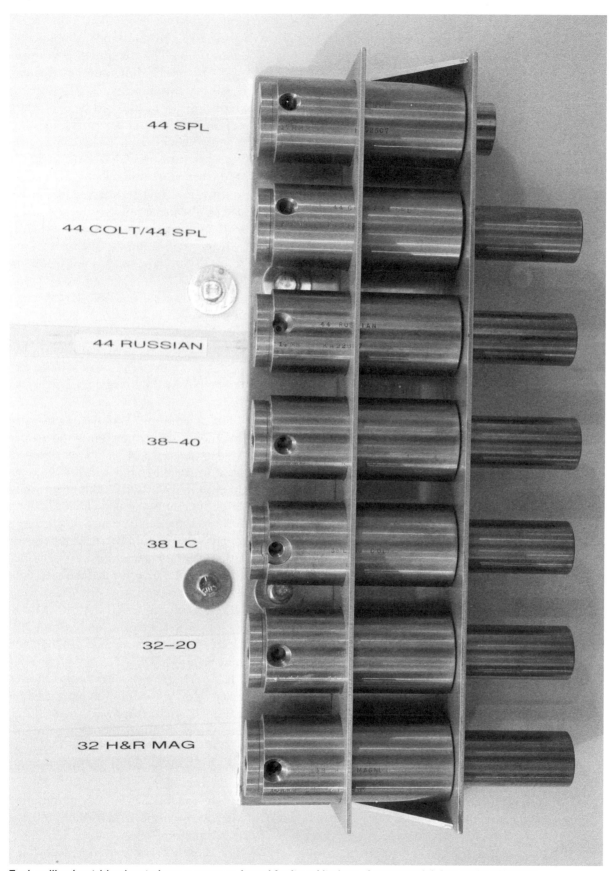

Each caliber/cartridge has to have a pressure barrel for it and it alone. A pressure lab has racks of barrels, stored against need.

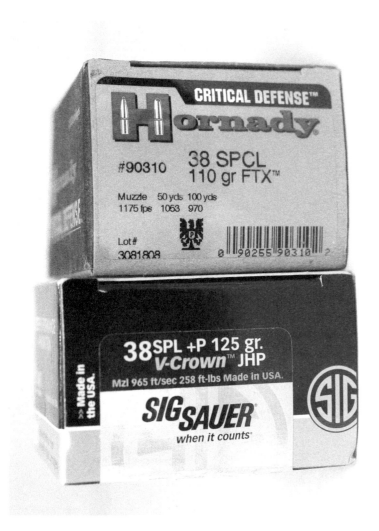

Pressure levels can vary, but only within the limits set by the industry.

charge, fast-burning powder, small case) or it may ignite the rear of the powder stack and burn forward. (That would be a rifle case, where you are igniting 25 grains of powder or more.)

The burning powder turns to gas, creating heat, and the gases try to occupy more space than is available. This is what we call pressure, and it is what drives the system known as firearms. The heat generated is an unavoidable by-product, and one that must be managed, since it can't be put to good use.

Once the pressure reaches a high enough level, the bullet begins to move. The timing of powder burn, bullet movement and peak pressure is important. It varies from cartridge to cartridge, and according to the firearm it is in.

Each publicly accepted cartridge is clearly defined by SAAMI, the Small Arms and Ammunition Manufacturers Institute. The maximum and minimum size of all dimensions is defined, as is the Maximum Average Pressure, or MAP. This is the allowed peak pressure for normal operation of that cartridge. When someone says, "The .38 Special has a pressure of 17,000 PSI," it is the MAP they are talking about. You could pressure-test every factory .38 Special load on the shelves of your local big-box store and not find one that came close to 17,000 PSI as the average for that lot. Your .38 Special ammo is not loaded to 16,900 PSI.

If only it were that simple, and that was all we needed to know.

Each round has its own pressure peak. The average is what we work with, but some will be over and some will be under. So, SAAMI defines the allowed data spread.

The Maximum Probable Lot Mean (MPLM) is defined as two standard deviations above the MAP. So, for instance, the .38 Special MAP of 17,000 PSI, given two standard deviations, gets us to 17,850 PSI. Using statistical calculations, having measured the peak pressure of a series of rounds, the ballistician will determine if the load being tested exceeds the defined MPLM. The limit (for those who love number-crunching) is that there is a 97.5% probability that the MPLM will not be exceeded by the load as-tested. If it exceeds that, it is deemed too high and must be lowered.

If lowering the pressure brings the velocity below the minimum permitted for that application, that load is rejected by the factory loading and testing as unsuited.

And they then go on to the next one on the list.

Each production lot of ammunition will have a statistically relevant number of rounds pressure-tested. (They'll even test on an hourly basis, with some loads.) If a round fails, the lot may be scrapped, the

Ammunition is made to fit a particular-chambered handgun. It fits properly, and if you use the wrong ammunition, it may not fit at all. There is no "one size fits all" ammunition, only what your handgun is made for.

components broken down, or the whole batch fed into a shredder and recycled.

When an ammunition manufacturer receives a new batch of powder they load it with standard, known components kept on the shelf for just this purpose. If the powder falls within the pressure specs the powder maker lists (every lot of powder varies slightly), then it will accepted, the variance noted for Production, and used to make ammo. If the powder fails, it is rejected and shipped back.

As a result, it may well be that a given .38 Special load, as developed by the factory, generates less pressure than the max allowed. If they can, for instance, get the 800 fps they want with the 158-grain lead bullet they are using, at only 14,000 PSI, why push it? What's to be gained by 875 fps? If they are loading a 125 JHP for defensive use, then they will push up to 17,000 PSI, but only if a given powder/bullet combination keeps them under the 97.5% level of confidence MPLM measurement.

Plus, the published specifications for a load must be met. If the company touts its 158-grain lead bullet as generating 800 fps in a .38 Special, they gain nothing by pushing it faster. So, they meet the 800 fps under the 17,000 PSI pressure limit, check for accuracy and, if all is good, haul it to the shipping department.

Each cartridge has its own MAP, MPLM and set of bullet/powder combinations that stay within limits.

But metallurgy has improved. The steel used in a .38 Special revolver of 2017 is in all likelihood much stronger than that used in a revolver made in, say, 1957. Or 1937. So, can we not do better? Yes, but only if we define things appropriately.

So, SAAMI carefully developed new pressures and definitions. Our .38 Special, at an MAP of 17,000 PSI, can be a .38 Special+P with an MAP of 21,000 and an MPLM of 22,050. This creates more terminal effectiveness (or so the hope goes) but it does so at the cost of more noise, recoil and a potentially shortened service life of the firearm in use.

The last part may not be significant. Let's just take as an example an S&W

+P+ ammo may perform better than the standard pressure ammo, but then again it may not, depending on the bullet used. A bullet pushed past its velocity limits may break apart, and that's not good.

M-60 and an S&W M-19. The 60 is a .38 Special and it might have a service life of only (not that I've put that much through any M-60) 10,000 .38 Special rounds. Or 20,000, or 30,000. The M-19, being a bigger, heavier and chambered in .357 Magnum revolver, could have a service life of 100,000 .38 Specials. (Me, I'd peg it more like 500,000, but let's stay in a graspable zone.)

Going to a steady diet of .38 Special+P, the M-60 might last only 5,000 rounds. The bigger and heavier M-19 would probably still last more like 40,000.

Do you know anyone who has put 5,000 rounds of .38 Special+P through an S&W M-60 or any revolver like it? If you do, don't be surprised if they won't shake hands. That's a lot of harsh recoil. Back in the old days, the joke was that most revolvers had a "service life" of six rounds. That's how much they got shot to make sure they worked, before they were reloaded and then stuffed in a nightstand drawer.

Even today, it is a rare shooter who goes through as much as 100 rounds a year. That's 50 years for our over-worked M-60.

No, most of the burden is put onto the shooter.

The velocity gain for a .38 Special+P over the standard .38 Special is 100 to 200 fps, depending on the barrel length and bullet weight.

+P+

So, what is this +P+ you sometimes read of?

There is no standard for +P+ pressures. That ammunition is loaded by big manufacturers for law enforcement. This is not a conspiracy. They will not offer it up into normal distribution channels for a good reason – there's no SAAMI spec for it. Lacking a SAAMI spec, the lawyers would have a field day if they started selling it "over the counter."

+P+ ammunition is loaded for law enforcement because the department or agency is willing to take the burden of liability. It works something like this: a department or agency asks for a given caliber, with a given bullet weight, at a desired velocity. The ammo companies test what they have, see if they can come up with the weight and velocity at a pressure they can live with. (Most likely, they consult their loading lab books, to see what they already have, or what comes close enough to test further. That's the benefit of detailed notekeeping over years of testing. It's all there on the pages.)

If the ammo, when tested, works for the agency, they order however much of it they need/want/can use/can pay for. The delivery is explicit: the manufacturer has no responsibility for the users' experience with it. Decreased service life of weapons? Not our problem. Too much muzzle blast and recoil for recruits to pass the qual course? Tell them to toughen up. Brass is rejected by commercial reloaders as used-up and only valued by its weight as scrap? What did you expect? You asked for it, you got it, stop bothering us.

And all that for maybe 50 to 75, at most 100 fps more than the regular +P ammunition.

Which can bring problems of its own. More speed means the bullets get worked harder. A bullet that worked well in the FBI tests at the "book" velocity might over-expand, and the resulting decreased penetration can cause it to score lower or even fail the FBI test. If an agency asks about that, the ammo maker has two options: explain the mechanics of the situation and offer the hope that spending money on bullet development will solve it, or "see above."

SUMMARY

Bullets are not a magic talisman. They are designed for a particular caliber, even cartridge, for a given velocity range. As an example, no matter how much a 9mm bullet expands out of a 9mm Parabellum, the same bullet loaded into a .380 case and fired out of a .380 Auto pistol is going to be seen as a failure, lacking to expand. The smaller, lower-pressure cartridge just can't generate enough speed to expand the bullet. The reverse is no better. Yes, you can take an 85-grain .380 Auto bullet and out of a 9mm Parabellum drive it to impressive velocities. At those speeds they will also fail, breaking up into shards and fragments in the ballistic gel.

A heavy, hard-cast semi-wadcutter will pass right through an anorexic drug abuser without doing much. Designed to penetrate three or four feet of big, tough, heavy-boned moose, it will hardly notice a meth addict. Especially at the 1,200 fps the moose application needs.

Similarly, a bullet designed to fully expand in the FBI tests will stop, fully expanded, against the shoulder bone of the moose, not even cracking one and resulting in the moose stomping you flat into the tundra or swamp. Good luck with that.

Bullets need to be matched to the caliber and velocity, as well as the application.

Bullets must be designed to fit a given case and operate within limited velocity parameters. You can't use a bullet that won't fit, and you can't depend on expansion if expansion happens at a velocity higher than the cartridge can generate.

3

WHAT IS "STOPPING POWER"?

CIVILIAN OR NOT?

A lot of police officers and departments use "civilian" as a term for people who are not them. This is incorrect, and those of you who have read my work before know that I am not nothing if not striving to be precise. A civilian is a person who is not subject to the Uniform Code of Military Justice. The UCMJ covers the conduct, duties and punishments for failing same, for military personnel. All who are not subject to it (and if you have not taken the military oath, you aren't) are civilians.

Yes, police officers are civilians. And, they are civilians even if they are military members, if they are not on duty as a military member at the time.

Using "civilian" to describe taxpayers who are not employed in law enforcement is attempting to drive a wedge between LE and the rest of us, where none ought to be.

Police officers are citizens who have been granted a certain authority and particular powers in order to better serve and protect those of us who have other jobs. The powers and procedures are carefully considered, limited by law and court decisions, and they exist solely to help officers do the job better.

The realities of some situations create a different decision tree for the rest of us than they might for a sworn officer of the law. For instance, once a fight has begun, a police officer is expected to continue until they subdue the individual. The rest of us? If we can disengage, flee and achieve safety, then the law counts that as a wise move. That option is not afforded (generally speaking) to an officer. The requirements and restrictions differ for the use of lethal force.

Keep that in mind.

What is "stopping power"? Simple answer: a myth, a dream, an aspirational statement. Fiction. What do people think it is? That is also simple: some combination of bullet weight, frontal area, velocity composition and construction; that when you shoot a person with it, they stop doing bad things right now.

I wish I remembered where I heard this, but a quote I recall sums it nicely: "Out there, someplace is a veteran with a true story of an enemy soldier who needed a second burst of .50 BMG before he went down."

Before we go any further let's make one thing clear, we are discussing lethal threat encounters. I'm not talking about a fistfight at a backyard barbeque, unless you live in a place where those things commonly turn into gunfights. Two children arguing over whose turn it is on whatever piece of playground apparatus is left these days is not our concern. We're talking a lethal threat, situations that fulfill the legal requirements for "I feared for my life, your honor," and nothing else.

The requirements differ, depending on the jurisdiction in which you live or find yourself at the moment, whether or not you are a sworn law enforcement officer.

Before we can even begin to try and wrap our heads and hands around a stopping power theory, we must have a grasp

Stopping power? Really? You want to argue stopping power, with your magnum and its 240 grains, against this 12-gauge slug, at 528 grains? (1.2 ounces, by the way.)

CHOOSING HANDGUN AMMO | 51

While some bullet makers are going all copper, others take a different approach. This Polycase bullet (left) does not expand, is not intended to, and never will. It does, however, stop in the same depth of gelatin as this expanding bullet, so there's something going on despite the lack of expansion.

of what goes on in a situation where we might use a firearm.

An understanding of the word "anecdote" is important to our discussion. An anecdote is a story, lesson or event that stands alone. A bad guy gets shot with a given cartridge, and he does or does not stop doing bad things. That event is an anecdote. It is important to keep in mind this important point: the plural of anecdote is not data.

In order for the event to be a piece of data, we'd have to know everything about it: the victim's mindset, chemical state (if any), plans and determination; the caliber, velocity and construction of the bullet; and the exact path of the wound track. Lacking all of the above, we cannot do more than call it an anecdote. The more of those variables we have, the better we can assign confidence in the information we have, and place it with the thousands of others we'd need to plot a reasonably accurate graph.

A theoretical example: a given police department issues two types of 9mm ammunition. One is a lightweight, high-speed bullet, the other a full-weight moderate-velocity load. The department tracks the results in shootings and finds that the X load is more effective than the Y load. This is useful if the ammunition is evenly distributed in the department and if it is evenly distributed in lethal force encounters. However, if the X load is issued to the SWAT team and the Y load is for general use, then to misquote the Spaniard in "The Princess Bride": I don't think that information means what you think it means.

If the SWAT team has a more frequent range schedule and is composed of officers who have demonstrated greater firearms proficiency, then the difference in effectiveness might be a matter of marksmanship and not terminal ballistics. If you do not know the differences between the two groups, then the information is anecdotal at best, and not data. This makes it difficult to measure the effectiveness of load X used in one department compared to load Y used in a different department.

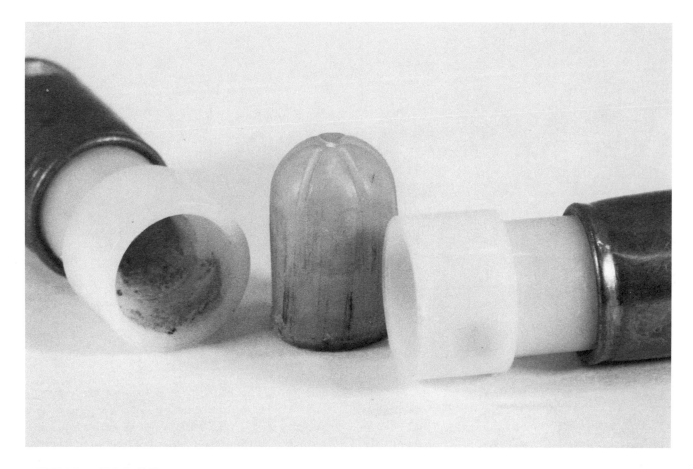

Not all ammunition is expected to penetrate, to expand, to be a "stopper." Here is a marking round, used in "sims" or simulated force-on-force training. All it is expected to do is break and mark. This one obviously failed.

LETHAL FORCE ENCOUNTERS

The requirements for use of lethal force for a non-sworn individual consist of four components: Ability, Opportunity, Jeopardy/Intent and Preclusion. Some jurisdictions do not require Preclusion, and it is wise to know the laws of your locale. (I'll assume, for the purposes of brevity if nothing else, that law enforcement officers who are reading this know the requirements of their department. If they do not, they must learn them.)

And let me assure my editors, the publisher and readers who are graduates of law schools, I am not offering legal advice. I'm telling you that which I have learned, and I strongly advise you to find a good attorney in your area and talk this matter over with him or her, preferably before you have need of their services.

And why are we discussing this, a subject that you can study in classes (which I strongly urge you to attend), watch videos, and read cases? Because wrong beliefs on the nature and details of the law can turn an otherwise "good shoot" into a prison sentence. Arguing with the IRS that you didn't know the law probably means a fine and penalties. Arguing you didn't know the law when someone got shot has the potential of much more serious consequences.

I'll bring this back around after a brief up-to-speed on the legal parts of the problem. They all hinge on your belief that you are imminently in danger of grievous bodily injury or death. Not that you were or were not actually in danger, but that you actually, factually, reasonably believed. That is what is known as the "reasonable man" basis.

ABILITY

Does the bad guy have the ability to inflict "grievous bodily injury or death"? Someone who holds a firearm obviously does. What else? Big knives, clubs? What

It cannot be stressed too strongly, you need velocity to expand a bullet. These were all fired into ballistic gelatin, out of target loads (loaded to be soft in recoil), and not one of them expanded.

about a molotov cocktail with the fuse lit?

There are gray areas. A 250-pound man, fit and muscular, who holds a club the size of a nightstick could be argued to satisfy the Ability component. Your 85-pound grandmother, holding a Louisville slugger and barely able to lift it, might be a more difficult argument to make.

A 250-pound man without a weapon might or might not have the ability. It would depend on the circumstances.

This leads to discussions of "disparity of force." One otherwise unarmed man? Maybe he's a lethal threat. Two men? That's worse. Three men? Now you might seriously make your case that they posed a threat of grievous bodily injury and even death.

This is something you need to talk about with your lawyer, because the threshold depends on the laws of your state and case law developed there.

Also, you have to reasonably believe he has the ability. A man standing in front of you with a concealed firearm has the ability, but he does not have the Ability, if you follow. He has the gun, but if you don't know it, you can't say you were in fear for your life because of the firearm. Follow?

OPPORTUNITY

The bad guy is holding a club, but he is on the other side of a busy road. You can run, and he can't run after you until traffic clears enough to not get run over. He does not have the opportunity. However, standing on the other side of the same road holding a rifle, he may.

The word itself gives you the clue you need: does he have an opportunity to use the particular Ability that you can see or know he possesses?

As with location, this can change in a moment's notice. If traffic clears and he starts to sprint across the road with his club, he certainly has the Opportunity now, where he may not have a moment before.

JEOPARDY/INTENT

Has he indicated his intentions to inflict this harm on you? He doesn't have to say so in so many words. A man walking towards you holding a knife, locking eyes with you and grinning in an unfriendly manner, in a time and place where you might well expect a knife-wielder to be, might well be taken as Intent.

If someone is standing next to a rifle or a shotgun in a rack or a handgun lying on

To speak of "stopping power" in handguns is to miss the point. If you really want to be stopping things - people, animals and vehicles - you need to drastically up your game. This 12-gauge slug is one ounce and travels at 1,600 fps. No handgun does that.

a table and they say, "I'm going to shoot you," that may indicate Intent, but the quick reader will ask, "Is there Opportunity?" Probably. Maybe. Is it Ability? Perhaps. But if he says it while standing stock-still, then you have to question the actual Intent, considering the totality of the circumstances.

In the example of a man with a club sprinting across the road, if he has spent the previous minute shouting threats and promises to injure you, then the sprint may well constitute proof of Intent. (The wise reader will ask why you stayed there for the previous minute, and didn't just leave. The Prosecutor, and then the Courts, will also ask that question.)

PRECLUSION

Is the application of lethal force the only possible solution to the problem at hand? In a lot of jurisdictions, before the rise of "Castle Law" doctrines, the courts (and statutory law, in some instances) held that flight was the first choice. Indeed, in some locations, flight was considered a viable option in almost all circumstances, and fighting was only an allowed legal option in the direst of situations. Some locales would even require that a person had to flee their own home rather than fight.

That has changed, with many states passing laws stating that, if you are in a certain locations, you need not flee before you fight. These rules also prevent bad guys from using your fight as a pretext for a civil suit, for injuries received, etc.

It is imperative that you know the laws concerning the use of lethal force in your jurisdiction.

For detailed discussion of these concepts, the book "Deadly Force: Understanding Your Right to Self Defense" by Massad Ayoob is an exceptional resource.

LETHALITY

Here's a conundrum for you: modern medical knowledge and physicians' skills are so good in the 21st century that four out of five people shot with a handgun survive the encounter. In fact, it is a much greater percentage if the victim arrives at the hospital with a pulse.

But, it is the potential for lethality that defines the tool you will use, not the actual. Your neighborhood kids, playing baseball, are doing so with objects that could, in different circumstances, be lethal

Top: Testing is one thing, showing off is another. There is no correlation between melons and people, and using produce to "demonstrate" a cartridge or load is silly. Bottom: However, demonstrations can be fun. This is that watermelon, struck by a 12-gauge slug, and those who stood too close smelled of vaporized watermelon for the rest of the day.

weapons. That does not in and of itself mean anything. The bad guy who just demanded your wallet, and upon receiving it is still winding up to strike you, has a lethal weapon.

We are not, however, concerned with lethality. Lethality is not our goal. A .22LR can be lethal. Indeed, people have died from lesser projectiles. We are not interested in lethality.

However, in defense with lethal force, we use force that may well be lethal itself. Until phasers set on stun are available to us, the only option remains the use of tools that are potentially lethal by their very design. That, or surrender. I thought not.

So, if stopping power is a myth, why do we search for it so enthusiastically? Because in a bad situation, we want every assurance that things will work out all right. And that leads us to the first step in understanding stopping power: most of the time it is mental.

There are two aspects to a fight, mental and physical. If someone is mentally prepared and psychologically attuned, they will be able to bring all their physical skills to the process. Those skills might not amount to much, but they can bring all of them to the table.

On the flip side, someone unprepared and/or psychologically untrained will react quite differently, regardless of physical capabilities. There is also the matter of prior conditioning. Mental state and expectation play a big part in the results of conflict.

On the physical side, there is good news and bad news. The bad news is that your opponent has, through evolution, been created as a difficult opponent. Key parts of his anatomy are armored, he has redundancy in critical systems. His body will adapt to injury and, if given even a short time and minimal care, he can heal and rebuild. He is equipped with fast reflexes, an adaptable central processing unit, and the decision-making processing power to change plans in mid-stream. He has strength, stamina, adaptability and agility.

The good news? That also describes you.

Physically, there are two ways to stop an opponent. You can deal a damaging blow to the central nervous system. You can cause sufficient blood loss that blood pressure drops below the operational level. Those are it, physically.

Let's take a look at a statistically significant number of lethal threat encounters. We'll start with a nice, round number — one thousand.

A thousand times, lawfully armed citizens find themselves in a situation where a firearm is needed. Of those thousand times, somewhere between five hundred and nine hundred will be defused by simply showing the gun. This is a subject and a number that has been greatly debated. The pro-gun side posits that the number is large, and perhaps unknowable, simply because most people in that situation do not report it.

You see, while concealed carry is more common and more accepted, there are still laws on the books in every jurisdiction against "brandishing." Brandishing is a complicated legal topic, worthy of study but beyond the scope of this book. Back to our one thousand.

Nine hundred incidents never happen, simply because the gun was there. Of the remaining one hundred, another fifty actually required it be handled. Of those fifty, shots were fired, and forty times everyone involved missed. I kid you not, people miss. They miss a lot. And that is usually not a bad thing.

An incident I watched on video is a good example. Detroit, the near West side. A cold winter night, and the homeowner has security cameras on the house, recording. Three guys try to enter the house by the back door. The door is locked, they threaten, they are told, "Go away, I have a gun." The lead guy kicks in the door and the three rush in. Shots are fired and three guys run out, down

Bullet design can influence the effectiveness of a bullet, but the difference may not be as marked as you might think. Velocity also plays a part, but it is the combination of all variables - weight, shape, speed and placement - that determines the outcome.

the stairs and into the night. One of them stops in the snowy driveway, turns and actually pulls out a gun and heads back in. The occupant, a woman, fires more shots, and the intruder wisely runs back out the door away into the night. (Later to be arrested.)

Quiz time. In the 950 incidents, including the one just described, how important was stopping power? Anyone who gave any answer other than "not at all" ought to go back and start over. The stopping power of the firearms used, or not used, was utterly immaterial.

Stopping power may be of importance in the remaining 50, but then again maybe not. Of those fifty, with shots fired, thirty of the bad guys run away as soon as they are hit. Hit anywhere. With anything. .22LR on the fleshy part of an arm, "I'm outta here!" A bigger bullet grazing a leg, a hand, knocking a hat off a head, "No more of this for me!" Twenty left. Ten of them take solid hits and flee. They will need serious medical attention, but they still have enough strength to get out of Dodge.

Ten are left of our original thousand, and they fight. Some not so well, others with ferocity and tenacity. Those are the ten we will spend most of the book discussing, but they are also the highlights that define our dilemma.

In another situation, relayed to me by a friend with decades of experience in a big city with a whole lot of crime, a bad guy breaks into the home, the homeowner phones the police and calls out, "I have a gun." Bad guy starts up the stairs, the homeowner the whole time shouting, "I have a gun," which is pointed at the bad guy.

Homeowner decides enough is enough, he shoots. The bad guy takes a full-power factory .44 Magnum underneath the left eye. Bad guy tumbles down the stairs, gets up and walks out of the house. When the police arrive they begin a search and find the bad guy around the corner, next to his car, keys on the ground, dead.

A council of experts could argue the question, "Was there enough stopping power?" on this one until the cows come home. On the "yes" side, the bad guy stopped doing what he was doing. On the "no" side, he decided to do something else instead, and could have spent that last minute fighting instead of fumbling with his car keys. And by the time we're done, you'll agree with both of them.

The dilemma of our book, our situation, our life's work in firearms is this – statistically speaking, caliber doesn't matter. 990 times out of 1,000, caliber didn't matter.

You can quibble with the actual numbers, but the point is this: the subset of potentially lethal encounters where stopping power becomes the determinate factor is very small. You are better served with proper situational awareness, having a plan, knowing the law and being proactive than in obsessing over a few percentage points on a theoretical scale of "stopping power." Put your effort where it will deliver the greatest return.

Also, if we were going strictly by statistics we wouldn't be carrying a gun. It is the job of the police to deal with crime, with violent people, and to be in harms' way. Or at least, potential harm's way. And there are departments full of officers who have not killed anyone with their

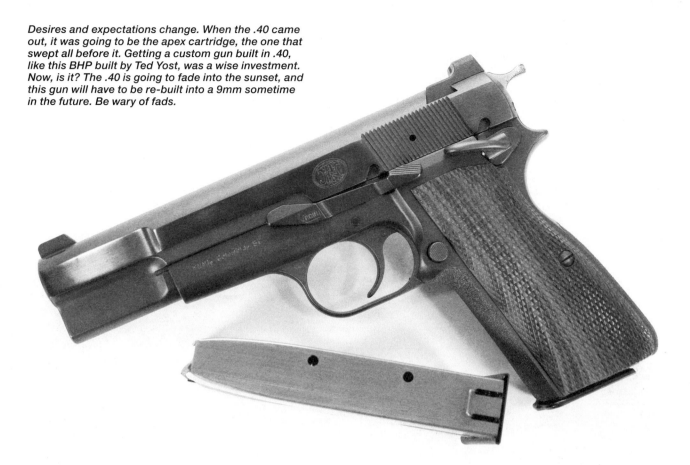

Desires and expectations change. When the .40 came out, it was going to be the apex cartridge, the one that swept all before it. Getting a custom gun built in .40, like this BHP built by Ted Yost, was a wise investment. Now, is it? The .40 is going to fade into the sunset, and this gun will have to be re-built into a 9mm sometime in the future. Be wary of fads.

sidearm. It is not unusual to find many departments where there is only one officer who has been in a shooting incident. The rest? They will wear a sidearm for their entire career and might, a dozen times, point it at someone, but never discharge it in their official capacity and retire having never been in a gunfight. If that's the police, what are the statistics for those of us who do not seek out danger as a professional requirement?

But, the third side of this two-sided coin is this: if you are one of those ten in the thousand, and you do not have a gun, there and then statistics mean nothing.

So, what is stopping power? When you find a final, true, convincing answer, let me know.

BELIEF

Science does not consider belief. You can craft any speculation, construct any hypothesis, and test it with an experiment to create a theory. What you believe has nothing to do with the end results. The law, however, does depend on belief in many instances; for our purposes, the reasonable man perspective. That is, given the facts at the moment, did you, and would any reasonable man, believe that you were in immediate danger of serious bodily injury or death (based on the four criteria listed above)? If so, you are accorded, under the law, the authority to use whatever means are at your disposal to prevent that injury or death. This includes lethal force. However, the law also requires that the moment that the danger to you is gone, you must cease your use of lethal force.

This is not the case in many places besides America. In Britain, for instance, the use of lethal force is reserved solely to the Crown and its designated subjects. If you are attacked, even with something potentially lethal, the use of countering

The 9mm cartridge came about with the Luger, because the German Army could not stomach the use of a .30 pistol. Then, and for a long, long time, the 9mm could be found only in FMJ loadings, or softpoints that expanded not at all. Today that is different.

CHAPTER 3: WHAT IS "STOPPING POWER"? | 61

lethal force can land you in a prison of the Crown.

Here in the States, if you live (or are located at the moment) in a jurisdiction that requires retreat before defaulting to the use of lethal force, and you do not, you could face prosecution.

But, and this is the important part, you must reasonably believe you are in danger, where all of the criteria of a lethal force encounter are met.

This is where a good class with an instructor qualified to teach on the subject, or a long talk with an attorney who is up to speed on the subject, would serve you well. And no, not every attorney is "up to speed" on the use of lethal force.

FORCE DYNAMICS

Along with the need to comply with legal requirements before applying lethal force, you have to balance the use with the cessation. Once you have lawfully exceeded the threshold for use, you must (if you are to make the probability of your survival as great as possible) apply as much force as you can bring to bear, for as long as it is necessary, and not a moment longer.

In movies and television, influenced by practical shooting competition (and mainly the movie Director Michael Mann, whom I have met and spoken with on a professional basis, nice guy) viewers expect a shootout to be composed of pairs of shots. Since this is what most competitors do in competition, who would think otherwise? Reality intrudes. You likely will shoot continuously until one or more conditions occur:

- You run out of ammunition.
- The bad guy stops doing what he was doing, that is, being a lethal threat.
- The bad guy disappears from sight.
- You lose the fight from a lucky hit by the bad guy, and cannot continue firing.

The attitude among students of small arms is not unlike the standing orders of an Admiral, early in the sea war with Japan: "Fire at the maximum rate weapons are capable of, until the target changes course, changes shape, or catches on fire." In a lethal force encounter, you do not fire two rounds, stop and assess the effect, and then continue "if you need to."

As a result of the imperative to shoot until the lethal threat is resolved, it is entirely likely that the bad guy will receive multiple wounds from your firing. It is also likely that you will be unable to remember how many rounds you fired. The first is important for the surgeons, the second is important for your attorney. (See above: talking to your attorney before the fact.)

We'll come back to this in a bit.

REAL ESTATE

You've heard the saying about the three most important details of real estate? "Location, location, location." Perhaps trite, but true. Well, the way we use firearms also has a part in the effectiveness of the firearms and ammunition we use. This has been an on-going learning process, in fits and starts, with occasional backward steps.

I have mentioned, and will mention again, the FBI shootout in Miami. Others have as well. But it is not the only learning experience, and not the only famous one. If we were paying full attention to every incident, everything can be a learning experience, but not everyone gets the word, and not everyone learns the same thing from it.

One such instance was the Newhall incident in California back in 1970. Four officers of the California Highway Patrol died there, and much was learned. Also, much was transformed into urban myth, such as "pockets full of empty brass."

What was learned then, and had to be lost, forgotten, not learned, and then re-learned, was that what you learn to do under stress, you do under stress. Learn bad habits (whatever those might be) and you will do bad habit things under stress.

The art of gunfighting is an ongoing

course of study, with new lessons added. Not all of them are relevant for all situations. What a USMC Fire Team learns, busting in steel doors in dusty places, using the tools the Corps gives them, may not be all that relevant to a homeowner trying to keep life, family and property safe in a crime-ridden urban environment.

What does matter is that where the bad guys are shot (speaking anatomically) can be much more important than what they are shot with. And this can color the impression of cartridge effectiveness. We have to keep that in mind when we discuss theories of stopping power.

STOPPING POWER THEORIES

The basic goal of the various speculations on stopping power is an attempt to predict the effectiveness of a given bullet, cartridge, velocity combination. The problem arises when each is either distilled to a clever one-liner, "they all fall to hardball," or pushed to the edges of effectiveness. That is, the ends of the data set.

If we take a hundred, or a thousand, or ten thousand shooting incidents, and we plot the results of each of them, we could construct a graph showing the information. We could plot it any of dozens of different ways, but what most people are interested in is simple: however defined, did the bad guy stop doing what he was doing, as a result of being shot? It's the definition that gets us in trouble.

Did he (not to be sexist, but most of the time it is a he) manage to move from where he was? Or if moving, keep moving in the direction he intended? If so, how far, how fast? Was he able to continue using his weapon? Some would say if he could still try, shooting him was a failure. Others would say that trying but not succeeding is a success for us, as he was stopped from completing his action.

The essence of a theory is that it predicts: a bullet of this diameter and this construction at this velocity will stop a bad guy X percent of the time.

But, that's not all of it. We have to assume, for the purposes of theory construction, that the person shot was struck in a reasonably effective area. No cartridge lopping off a pinky finger can be counted on as a stopper.

PLACEMENT

What matters most, and what someone will invariably bring up in any discussion of stopping power, is placement. A hit to the correct spot works faster, and a hit to a non-correct spot works slower, if at all. There's a classic cartoon on this from the cartoonist Gary Larson, in one of his The Far Side cartoons. The scene: a mammoth, on its back, all four feet in the air, with an arrow sticking out of it. One caveman says to the other, "We should write down that spot."

It is obvious that placement matters, but where is the best location (if we can use "best" in this context) and how much does it matter? To get a handle on that, we have to consider wound formation, which we'll do in the next chapter.

WHAT MATTERS IN A FIGHT, AND HOW BULLETS WORK

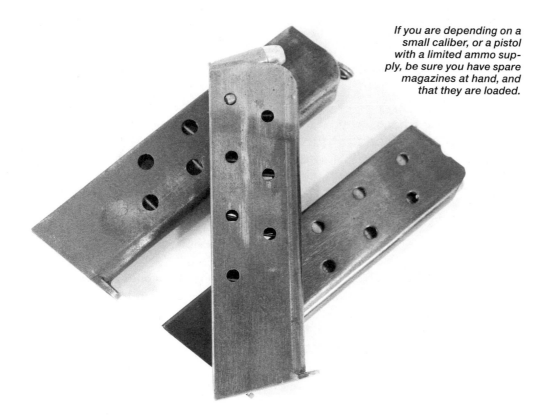

If you are depending on a small caliber, or a pistol with a limited ammo supply, be sure you have spare magazines at hand, and that they are loaded.

The wound formation process is at first glance a matter of simple mechanical dynamics. A bullet enters an object and the velocity of the bullet displaces the existing tissue. That force is also acting on the bullet to slow its progress. This is Newton's First Law, an object at rest will remain at rest unless acted upon by a force. An object in motion will continue in motion unless acted upon by a force.

So, the energy of the bullet is diminished by the act of pushing aside the tissue through which it travels. Additionally, the bullet's motion is diminished by the heat generated by friction (admittedly, a trivial amount in this exercise) and by any change in the shape of the bullet itself. The energy needed to expand an expanding bullet has to come from someplace, and the only place it can come from is the energy the bullet brings along with it.

This is a compound problem, as the energy to deform the bullet comes from the bullet velocity, and the expanded bullet now creates more friction, or drag, and thus slows down more. Once the energy of the bullet has been completely used in damage to the body, expanding the bullet, it stops.

With less deformation, less energy is taken from bullet velocity. Extreme deformation, or breakage, of the bullet creates so much drag that penetration is greatly limited. For those who want a PhD level education in the physics, fluid dynamics and results of bullet penetration, you need to find a copy of Duncan MacPherson's "Bullet Penetration." Fair warning: you may want to tune up your physics, math and mechanical engineering basics to keep up.

The bullet creates two wound tracks, caused by tissue displacement along the axis of travel. It is important to focus on the essential word here, displacement. First is the permanent wound cavity, the tissue directly impacted by the bullet that cannot move out of the way enough, or fast enough, to avoid damage. The second track, which encompasses the Permanent

If you plan to read and learn from MacPherson's book, be sure you have on your math hat.

track, is the temporary wound cavity. The temporary cavity is the tissue moved aside, impelled by the kinetic energy delivered to it by the bullet, and the tissue being displaced by the bullet.

The temporary cavity can be quite impressive, as seen in high-speed video of shots into ballistic gelatin. Looking at a video of a high-velocity (relatively speaking) handgun bullet, watching the gelatin swell, jump, bounce and thrash on the table, you'd think the temporary cavity would be very, very important. It isn't. To understand why, we have to look at human anatomy.

WHAT WE'RE MADE OF

Romantically, and in terms of physics, we're made of star stuff. Mostly we are made of water. The additions, like the alloying constituents of iron, make all the difference.

The structure of the human body, with a very few organs aside, is made of fibrous, flexible, not-really-anchored parts. A lot of the parts of the body can be moved about inside the body, with minor disruption and damage which can be repaired by the body. A bruise? That is the result of broken capillaries, tiny blood vessels, that then clot, repair, and absorb the leaked blood.

The bones are anchored in place (they are, after all, the structure from which everything else is hung) but they are also harder than concrete. The brain and the liver are inflexible, non-compressible and easily damaged by impact or penetration. The rest? They move when pressed.

When a bullet enters the body, the blood vessels that are in the way twist and bend, flex and roll, and get out of the way. In order for the bullet to cause leakage, a blood vessel must be impacted directly, at high enough speed, by a sharp-enough surface or edge, that it cannot escape and gets nicked, cut or severed. Crushing doesn't do much, either, as the clotting of the blood happens almost immediately after an injury. If the clotting works faster than the flow rate, the wound seals.

Time for a visual aid. We've all seen a ream of three-hole punched paper, right? The stack of sheets of paper, with a tunnel of air down the stack for each hole? That's not the hole your bullet makes. Punch a ballpoint pen through a single sheet. Then press the edges back into the hole. That's more like the hole your bullet makes.

The permanent wound thus looks more like a weed-choked ditch, with pieces of automobiles from crashes and discarded appliances along its length, than a smooth, concrete-lined storm chute. Blood will not flow smoothly or quickly through the wound unless a major artery is severed, and the cluttered

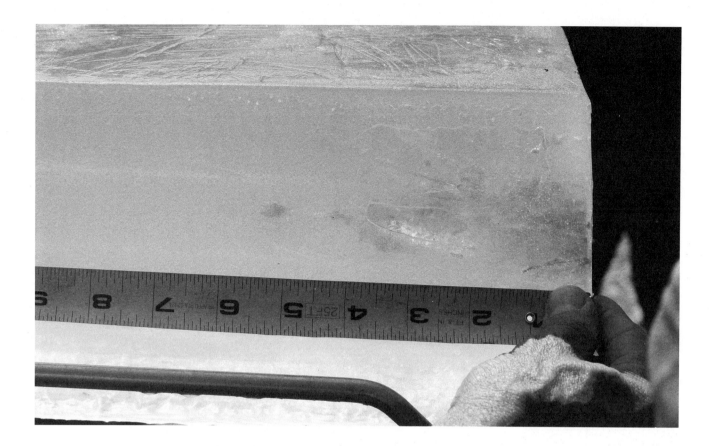

This bullet only penetrated 5.5 inches. It did, however, go through a barrier before. Is this good enough for you? That depends. Will you be shooting bad guys who hide behind walls?

tube can be pressurized.

There's a medical formula for how much IV fluid you can administer to a patient. It is called Poiseuille's law. Empirically derived by Jean Léonard Marie Poiseiulle back in 1838, it tells us, in the short form, that the flow of a fluid through a tube is related to the fourth power. That is, if you double the diameter of the tube, you can produce sixteen times the flow. Wow. You'd think this was an amazing fact, and one of great importance to wound ballistics. Alas, it fades in importance as you look at it.

First, Poiseuille tested this with a smooth pipe and a uniform fluid. It depends on laminar flow, which is where the fluid (or gas) in question flows in smooth layers, with no disruption or interference between the layers. This means the fluid flows slowly at the walls, but faster at the center. There is no turbulence. Thus the larger the diameter, the more water, gas, blood, whatever, is far enough from the tube walls that it doesn't experience the drag experienced by the layers closer to the wall.

Viscous fluids (and blood is nothing if not viscous) do not experience laminar flow. That is, each layer does not flow at its maximum pace, undisturbed by the layers adjacent. Also, the chemical reaction of the body to damage puts systems on high alert, and at the first blush of atmospheric oxygen blood begins clotting. Flow will not necessarily be smooth, even, or at all behaving like Poiseuille predicted.

The organs and other body parts rudely shoved aside by the formation of the temporary cavity may have broken capillaries, and will in essence be bruised as a result, but they will not bleed at anything like the rate needed to cause immediate cessation of hostile activities.

Let's circle back to the need to continue shooting until the threat is gone. Take two extremes: one is a cartridge, bullet and placement where one solid shot causes the bad guy to drop and stop fighting. If he survives until EMS arrives,

CHAPTER 4: WHAT MATTERS IN A FIGHT, AND HOW BULLETS WORK | **67**

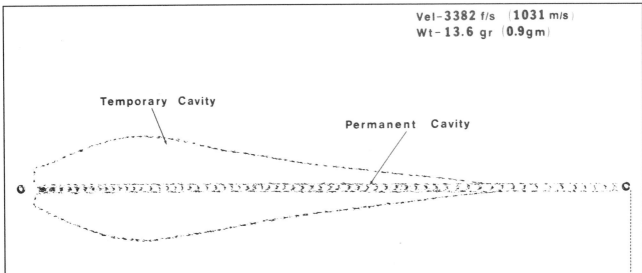

Fig. 2. Wound profile produced by a steel sphere. Observe that little or no cavitation occurs in the last 15 cm of penetration. This last part of the sphere's path corresponds to what is observed in battlefield casualty, yet most wound ballistics researchers who use this projectile concentrate exclusively on the initial part of the path. The cavitation effects of the first part of the projectile path are not seen in fragment wounds of the wounded combat casualty and the cavitation effects produced by rifle bullets occur at a deeper depth of penetration. Although the sphere does produce easily repeatable results, unfortunately these results do not reproduce battlefield type wounds.

Bullets (in this instance a sphere) displace water. The temporary displacement is not usually useful, in handguns. Image courtesy the late Dr. Martin Fackler.

he'll likely survive to the hospital. And if he's still alive when they wheel him into the OR, his chances of surviving are better than nine in ten. The surgeons have one wound to probe, diagnose, repair and close. And that wound is likely to have a bullet at the end of it, a bullet the surgeons can extract, leave in place, or put a hold on for later removal.

At the other extreme we have a cartridge and bullet that didn't stop well, and thus required a dozen hits before the bad guy stopped. (We can safely say this was an FMJ or LRN (lead round nose bullet).) First, this takes longer to occur, and until he stops fighting the EMS can't come and start plugging leaks. Second, he has a dozen wounds and each is most likely a through-and-through, that is, they entered and then exited. EMS techs will have to basically swaddle him with every piece of gauze, dressing and bandage they have on the truck to try and plug all the holes. In the hospital, even if none is a major artery-severing event, he is bleeding from a dozen places and only two surgeons can reach in and work at any given time.

One could rationally argue that a massively expanding bullet is a better stopper, less lethal (not in the sense of pepper spray or a Taser) and more humane.

What matters in a fight is that the bullet(s) you launch strike an important-enough part of your opponent and cause him to stop doing whatever he was doing when you found it necessary to shoot.

HOW DO BULLETS DO THAT?

We have discussed the permanent and temporary cavities, but only as they pertain to stopping-power theories. What we need to know is, how do bullets do their work, and what matters in that process?

Water is what's known as an "incompressible medium." It cannot be compressed into a smaller volume. It is not

Ammo selection depends on the situation. If you lived in a house built like this church in Greece, (like every other house in that small town) there is nothing you could own that would shoot through those walls. If, however, you live in a frame house in suburbia, over-penetration is something to consider.

alone in this (the other being the metals of which your bullets are composed), but it is one that matters at the moment. Humans are mostly water, something you might remember from science class. There are greater densities than water, and some lesser, in the human body, and there are structures that are stronger and more brittle than water. But, keep that in mind that fact that we are mostly water as we discuss the effects of bullets on and in water. We'll use water as a first approximation to understand bullet dynamics.

When a bullet strikes water, the water moves. However, the water has mass and experiences inertia. It takes time for the water to move. This resistance to movement potentially does two things to the bullet: slows it down and deforms it. Now, a stoutly constructed full metal jacket bullet (FMJ) will resist deformation. It was built to do exactly that, in order to increase penetration. The bullet also pushes water ahead of it. Water, being a fluid, will then move aside, out of the path of the bullet.

The inertia of the water as it moves creates a compression gradient in front of the bullet. This is not compressed water as in a smaller volume, but compressed as in a more-resistant-to-movement substance. It is also a pressure gradient that can break things as it passes through them. (Don't celebrate just yet.)

With the bullet moving forward, the pressure gradient appears as a cone, expanding from the source but trailing the bullet in its path. Exactly like the sonic boom or shock wave you may have seen in illustrations of planes or bullets moving through air.

The lack of movement of water creates drag on the forward movement of the bullet. This drag is what brings a bullet to a stop in sufficient water, or sufficient person.

The inertia of the water also can deform the bullet, if the bullet is constructed to deform or is not strong enough to withstand the forces acting upon it. A hollow-point bullet (HP) or a jacketed hollow point (JHP) bullet is designed to expand.

An example of a bullet not designed to expand, but which cannot withstand the forces working on it, is the 55-grain full metal jacket boat tail (FMJBT) used in the .223 Remington or 5.56x45. The FMJBT is used in rifles with a certain twist rate.

CHAPTER 4: WHAT MATTERS IN A FIGHT, AND HOW BULLETS WORK | **69**

They are stable in air, but they are not gyroscopically stable once they enter a denser medium, that is, water. The bullet begins to yaw (turn sideways, essentially) and is not strong enough to withstand the forces acting upon it as it travels sideways. It breaks in half at the cannelure (a ring impressed around the bullet as a location for the case neck to be crimped).

This dynamic is not available for the handgun cartridge. Handgun bullets do not travel at nearly the speed needed to cause them to fragment after yawing. Plus, their rotational speed is so great they cannot yaw quickly enough to matter in a defensive application. Finally, they are not long enough, as a ratio of their diameter, for them to break when traveling sideways, should they yaw.

So, they can only expand if specifically designed to expand. Compressed water on the front face of the bullet cannot move away from the bullet quickly enough, and the water thus acts as a barrier upon which the bullet upsets itself, dissipating the energy that is "trapped" in the space at the front of the bullet. The water, compressed but not diminished in volume, exerts a force upon the bullet and the force can only act in one of three ways: movement of water, movement of metal, and heat.

Why, then, do FMJ bullets not upset or have their noses pushed back? The angle of the interaction between water and bullet allows the water to slide aside. Plus, the surface area at the tip of the bullet is far too small to act as a lever upon the tip of the bullet, and begin deforming the metal there.

As a bullet expands, it offers more and more drag to the movement of the water and deforms more, until as the velocity drops, the compression at the interface falls below the level needed to deform the bullet metal. At that point, the only force left to act is drag, and bullet slows to a stop, having deformed as much as it will earlier in its path.

The earliest expanding bullet designs suffered from several problems. The designers were familiar with the performance of bullets in rifle applications. How to make a .30-30 bullet expand on a deer was a problem solved well before WWII. Doing the same for handgun bullets didn't happen for another half century. Those early designs also lacked velocity and customer demand. A .38 Special bullet, to take one example, was

We all practice "house-clearing" because it is fun and teaches valuable lessons. The most valuable: don't do it. Phone the police, get behind cover, and wait for them to arrive. Only the direst of circumstances will require that you go out and find the bad guys.

not exactly fast. A 158-grain lead round nosed bullet (LRN) in a .38 might go 700 fps, back in the old days. Putting on a stout jacket and adding a hollowpoint was not going to make that bullet expand, not at 700 fps. Even making the jacket thinner wouldn't help until the hollow point dimensions and angles had been experimented with, to discover what worked. That and going with a lighter bullet, one that could be driven faster.

Drop the weight to 125 grains, up the velocity to nearly 1,000 fps, and make the nose angles and jacket the appropriate dimensions, and expansion is much more consistent and much more likely. Taking a bullet of that weight and putting it into a .357 Magnum, where it can be fired at over 1,200 fps, assures expansion.

Therein lies the trap that many fall into. The trap is the thought that velocity, being necessary for expansion, is a good thing in and of itself. By adding velocity, you always add terminal effectiveness. Not so.

The inertia of moving water pushes aside the water adjacent to it. This creates the temporary cavity you see touted in high-velocity loadings.

The amount of pounds per square inch (PSI) in the compression wave varies, depending on the shape of the bullet and the speed of impact. A smooth, rounded, "pointy" round-nose bullet will efficiently and smoothly push the water to the sides, and thus will penetrate more deeply. This is the very definition of the 9mm bullet in many loadings. It is pointy for a number of reasons. A pointy bullet is easier to fabricate, as it will come out of the nose-forming dies more readily. It will be longer for its weight, and this makes the loading ballistician's job easier. A longer bullet, limited in overall length, creates a smaller combustion chamber. This provides a space that requires less powder and a more-consistent ignition. Less powder matters? Yes. If you load a million rounds, and you have "only" decreased the powder charge by two-tenths of a grain due to the smaller combustion chamber, in the course of loading a million rounds you will have saved almost 29 pounds of powder. If, as a commercial loader, you can buy powder at the cost of $8 a pound, that's a savings of $230. If you say, "$230 dollars in a million rounds isn't much," you just failed your job interview to work in an ammunition plant.

The pointier bullet also feeds more reliably in pistols. When customers blame anyone but themselves for a failure to feed, the last thing an ammo maker wants

Round-nose bullets push fluid aside. The wider the flat, and the sharper the shoulder, the less-gently fluid is shoved aside, thus increasing wounding.

A semi-wadcutter (SWC) has a nose, long or short, and a bore-diameter shoulder.

is a reputation as a lousy ammo maker.

A pointy bullet causes the water to move aside more smoothly, and the curve of the compression wave is a sharply angled cone, where the tip is a small rounded cap.

So, pointy bullets penetrate deeper. That's not necessarily what we want.

A flat spot on the tip of the bullet, known as a meplat, changes the shape of the compression wave. The flat makes the rounded cap of the compression cone widen and less rounded. The larger the flat, the greater this effect. The compressed water ahead of the bullet offers a greater force to create deformation of the bullet and increased drag to stop the bullet sooner in the water. The way to make bullets perform better when they do not expand is to create a flat spot (the meplat) on them, and the larger the better.

This leads to the inevitable question: does that mean a full wadcutter is the best in this regard? Yes, it is. Then why not make all bullets with full wadcutter profiles? Because pistols won't feed them, and reloading them into revolvers under stress is not easy.

What about semi-wadcutters (SWC)? SWCs have a long nose, a flat top, and a ring or shoulder around the long nose, just above the case mouth. SWCs work, but the nose does all the work. The shoulder does not, as the compression wave has been created ahead of it, and as a result there is a vacuum between the nose and shoulder, or at the least, a normal-pressure area that is not adding to the compression formation or damage to the water.

Then why the SWC? The shoulder does two things for the SWC bullet and the cartridge in which it resides. First, by providing a bullet-diameter ring ahead of the case, the bullet is already resting into the forward part of the revolver chamber and filling it. The bullet does not have to slide forward out of the case to enter that area, part of it is already there.

The second thing the shoulder does dates back to Elmer Keith and the development of the .44 Magnum. By making his bullets in the SWC shape, he gained the above advantage for accuracy, but he also put more of the bullet weight out of the case, enlarging the combustion chamber. "But, the chamber is better smaller, you said so above." Yes, there. But what Keith was trying to do, back in the 1920s, was use rifle powders in his .44 Special cases. Those powders had a slower burn rate than handgun powders,

but they were also bulkier. He needed more room in order to use those slower-burning powders and generate the velocity he was looking for.

The end result of the "long, heavy bullet, with a flat point" is the line of bullets designed by Veral Smith, with combinations of Long, Wide and Flat in their designation. Where a standard LRN in the .44 Special, back in the 1920s and until today, weighs 246 grains, Keith got his bullets to be 250 grains, but more of the shape, and thus the mass and volume, was out of the case. A Cast Performance Wide Flat Nose Gas Check bullet, in .44, weighs as much as 320 grains, and out of a strong-enough handgun can be accelerated to over 1,000 fps. The "lightweights" in the .44 line are a mere 255 grains, but they are wide on the meplat.

Curiously, while the large meplat does more damage to the water, it does not seem to decrease penetration much, if at all.

As an example, I have fired a lot of handgun bullets into ballistic gelatin and Clear Ballistic gel. I have not yet been able to capture the deepest-penetrating handgun bullets in a pair of rifle blocks. Those are the ones that measure 8x8x18 inches. A .45 ACP loaded with H&G 68 bullets, a 200-grain, hard lead SWC, does not stay inside of the 36 inches of gelatin those blocks represent. The velocity doesn't matter, unless I load them way down. At standard USPSA/IPSC velocities (850-900 fps) they exit the back of the blocks. The vanilla-plan and common load for the .40, a truncated cone of 180 grains, at 900 fps, does the same.

An expanding .45 or .40 stops inside of a handgun block, which measures 6x6x16 inches.

What stops the expanding bullet? Increased drag. An expanding .45 bullet, for example, that goes from .451 inch in diameter to .600 inch (not uncommon, today) has increased its frontal area by 75%.

But, what matters is the damage done to the water.

TISSUE DAMAGE

Now let's stop using water as a euphemism and get back to the task at hand: wound creation.

The human body is composed of various tissues, most of which are quite flexible, fibrous and tough. Were it not, the massage you get at the spa could be fatal. If pushing your parts out of normal placement and letting them move back was damaging, your physician couldn't touch you. So, it is not the temporary cavity

The heavier the bullet, the more momentum it delivers. The wider the meplat, the more it wounds. In terminal ballistics, more is more.

The idea with a handgun is to create as much tissue disruption as possible, within the depth of the human body. Energy, momentum, whatever, that the bullet takes with it when it exits is generally viewed as wasted.

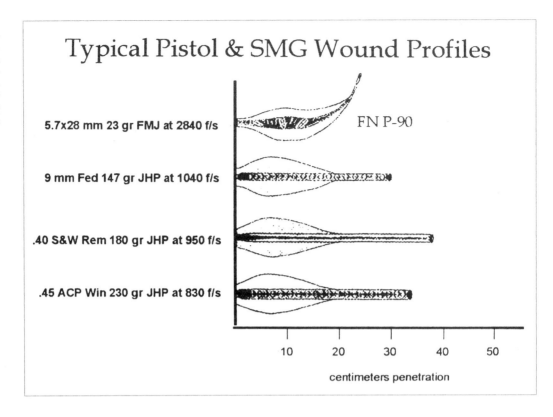

that matters, but the permanent one.

Now, some structures cannot be moved or subjected to more than minimal stress. One is the liver, which is not all that flexible. It is, however, composed of five lobes, and you can apparently damage four of them, have them surgically removed, and grow back the missing mass. Wow. The brain is another, but it is not so amenable to damage. It is, however, enclosed in a very strong structure, designed to shield the brain from injury. That's the skull, and reference articles books and medical literature are filled with examples of patients who received a gunshot to the head, only to have the bullet skid off the skull.

Bones are another brittle structure, but bones are not always a vital factor in staying in or leaving a fight.

The vital structures are the arterial system and the brain stem. With sufficient blood loss a human body will cease activity, regardless of the wishes of the occupant. That is the primary reason defensive trainers, police and others insist on a larger caliber. It is a simple matter of physics: a bigger bullet makes a bigger permanent cavity, and that increases the likelihood of striking a major artery and inducing rapid blood loss.

As mentioned earlier, Poiseuille's law dictates that a larger permanent wound will dramatically increase blood loss, but only if the wound edges are clean and it strikes an artery. In this instance, close does not count and you do not get partial credit.

The wound is created when the local compression wave, in front of the bullet, is great enough to break the cell walls of the tissue in front of it. Just as your organs are tough, so are your cells. They can withstand a certain amount of pressure before the cell wall breaks and the important parts turn into goo.

If the pressure is below that threshold, the cell is simply compressed, rebounds, and continues on. Tissue and cells far enough from the axis of the bullet path will not be compressed enough to be damaged. They will be displaced, but not broken. (With the exceptions we've already mentioned.) Once the bullet slows

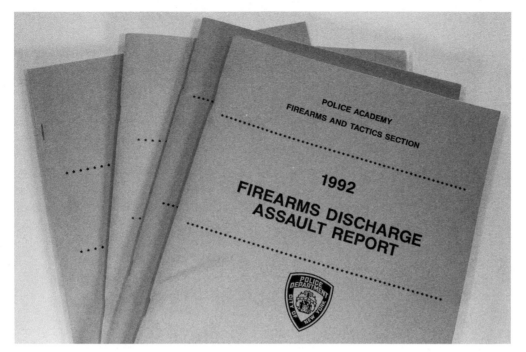

There was a time when you could get the NYPD shooting reports summaries just by asking. Now, need a contact in a police department, and even then NYPD would be annoyed if they found out how you got your copy. Useful information, but remember, these are the results of law enforcement, not home defense.

down enough to drop the compression wave below the disruption threshold, damage ceases. As with the displacement, the bullet then slides the last part of its path, pushing tissue aside but not crushing the cells of which it is composed.

Structural and operational components, such as arteries, veins and bones, are similarly treated. An artery or vein is not severed unless the bullet strikes it directly enough that it cannot twist out of the way. Otherwise, it will twist, bend, move and not leak afterwards.

Bones, with a much higher threshold of strength, require a great deal of force. Imagine a car on the freeway, veering off the road and hitting a bridge post or pier. If the car strikes a glancing blow to the concrete pillar, there may be only cosmetic damage to the bridge support. The car, on the other hand, will be mangled, and you might think, looking at it, that the concrete pillar was also damaged that much.

The vehicle must impact the pillar directly, and with great force, to damage the pillar. And even then, the bridge will stand.

Bones are much the same. Not many handgun cartridges generate enough force to break bones, especially the largest bones. And a broken bone, while no picnic, is not enough to keep you out of a fight. (Personal experience tells me that.)

Only tissue that is damaged counts. And the nature of the damage influences the potential blood loss as predicted by Poiseuille's law. Remember all the ruptured cells, along the bullet path? They act to block outward flow. Unless you sever an artery, which can generate enough pressure to push the blood out, the wound track of a gunshot is more likely to be an oozing mess than a clean pipe jetting blood out into the air.

Wounds such as those do not help to stop a threat; we need hits to vital areas. But, where are they?

WHERE TO HIT?

The problem is one of probabilities and not marksmanship. You see, we can make the "A" zone on a target any size we want and that won't change the essential randomness of a firearms-involved personal altercation.

The goal is simple: to make the bad guy stop doing bad things, as quickly as possible. When it comes to marksmanship and target design there are two approaches, and their adherents are not of a mind to compromise. One is the "real world" target design approach. That is, to make the important parts of the target smaller than we'd like for personal gratification, in some instances to make them "anatomically correct." The other is to use a size that seems reasonable, and to improve speed, to the point of seeming out of control when shooting.

The anatomy-oriented designers delineate the heart, aorta and the major arteries on the target. Miss the half-inch-wide superior vena cava on the target and your score on the shooting exercise is marked as "Fail." Anyone care to point out the problems with this? That's right, the SVC is not marked on a human being. And, it is not in the exact same place on each of us. Plus, the angle at which you shoot the target/person/felon/whomever determines if the SVC is actually on the line of the wound track or just slightly off of it.

Finally, you could very well have placed your shot exactly on the surface, directly axial to the SVC, and the bullet veered ever so slightly off the line and missed the superior vena cava. Oops.

Anatomical targets present a false sense of precision. Plus, they encourage slower shooting.

The other approach is to provide a "good enough" scoring area and encourage a faster shooting pace. As a result, more shots fired increase the chances of hitting something important.

The idea is that probability will stick a great big oar into your efforts; that your perfectly-aimed and fired shot, meant to directly strike the superior vena cava, will be thwarted by a last-second movement of your opponent. Or diverted just slightly by the cheap, disposable, ballpoint pen in his pocket. Since you cannot count on any one shot being sufficient, you fire enough shots to make up for the muddying effects of probability and expect that at least one of them will work.

This also accounts for the fact that not all human bodies are the same, nor have the same effect/reward for your efforts. However, there are other external variables at work.

A suitable target might be, for instance, a 3"x5" card, placed on a human outline to represent the upper center of the thoracic zone. That's good idea for an effective level of marksmanship, until you as the instructor/range officer find that 75% of your department's officers can't hit it under even the slightest stress or even partially limited time. The Chief/Sheriff is not going to be happy about the time and effort needed to get them all up to speed and keep them there. And the city or county isn't going to be happy about the money (both in ammunition and time of officers/deputies off work and on the range) that your level of marksmanship requires.

This is how the common police targets, such as the federal "blue man" target, end up being so large. The larger allowed area considered "good enough" encourages and rewards a faster shooting pace. Made too large, it encourages and does not penalize sloppy shooting.

Make the target too small, and the shooting pace becomes too slow for real-world applications. How large, and what shape should the target be? That's a question outside the scope of this book, but my take is this: anything larger than half a sheet of copy paper is too large, and if it isn't placed so it sits with the top edge at or above the collar bones, it is too low.

Shot location can make a difference in the short term, as well. In the Miami shootout, Matix received a head shot from Agent McNeill. This shot, from the FBI 38 Special+P load, fractured Matix' skull in several places and stunned him through most of the fight. He did recover consciousness well enough to exit the car, but not well enough to re-join the fight.

To circle back to an earlier discussion, does this count as a "stop" or not? Matix had enough function to move, leave

We all like to think we will only use the best to be had. However, not everyone has the luxury of expensive guns for defense. This Davis .380 will work for its owner, as long as the owner doesn't require thousands of rounds of practice a year. We can't recommend "a magazine a year of shooting" as a practice routine, but a lot of people do just that. Or less. Ammo costs money, and some people don't have much. They should have the tools of defense, also.

the driver's seat, exit the vehicle, but not fight. Was it because his vision kept him from seeing well enough to engage? Could he, in a befuddled state, just not decide what to do?

We'll never know, but even "effective" hits are not always enough.

ENERGY

The proponents of energy, and by extension, temporary cavity, talk about "hydrostatic shock" and shock waves. The idea is simple. The displaced tissue, being mostly water, causes a compression wave to travel through the body. This compression wave disrupts the body's systems, or causes damage, or displaces organs, causing pain and damage.

As one who has personally found that pain is not a compliance tool, pain caused by a wound has to be off the charts before I would depend on it. Compression waves are an inefficient way of transferring energy to the body. As a flippant example, kidney stones are shattered by sound waves, and no one who has had their kidney stones broken by the Lithotripter has been so stunned by the sound that they are incapacitated.

The velocity handguns can generate is insufficient to produce shock by velocity. The best you could ever do, if you hot-rodded something like a Soviet 7.62x25 cartridge, would be to boost that little 86-grain bullet to just under 2,000 fps. The early smokeless rifle cartridge did that. The classic for us is the .30 Krag, the .30-40 or .30 U.S. Army.

A contemporary was the Spanish 7x57, which was used by the Spanish troops in Cuba and the Philippines. None other than Teddy Roosevelt mentioned the lack of stopping by the Mauser, as mentioned in Phil Sharpe's book "The Rifle in America": "The [7 mm] Mauser bullets themselves made a small clean hole, with the result that the wound healed in a most astonishing manner. One or two of our men who were shot in the head had the skull blown open, but elsewhere the wounds from the minute steel-coated bullet, with its very high velocity, were certainly nothing like as serious as those made by the old large-caliber, low-power rifle. If a man was shot through the heart, spine, or brain he was, of course, killed instantly; but very few of the wounded died even under the appalling

Expensive, rare, or competition-oriented handguns can be used for defense, but don't get them because you think you "need" them. A hi-cap pistol, a titanium-framed one, or a rare German police trade-in should not be among your first choices.

conditions which prevailed, owing to the lack of attendance and supplies in the field-hospitals with the army."

Much the same phenomenon was seen with the U.S. Army use of the Krag in the Philippines. Unless a Moro was hit in the spine or head, the 220-grain round-nosed FMJ bullet of the Krag would poke a hole straight through and the Moro would not stop.

The change happened as much through inadvertence as anything else. The change here in the U.S. mirrored that of other countries. The .30-03, with a 220-grain bullet with a muzzle velocity of 2,300 fps (book value, probably more like 2,150), was changed in 1906 to a 150-grain spitzer, at a velocity of 2,700 fps. The new bullet had a flatter trajectory, allowing a greater effective range with fewer problems from errors in range estimation, but best of all, better stopping. The pointed shape of the spitzer puts the center of mass behind the center of form, and as a result, when the bullet strikes tissue, its own unbalanced shape causes it to yaw, or tumble.

Alas, this is a form of wounding and energy transfer that is unavailable to handgun users. Bullets cannot be made long enough, and cannot be pushed to fast-enough velocities, for this to be at all useful.

Keep this in mind when assessing the performance of a cartridge or bullet; the permanent wound cavity is the only one that counts.

URBAN MYTHS ON BULLET PERFORMANCE

HEAT
We've all heard the description "hot lead" referring to bullets. Yes, they are heated by the experience, but the amount of heat they deliver is utterly inconsequential to the wound they create. Do you really think that the equivalent of a first-degree burn (which is about all a bullet might muster) is going to make any difference in a wound track that is a foot or more deep, and half an inch in diameter?

It isn't.

ROTATION
I've read over-wrought descriptions of hollowpoint bullets by anti-gunners who really don't have a clue about the technical matters of firearms. Let's use a high-speed 9mm as an example. At a speed of 1,150 fps and a twist rate of one turn in ten inches (the fastest you're going to find in a 9mm, most will be one in sixteen), the bullet will be rotating at 69,000 rpm. That sounds perfectly horrible, as a wounding mechanism.

And yet. Don't look at it as a function of time (rpm) but as a function of distance, the twist rate. It will rotate, if it is not hindered, one time in ten inches of wound travel. All of a sudden, imaginative mental images of a high-speed 9mm drill bit disappear. And, it can't rotate the full turn in nine inches of travel if it is experiencing resistance from the medium through which it is traveling.

LEAD POISONING
Yes, lead is bad for the body. But a bullet left in the body is not a slow poison. The body encapsulates foreign objects that cannot be expelled, and surgeons know this. If a bullet left in place will cause no further damage, or less damage than the cutting to remove it, they'll often leave it in place. The number of people walking around with bullets, bullet fragments, etc. left in their bodies might surprise you.

5
HISTORY OF STOPPING POWER FORMULAS

When smokeless powder came about, a lead bullet of 85 grains was going 800 fps. With a smokeless boost and a jacket, it could now go 1,200 fps. Was that useful, or a distraction? We've spent a century since trying to figure that out.

I know I just threw cold water all over the very idea of stopping power, but if you're going to have a clue about the arguments that will rage at the gun shop, the gun club, gun shows, and Internet forums, you need a bit of history. And messy it is. This all pretty much started with the advent of smokeless powder. Before smokeless powder, you had one choice if you wanted to improve your odds — go bigger. Black powder, simply due to the way it combusts, has an upper limit on velocity of about 1,400 fps. No matter how much more powder you used, that was as much as speed as you got.

So the Revolutionary War, just to pick a historical mile marker, was fought with smoothbore muskets, .75 inch and shooting round balls of lead. That's right, if you read about George and the crew they were fighting with what amounted to 12-gauge shotguns, loaded with deer slugs. Guns that they had to load one shot at a time. Rifles were smaller-caliber, a lot slower to load, and offered accuracy. A "small bore" rifle might be a .40 or .45.

What about the accuracy difference? A smoothbore musket fired at a man standing 100 yards away might hit him one shot out of ten or twenty, depending on how tightly the ball in its paper pouch fit the bore, how often the bore was cleaned, and how uniformly the bore and the ten or twenty balls had been made. A rifle could be counted on to hit him five or six times out of ten, more if you scrubbed the bore frequently. Then why muskets? A trained soldier could load and fire two shots a minute from a musket, three if he was really good at it. A rifle? Most were lucky to do one a minute. So, how long does it take you to sprint 100 yards, bayonet extended? Wars then were fought between infantry units with mass volleys followed by a bayonet charge.

By the time of the Civil War, calibers had gone down and rifling had been adopted en-mass. A rifled musket of the time was .58 caliber, but still one-shot, muzzle-loaded, and produced billows of smoke. The Minie ball, a hollow-base bullet that expanded on firing to grip the rifling, made it as fast to load as a musket

CHOOSING HANDGUN AMMO | **81**

and as accurate as a rifle. In the Civil War (American version), it was not uncommon for units to stand fast in formation, 100 or 200 yards apart, and pour accurate rifle fire into each other. The first one to break and charge usually lost.

Just before smokeless powder was invented and adopted, military rifles had gotten down to the range of bullet in .40 to .45 inch in diameter, using fixed cartridges, and some experimenters were working on repeating mechanisms. It took almost 200 years to go from a reliable smoothbore flintlock musket to a repeating cartridge rifle, from the early 1700s to 1880-90. In the ten years after the invention of smokeless powder, almost all armies of the world switched to the new stuff. Those at the tail end of that change were so hidebound or strapped for cash that they took longer, but only by a few years. Soldiers and armies had six generations to learn the tactical use of big-bore black powder arms. A West Point cadet graduating in the year Custer disappeared underneath a surge of Indians would, before he retired, see black powder and single shot rifles disappear, replaced by repeating, smokeless powder-using rifles and belt-fed machine guns in service.

The velocity of the earliest smokeless powder rifle loads was 2,000 fps. Later, bullet design and further powder changes would bring that up to as much as 2,700 fps. But those were rifles. What about handguns? They, for the most part, stayed in the exact same velocity ranges when transiting from black powder to smokeless. Why?

The main reason is chamber pressure. Generally speaking, the maximum chamber pressure a black powder cartridge can generate is in the 14-15,000 PSI range. When smokeless powder came about, rifle actions could contain those pressures, in the 40-45,000 PSI range, that those cartridges produced. Improved steels and improved designs kept them intact at the higher pressures, which later moved even higher. Handguns, however, could not. It was relatively easy (though it didn't seem so at the time) to design a rifle to contain 45,000 PSI. After all, you've got eight pounds or so of steel and walnut to work with. Handguns, on the other hand, are useful because of their compactness and portability. An eight-pound handgun isn't either of those.

Improvements in steel and design allowed some increase in useable pressures, but not much. The magnums and hot numbers such as the 9mm Parabellum operate with a pressure ceiling in the mid-30,000 PSI. There's also the matter of felt recoil. Yes, handguns can be designed to contain pressures in the 40,000+ PSI range, but they face a procrustean choice: if they stay medium-bore, 9mm or so, they simply add velocity.

If you take, as an example, a 9mm Parabellum handgun driving a 125-grain bullet at 1,150 fps and increase the pressure, you can net yourself another 200 fps or so. 1,350 fps is brisk, but not earth shattering. If you take a .45 ACP (with a pressure ceiling of 23,000 PSI in +P trim) and up the pressure, you can lift a 230-grain bullet from 850 fps to 1,000 or 1,100 fps, at which point it becomes a difficult handgun to learn and master. A 230 at 1,100 is just below the bottom of the .44 Magnum range in performance, and the .44 isn't exactly the first choice of EDC handguns, outside of the bear-thick regions of Alaska.

As a result, while a handgun is comforting as a back up to a shotgun or a rifle, by itself it was a pretty weak reed,

Bullets do what physics require. You need velocity to expand bullets. This most-excellent JHP was found next to a 300-meter target (yes, we were shooting at it) and it is unexpanded. At 300 meters, it had lost enough velocity that the soft soil it impacted did not make it expand. Regardless of whatever else you have, you must have enough speed.

by comparison. This explains the intense interest in measuring "stopping power." If you have to depend on a not-too-powerful tool, you want it to be the best of the poor choices offered.

And to keep the details in mind, a reminder: turn-of-the-century smokeless powder pistol cartridges often favored speed over mass. The .30 Luger (aka 7.65 Luger) fired an 86-grain bullet up to 1,200 fps. The 7.63 Mauser used the same bullet, but at over 1,200. The later 7.62x25 Tokarev upped that to 1,300. The 9mm Parabellum was a 124 at 1,100, the Browning-designed .38 Auto a 130 at 1,100. They were all in much the same workspace: a .30-32-inch diameter bullet, weighing under 90 grains and going over 1200 fps; or a .38-9mm bullet in the 115 to 130 grains weight range, at around 1100 fps.

They were soft in recoil, shot flat, and fast to reload. But did they "stop"?

THEORIES, SCALES AND CHARTS

The idea that we can test and rank various calibers and bullet designs on a scale and determine which is "best" is very alluring. In the early days it was easy. How big was it and how big a powder charge did it use? In fact, the first rifle cartridges were named in exactly that way. Well, at least the Winchester ones were. The .45-70? A .45 caliber bullet using 70 grains of military powder. (There was only black powder back then, so there was no need to call it "black powder." Now, we have to.) And so on, with the .44-40 and .38-40, both handgun cartridges but also used in rifles, as well as the .32-20, .45-75, .40-65. You get the point.

Once velocities exceeded the usual black powder ranges, diameter and weight were just part of the effectiveness of a cartridge. But, how to account for the effects of velocity?

The military was much taken with smokeless powder, and not just because of the loss of smoke. Higher velocities meant flatter trajectories. Where before, even with a rifled musket, a range of 300 yards was the maximum for a standard service rifle, now there could be much more. A good rifleman could command open ground out to 1,000 yards, and with a flat-enough trajectory the inevitable small errors in range estimation didn't matter.

Handguns, on the other hand, were still used almost entirely inside of 50

Knowledge is good, knowledge is powerful, but not all knowledge is equally useful. Elmer Keith was a master and pioneer, but what he learned about big-game hunting does not translate to home defense. Hatcher was brilliant, but the latest info he provides is over three-quarters of a century old at this point. Be careful of your sources.

yards. And the vast majority of those uses, even military, would be at ten yards and less. The flatter trajectory of a 7.63 Mauser cartridge out of a pistol meant nothing at those distances.

In collecting information over the decades, I've come across a number of books and magazine articles detailing the various theories. In talking with others I've heard even more, and there are, depending on how you differentiate the various approaches, around two dozen theories of how to calculate stopping power. The approaches run the gamut. Duncan McPherson looks at it from the viewpoint of a literal rocket scientist, with Bachelors and Masters degrees in Mechanical Engineering. Evans and Sanow look at it from street level, collating data. Others take a more theoretical approach, attempting to assign various weights in effectiveness to diameter, bullet shape, velocity, expansion and more.

The fault lines of stopping power theories can be seen in almost all variables. There is the energy vs. momentum split. There's the caliber split, with bigger being better, except when it comes to number of shots available. There's the bullet weight matter, again with bigger being better, but opponents object to excess penetration. With bullet shape, proponents of large meplats are pitted against hollowpoints that now work. And, back to bigger is better, the smaller-caliber mention of expansion is met with, "A 9mm can expand, but a .45 never shrinks." A lot of the division is driven by two things: turf and clinging to assumed facts or singular incidents.

Someone who has had a singular experience with one or the other will be loath to give it up. If a police officer, for example, has used a 9mm (or his partner, or shift buddy, or fill in the blank) and on that instance the single shot put the bad guy down like a bolt of lightning, then well, you know what his opinion is going to be. Someone who is struck by a given design or numerical factor as their initial learning experience in a subject is also going to use it as a guidepost. It is simple human nature.

Let's look at a rundown in more-or-less historical order of the various theories, and then review their shortcomings. With that as background we'll move on, and you will have a bit of knowledge about each of the theories, so when the subject comes up you know what's what.

Now, when you study a theory and then tell those involved where they were wrong, you get a certain amount of pushback. My approach to this, and a lot of other areas, is simple: I don't have to be a CPA to know when a checkbook balances or not. I don't have to be a graduate of a musical conservatory to know when someone hits a wrong note. And if you must have actually shot people in order to have a say in what stopping power is, then there will not be many approved theorists.

That said, let's go back more than a century and see where it all started.

THOMPSON-LAGARDE & HATCHER

Late in the 19th century, the U.S. Army had succumbed to the lure of the .38 and found it wanting. The blame is usually laid at the feet of the Philippine Expedition and the Moro warriors who were on the other side in that conflict. The .38 then in use, the .38 Long Colt, was a 150-grain lead round-nose at a nominal 750 fps. It probably didn't really deliver 750 fps, and while not exactly a brick, it was not nothing. The story goes that Moros would "soak up" many hits and not stop.

At this point I have to wonder, half a century before, the Civil War was fought in great part with .36-caliber cap-and-ball pistols. Their ballistics were, you guessed it, pretty much the same as the .38 Colt. So all of sudden in the 1890s it isn't enough? And it isn't enough on smaller combatants than those involved in the Civil War? Ah, but they were "on drugs" and "worked themselves into a frenzy." Previously retired .45 Colt revolvers were pressed into service, and the troops were much happier.

I suspect we were seeing the first documented case of "placement is what counts" in action. I've read some of the accounts. Yes, a Moro would take all six hits from a revolver, but many or all would be peripheral hits. The rifle used then wasn't a big help, either. The Krag rifle, firing the .30 Army or .30-40 Krag, used a 220-grain, FMJ round-nosed bullet at about 2,000 fps. Think high-speed knitting needle. Now, place yourself in the shoes of a trooper armed with a Colt SAA instead of a Colt .38. A screaming Moro is charging you, machete poised overhead. You've got time for one shot and no time for a second. You'll focus on the front sight and put that 255-grain lead .45-caliber bullet right through his sternum. Will he be stopped? The odds are pretty high, right?

The Cavalry also drove the change. Cavalry was the branch of service back then closest to what the Seals/Socom/SF/Rangers are today. It was the prestigious arm of the service, and back then they had one goal – to stop the other side's cavalry. (Not so much today, but then, not many horses are seen in combat these days, either.) If you want to bring down a mount, a .45 is a lot more useful than a .38. The Cavalry wanted a .45, so the Cavalry got a .45 in the upcoming pistol trials. But, someone had to prove that it was superior. Enter Thompson and LaGarde.

In 1904, Colonel John Thompson (yes, of Tommygun fame) and Major Louis LaGarde set about terminal ballistics testing. Thompson, Infantry, and LaGarde, Medical Corps, visited a Chicago stockyard/slaughterhouse with essentially a sack full of handguns. Fair warning: if you are squeamish, love animals and read with relish the end of the movie credits where no animals were harmed in the making of the movie, it might be best if you skip to the next chapter. Or at least skip the next few pages.

The question to be answered on that visit was this: were the new, high-velocity, full-metal-jacketed bullets used in some cartridges as good as the old designs of lead? And was small and fast as good as big and slow? And finally, would a bullet shape other than a round-nose work better?

The cartridges tested were 7.65 Luger FMJ, 9mm Luger FMJ, .38 Long Colt LRN, .38 Auto FMJ & JSP, .45 Colt blunt-nose lead, the hollow-point .476 Eley LRN and a .455 Webley with a "manstopper" bullet. The last is essentially a hollow-base bullet turned 180 degrees, with the hollow point being the full diameter of the bullet. Interestingly, despite the Hague Accords (the U.S. was not, and remains not, a signatory), they were testing hollow-point bullets.

Testing consisted of selecting cattle at random and shooting them through the lungs with the various calibers and bullet styles. The unsuspecting cattle were then observed. If the animal appeared to not be expiring in due time, a slaughterhouse worker dispatched it by the slaughterhouse's usual method, a hammer to the forehead.

They were not all shot with a single round, some were shot multiple times. And the bullet placement, wound track and tissue damage could not possibly have been the same for all.

The second day (yes, two days worth of cattle-shooting), the plan was different. This time, they would shoot as many times as they could in rapid fire until the animal expired or they had expended ten rounds. The rates of fire were not the same; some of the firearms malfunctioned, slowing the firing rate, and animals had to be finished off by slaughterhouse workers.

Finally, they shot the test rounds into cadavers suspended from frames and measured the movement observed when the torso or the limbs were struck.

The only place the author has managed to find a complete copy of the Thompson LaGarde tests is in Potocki's book on the 1905 Colt.

All told, the count was ten cadavers, sixteen "beeves" and two horses. Grim work today, and probably not a day in the park back then, either.

Where to begin? First, the tests were undertaken in 1904 and we have the results of them in LaGarde's book "Gunshot Wounds," which was first published in 1914. I'm sure there was some distribution of the tests results before then, but the first from less-ephemeral enough to survive sources were his 1st and 2nd Editions. As far as I can tell, reading the results from LaGarde, and summaries two decades later by Hatcher in "Textbook of Firearms Identification," the cattle were not dissected and the wound tracks were not studied or analyzed. The cattle, having deceased and thus served the purpose of the moment, were conveyed into the slaughterhouse and butchered.

The War Department apparently didn't think it useful enough to add an extra officer or some enlisted men to look over the shoulders of the butchers and ask questions about what happened inside the unfortunate "volunteers." There was just Thompson, LaGarde and the unnamed sergeant who was doing the shooting.

However, the cadavers were analyzed. Thompson did the shooting and LaGarde the observation and note taking. The impact of the various bullets on various locations was noted, and the wounds were x-rayed and dissected for study.

By today's standards the tests were both brutally callous and shockingly casual. There was no scientific method about the tests. Were you to do such a test today, besides having PETA and all manner of animal activists raining abuse down upon you (and rightly so), your resulting report would be laughed out of the professors office and you would be given a failing grade. But, they got the results they and everyone else wanted: the .45 bullet diameter was proven superior.

Curiously, in all the literature I've read, finding a copy of the report has not

86 | GunDigest.com

Table IV. The Estimated Stopping Power of Popular Pistol and Revolver Cartridges

(Based on the momentum of the bullet times the sectional area times a factor to compensate for shape and bullet material.)

Cartridge	Momentum, pounds—feet per second	Sectional area of bullet, sq. ins.	Factor for shape and material.	Relative stopping power.
.22 Long Rifle Outdoor type	.083	.039	1000	3.3
.22 Long Rifle Hi-Speed	.097	.039	1000	3.8
.22 L. R. Hi-Speed Sharp Shoulder	.097	.039	1250	4.7
.25 (6.35 MM) A. C. P.	.083	.049	900	3.7
.30 (7.65 MM) Luger	.246	.075	900	16.6
.30 (7.63 MM) Mauser	.249	.075	900	16.8
.32 (7.65 MM) A. C. P.	.147	.076	900	10.0
.32 Smith & Wesson	.118	.076	1000	9.0
.32 Smith & Wesson Long	.165	.076	1000	12.5
.32 Colt New Police	.164	.076	1100	13.7
.32-20 (.32 Winchester)	.244	.076	1100	20.3
.380 A. C. P. (9 MM short)	.177	.102	900	16.2
.38 A. C. P. (Super .38 automatic)	.347	.102	900	31.8
.38 (9 MM) Luger	.288	.102	1000	29.4
.38 Smith & Wesson	.233	.102	1000	23.8
.38 Colt New Police	.240	.102	1100	27.0
.38 S. & W. Super Police	.273	.102	1050	29.2
.38 Long Colt	.272	.102	1000	27.7
.38 S. & W. Special	.302	.102	1000	30.8
.38 Colt Special	.302	.102	1100	33.3
.38 Special Super Police	.338	.102	1050	36.3
.38/44 S. & W. Special	.386	.102	1000	39.4
.38 Colt Spl. High Velocity	.386	.102	1100	43.3
.38/44 Spl., Keith bullet	.386	.102	1250	49.2
.38-40 (.38 Winchester)	.380	.126	1100	52.6
.41 Long Colt	.305	.129	1050	41.8
.44 S. & W. Special	.416	.146	1000	60.6
.44-40 (44 Winchester)	.408	.143	1100	64.2
.45 A. C. P.	.420	.159	900	60.0
.45 Colt, 770 f. s. velocity	.428	.163	1050	73.6
.45 Colt, 910 f. s. velocity	.505	.163	1100	87.4

The Hatcher Scale, in all its glory and messiness. Look it over and see what anomalies you spot.

been that easy. The one place I managed to find the complete 40 typed pages is in a book on the 1905 pistol by Potocki.

The squeamish may now resume reading.

HATCHER SCALE

In his textbook, Hatcher took this information and, over the three decades elapsing since the tests, came up with his estimate of stopping power. The formula was simple and appealing. Take the sectional area in square inches of the bullet. Multiply that times the muzzle energy in ft-lbs. Then, multiply that with a "form factor" which takes into account the shape of the bullet.

An example: a 9mm Parabellum with 300 ft-lbs of energy has a sectional area of .099 square inches. The form factor for a jacketed FMJ was 1.00, so we end up with a Hatcher RSP of 29.7. Hmm. The same calculations for a .45 ACP gets us an RSP of 48.6. A .380 Auto earns an RSP of 13.5.

Back in 1935, this all seemed reasonable. Today, we can take a quick look and agree it doesn't pass the reality test. Yes, a .45 is better than a 9mm, but twice as good? And four times as good as a .380?

A detail I find curious was that in 1935, while Hatcher was developing and publishing this theory, the two most common daily carry calibers to be found were the .32 Auto and the .380 Auto. Users of the time clearly thought that a .380 FMJ (there was nothing else to be had) with an 85-grain bullet at perhaps 800 fps was good enough to take care of business. It would be decades before there was much interest, outside of the caliber mavens, for anything much better than what we would consider today the "lowly" .38 Special: a 158-grain lead round-nose at 750 fps.

But, the test was the test and the scale was the scale. And Hatcher was such an authority that the RSP stood for decades. The problem with the RSP is that it is all a pile of estimations and assumptions. Does shape matter? And if it does, is a JRN only 90% of an LRN? If so, why does Hatcher assign a .90 shape factor to the 30 Luger, .30 Mauser and .32 ACP, but a 1.00 to the 9mm Parabellum? And is muzzle energy, mass times velocity squared, a valid weight for that particular variable?

In a time before high-speed video, ballistic gelatin, inexpensive chronographs, computer calculation and modeling, and rapid communications (to collect re-

The Taylor KO scale, which may have been useful for his time and place, but really doesn't tell us much about handguns in the 21st century. It probably didn't much in the 20th, either.

BALLISTICS OF LARGE-BORE RIFLES

Rifle.	Weight of Bullet in grains.	Pressure in tons per square inch.	Velocity in ft. per sec.				Energy in ft.-lb.				Knock-Out Blow. Values.	Approximate Weight of Rifle in pounds.	
			Muzzle.	100 yd.	200 yd.	300 yd.	Muzzle.	100 yd.	200 yd.	300 yd.		D.B.	S.B.
.600	900	14.0	1,950	1,690	1,450	1,250	7,610	5,720	4,210	3,130	150.4	14–17	12–13
.577	750	14.0	2,050	1,730	1,450	1,210	7,020	5,000	3,510	2,440	126.7	11½–14	11
.505 Gibbs	525	15.0	2,300	2,020	1,790	1,550	6,180	4,760	3,740	2,810	86.25	—	10½–11
.500 Rimless	535	16(?)	2,400	—	—	—	6,800	—	—	—	90.3	—	10¼
.500 3	570	15.5	2,125	1,880	1,650	1,440	5,730	4,490	3,450	2,640	86.5	10–12	9–10
.476	520	16.0	2,100	1,890	1,680	1,490	5,100	4,130	3,260	2,570	74.2	11	9½
.475 No. 2	480	15.5	2,200	1,960	1,730	1,510	5,170	4,100	3,200	2,440	71.7	11–12	10½
.475 No. 2 Jeffery	500	?	2,000	1,818	—	—	4,450	3,670	—	—	67.8	11–12	10½
.475	480	15.0	2,175	1,930	1,700	1,490	5,030	3,970	3,090	2,360	70.8	11–12	10½
.470	500	14.0	2,125	1,910	1,700	1,500	5,030	4,060	3,210	2,500	71.3	10½–11½	9–10
.465	480	14.0	2,125	1,920	1,720	1,530	4,820	3,940	3,150	2,500	67.7	10¼–10¾	9–10
.450 No. 2	480	13.0	2,175	1,900	—	—	5,050	3,700	—	—	67.1	10½–11½	9–10
.500/.450	480	15.5	2,175	1,990	—	—	5,050	4,220	—	—	67.1	10¼–11½	9–10
.450	480	17.0	2,150	1,960	—	—	4,930	4,100	—	—	66.3	11–11½	9–10

ports of shootings as confirmations), the Hatcher Scale was as close as could be estimated without requiring slide rules and charts. Too bad it doesn't seem to correspond to what happens in the real world.

JOHN TAYLOR

Post-war another scale was developed. This one is wildly off the mark for our needs, despite being quoted from time to time. It is the Taylor Knock-Out factor, or Taylor KO factor. John "Pondoro" Taylor was an African hunter (and sometimes poacher) who developed this scale over the course of shooting thousands of animals over several decades. The result of his formula is a relative scale, a numerical figure allowing comparison of one cartridge to another.

He was certain it corresponded with real-world results. However, his world is not our world, and its applicability for our needs is pretty limited. First of all, he was dealing with rifles. Second, he was shooting moderate to large game. Third, he used for the most part full metal jacketed bullets, called "solids" in that context, thus no expansion and lots of penetration. None of those apply for us, with the exception of FMJ bullets, where we may not be allowed to use them. (New Jersey, I'm looking at you.) His shooting was what has come to be described as "left of bang." Hunters do not turn a corner and find themselves being robbed and needing to shoot. They shoot first, without warning to the prey. In essence, a good hunter ambushes his quarry, and rightly so. It would be a rare self-defense situation where you would be in the right to essentially ambush a felon.

He also considered only two types of shots as being situationally correct: headshots on the largest of game, and shots directly onto the shoulder to "anchor" the animal and greatly diminish its ability to escape wounded.

We are interested in none of those. We are using expanding bullets from handguns, "right of bang" (after the incident has been initiated upon us), and we shoot what we can shoot and hit where we can hit.

However applicable the Taylor KO Factor may be for rifles used hunting in Africa, stretching it into the realm of self-defense handgun ballistics is just too far a step.

RII, OR COMPUTER MAN

In 1975, the National Institute of Justice published its grand study. It would be worthy as a case study in an engineering school for how you can get everything wrong, but it would probably prove too onerous a burden for the students.

The RII is perhaps the first instance for the shooting public to see first-hand the computer acronym of GIGO and its results. GIGO? Garbage in, garbage out. How was this accomplished?

They used 20% ballistic gelatin and test-fired various calibers and bullet designs into it. That was the first mistake, 20% is too dense to be a suitable test media. The second mistake was to use high-speed photography and measure the size of the temporary cavity. Remember, when you shoot ballistic gelatin (in fact, pretty much anything) the bullet shoves the gel aside. The momentum of that push causes the hole down the length of the gelatin to expand to a large degree, so large in some calibers that it breaks the gel block. The gel then collapses back to its original size, and there is a hole left by the passage of the bullet. Recall that the initial expansion is called the "temporary cavity," and the hole remaining after the gel collapses back to its original size is the "permanent cavity."

The mistake the NIJ made in the RII was designating the temporary cavity as the volume "destroyed" by the bullet. Now, there are two organs in the body that do not deal well with shocks and do not readily move aside and then move back. Those are the liver and the brain. Everything else is flexible enough that, when shoved, it moves and then moves back. Surgeons routinely re-arrange

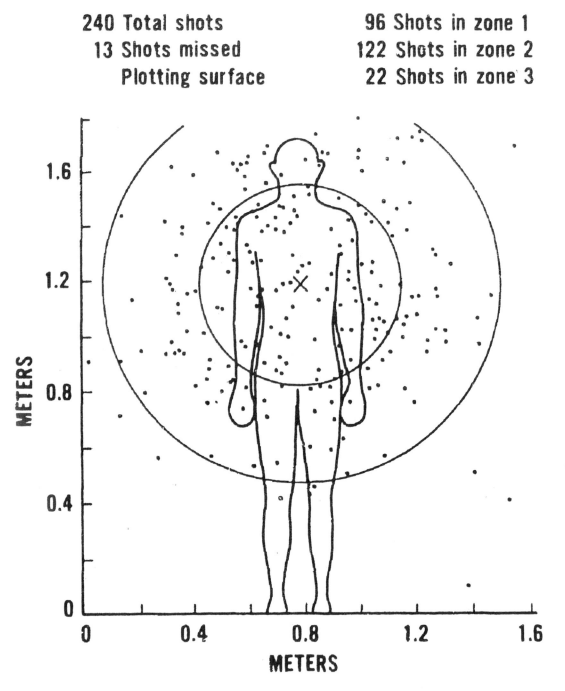

FIGURE 4. *Group A hit distribution superimposed on a computer man silhouette at 12-m range.*

Charts showing the distribution of hits and misses were subsequently used to "calculate" the "stopping power" of the cartridges tested. To seven decimal places, no less.

things while they are at work, and then put the pieces back more-or-less where they originated, if I may be so callous.

Only the permanent cavity is, well, permanent.

But the NIJ assigned the designation of "destroyed" to the temporary cavity.

The third mistake was an outgrowth of the first. 20% gelatin is less flexible than 10%, and shows greater damage than 10% would as velocities rise. This had the effect of exaggerating the effectiveness of high-velocity bullets, regardless of design or caliber. One might argue that 20%,

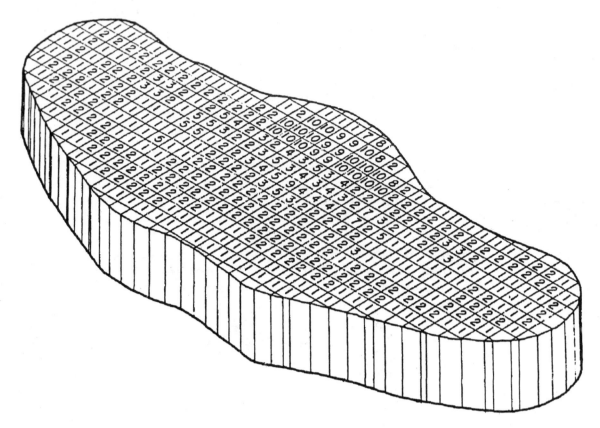

FIGURE 6. *Top view of typical cross section of the Computer Man (shoulder region).*

being stiffer, will show a smaller temporary cavity than 10%, but this does not offset the additional cracking and splitting that happens in 20%.

Then things got really strange. They used inexperienced volunteers who shot a single shot, at a given short time, on a silhouette, as fast as they could. The bullet hole locations were then plotted for each caliber.

Independently, the NIJ had a team of physicians look at a computer-generated 3D model of a human being. The model was divided into 15 thousand small cubes, and the doctors assigned a value to each cube according to where it was in the body and what organ it contained. The score was the effect that would occur, should that particular cube destroyed in an event.

If you're still following me, the NIJ then took the plotted bullet locations for each caliber, laid each temporary cavity model along it, and calculated (or rather, the computer did) the score of tissue destroyed. More temporary cavity, more tissue destroyed. More hits at vital points, more vitals tissue destroyed.

The scores were then ranked, and *voila*, soft-recoiling, high-speed bullets scored higher than heavier, bigger ones, in part because the softer recoil meant more center hits, statistically speaking. By the RII scale, the 9mm 115 FMJ was a better "stopper" than the .45 ACP 230 FMJ.

Whatever you might think about the relative merits of those two rounds, that is a result that is simply not in keeping with reality.

The errors build on each other. Using relatively untrained shooters, less recoil for a given caliber/load in a given platform means it is more likely they will score hits in vital areas. So a soft-recoiling load, even if it is a less-effective bullet impacting, gets an elevated score simply

This plate shows the distribution of the individual cells and their numerical value. The computer then crunched this data and spat out, well, nonsense.

CHAPTER 5: HISTORY OF STOPPING POWER FORMULAS | **91**

because there are more center hits.

"But, center hits matter. If a particular cartridge gets you more hits, then isn't it better?" Yes, but that isn't the question. You can also get better hits with proper training. If we're looking for the most hits with little or no training, we'll be limited to .22LR and .32 Auto as our candidates.

We're trying to determine the effective, no, the relative effectiveness of calibers, cartridges and bullets, independently of their shoot-ability.

STRASBOURG TESTS

More gruesomeness now, and the squeamish really need to move on to the next section. The Strasbourg tests (which remain the subject of quite some controversy) involved goats, French Alpine goats, to be precise, each weighing approximately 160 pounds. The tests involved some 600+ of them, if we are to believe the reports. Each was treated to a surgically implanted needle transducer in the carotid artery. Once recovered from the surgery, they were hooked up to electrodes for brain scanning and lead to a stall. The stall was fashioned in such a way that, to eat the food presented, each goat had to stand in a precise spot and angle for the marksman to shoot it. The results were recorded with video, photographs and observers notes. When dead (if it did not expire quickly enough, it was dispatched) an autopsy was performed. This allegedly took 18 months to perform, back in 1991.

Once the data was analyzed, the Average Incapacitation Time was determined from the goat's reaction (or lack) to being shot. While the numbers indicate that velocity matters, the published numbers do not indicate that the extra noise and recoil of extreme velocity are worth it.

Since the tests were performed in secret, the raw data never published, and the people conducting the test never identified, many researchers file it in the "never happened" category.

As an aside, one of the hallmarks of the scientific method is that the data set is available. Once you publish, you make available the raw data, the exact numbers (all of them, not just the "clean" ones that you culled to use for results), process and conditions under which your experiment was performed. The curious can crunch the numbers for themselves and decide if they agree with your results. The dedicated can replicate the test and see if they get what you got.

I have talked to industry insiders who are of the opinion that it did happen, but no one has come forth with the raw data or to say, "I was there, I saw it happen." The problems with it are many, besides the many goats being killed. The shots were specifically aimed to impact the lungs, and only the lungs. The medical measurements of carotid artery are interesting, but no correlation was made between that and incapacitation.

Until we can see the raw data, the test and the conclusions that come from it must be filed in the "curious, but not relevant" folder.

MARSHALL & SANOW

Evan Marshal was a police officer and detective with the Detroit police department. I met him at my first IPSC match (which I won, beating Evan, something I am perhaps too fond of recounting) and we've had a nodding relationship ever since. Ed Sanow was a sheriff's deputy out of the Great Plains. As far as I know, neither of them has ever had to shoot someone, but Evan was with DPD at a time when shootings were common. Heck, back then you could regularly hear gunfire across Detroit as the traffic died down after rush hour.

They took an entirely different tack toward constructing a scale of stopping power. They decided to do it entirely empirically. One way to set up an experiment is to determine what you will test, conduct the test, record the results and clean up. You then repeat the test, changing one variable in a noticeable but not overwhelming amount, and record the results. And repeat, repeat, and repeat, changing only one variable each time.

An empirical study does not change anything. You simply observe what happened, try to parse out the variables as they change on their own, and record the results. An example? Hmm, okay, try this: you think a certain drug will cure a certain disease. The experimental method would be to inject a lab full of rats with the disease, then give them different amounts of the new drug. How much works, if it works at all? The rats will tell you.

You want to test that drug on people? Good luck deliberately injecting people with the bacteria or virus. (And staying out of prison, even if you do it with them volunteering. Involuntary? You're going to prison for a long time.) So, you find people who already have the disease and talk them into volunteering for your test. You then have to parse out the effects of dosage, age, other health considerations, etc. That's an empirical study.

So what Evan and Ed set out to do was collect all the shooting incident reports they could from their contacts across America in law enforcement. As far as that goes, it was a noble attempt, but there were real problems with the approach.

First, unlike the lab rats or the medical volunteers who were already infected, the results, causes and fault determination of a shooting are not dispassionately studied, even more so in cases with law enforcement involvement. You can get a group of doctors to agree that someone had a particular disease. You can even get them to agree to how many were cured or not cured when given a certain dose of a certain drug. But a shooting? Even if it was entirely a "good shoot" in the LE parlance, everyone involved will come to its review with an agenda. (It pains me to say so, but even a dispassionate LE investigator will arrive with a perspec-

Marshall and Sanow tried, they really did. But the reality of politics and human nature were against them. Still, it was a good try and it did advance the field.

tive, based on experience, training and department.) As a result, the hard facts of a shooting incident will be fought over, analyzed, protected, projected, rejected and argued over again.

Plus, much of the information will not be available for a long time, months or even years afterwards. If a department is sitting on a report, not revealing details until all possible court action has been concluded, then that shooting would not be available to our pair. When it was, it would have been long in the past, and asking follow-up questions would be difficult. The answers might even be colored in memory by the experience of defending the shooting in the legal process.

This is not a way to get what is known in scientific endeavors as "clean data."

The second problem with this also flies in the face of the scientific method: all the sources, names, dates and locations had to be kept secret. Again, in our litigious society (and this was a couple of decades before "Hands up, don't shoot" became a societal flashpoint) having a shootout analyzed, debated, perhaps even litigated and settled, only to have it in the press again because of "a damned gun book" is more than a police administrator would be willing to tolerate. So, they had to remain secret.

This poses problems. Not that I have any thought that Evan and Ed would be underhanded, not at all. But, if you are studying data and you want someone else to make sure you haven't glossed over or given perhaps an improper weight to some, you have someone else look at the raw data and they then report their study/conclusions. If the raw data must remain secret, that isn't possible.

The limitations of the data sources then added further constraints. E & E decided to accept only single-shot, torso hit shooting reports to the study. Why? Because that was a limit to the volume of data, and volume was making things difficult enough. One shot, one hit, and what did the shooting victim (used solely as a descriptor of the person being shot, not a value/legal judgment of their status otherwise) do in the next few seconds?

This means otherwise useful or indicative data is left out. A bad guy who got shot twice in less than a second and fell to the ground without moving is left out of the data set. A felon in his job pursuits, shot through the thighbone and femoral artery, who took one step, fell and quit, isn't counted.

And multiple hits in the torso? Well, how do you determine which one of them was the first, second and third? Which of them caused the cessation of criminal activity? In many cases, it would have been impossible to tell the order, timing and thus effectiveness of multiple hits. So Evan and Ed left them out.

Even today, simply mentioning their names can bring some critics to frothing-at-the-mouth rants. I don't find the results derived from the inquiry to be useful to the full extent of the conclusions provided. Assessing calibers and loads to a fraction of a percentage point in their rankings and ratings strikes me as being far too precise, with the muddy data presented.

There was also an attempt in certain circles to assess the data strictly from a statistical point of view. By conducting a numerical analysis, not of the cartridges, but of the numbers posted for the effectiveness of the cartridges, some objected to a "too clean" result. By too clean, the objections concerned the plotting and agreement of the data. If you were to plot the results on a graph, you'd end up with a cloud of dots. Well, statistically, there is a way to find the center of the cloud, draw a line through the cloud and say, "This is the result." That line also comes with a "confidence factor." That is, and you've likely seen this before, "the result of this test is an 85% correlation, with a confidence factor of 10%." (Actually, it would be an 85%, plus or minus 5%, with a confidence factor of "X", but let's not get too technical just yet.)

The objection came down to the confidence factor being higher in the results presented than could reasonably be calculated from the variables. In other words, the data was muddy, but the end result was too clean. That makes people who are statically trained suspicious, since you cannot generate cleaner results than the data you have.

But, the effort is now a couple of decades old and the ballistics world has pretty much moved on.

WHAT HAVE WE LEARNED?

Basically, we've learned that people are very tough, mentally and physically. Handguns are low-powered tools when it comes to making bad people stop doing bad things, which is why the militaries of the world consider a rifle as the most basic tool to fight with and move up from there.

Can we construct a theory of stopping power? Maybe, but first we have to agree on just what it is that we call "stopping power." Until we have a handle on that, we can't even begin to measure cartridges.

# 6

IWBA BEGINNINGS
AND HISTORY

The International Wound Ballistics Association (IWBA) was essentially Dr. Martin Fackler, until he became so successful at putting forth his process that it wasn't necessary for him to do so any more. Dr. Fackler got his start in this subject as a trauma surgeon in Vietnam. Serving as a field surgeon in Naval Support Hospitals, he worked on soldiers, marines and other combatants wounded and straight out of the combat zones. He had a first-hand education in the wounding results of small arms fire, shrapnel and explosives.

He later served in the U.S. Army Medical Corps, and while there worked on developing terminal ballistics simulants. What he discovered through experiment was that 10% gelatin, cooled to a specific temperature, most closely simulated the effect that bullets had on pig muscle, and those of pig muscle on bullets.

One of the interesting facts of medical science is that, of the entire animal world, pigs are in many aspects the closest to us in biochemistry, organic function, structure and size. Indeed, it is a current area of medical research to see what pig organs can be safely transplanted into humans, for how long, and how to make them last longer. (Sometimes the 21st century just gets scarier and scarier.)

As we've covered elsewhere, there were a lot of test mediums tried through the years, but this one is so far the closest simulant.

Before we go any further, we have to address an argument. There are those who argue against gelatin because it isn't tissue, and that bullets pulled from game animals and people do not look like the bullets pulled from gel. True, absolutely true. Ballistic gelatin doesn't have bones, connective tissue, tendons, cartilage, etc.

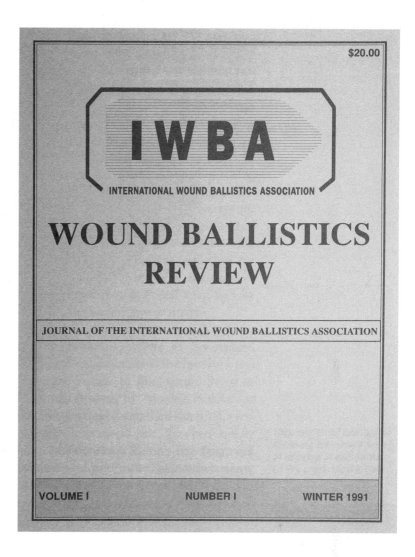

The first issue of the "IWBA Journal," information that changed small arms terminal research.

The important word to focus on here is simulant. We are simulating tissue, not duplicating it.

A brief aside here: if I can find a way to teach my spell-checker that I really do mean simulant, and not stimulant, I'll be happy. Even adding it to the list doesn't prevent the change, I have to check every time. Software rant over.

By using a simulant, we don't have to shoot 100 pigs, we can shoot five gel blocks. And, we know the results will be the same. Which leads me to the scientific answer to the question, "Why gel?"

THE BEAUTY OF BALLISTIC GEL

The process to manufacture ballistic gelatin for testing of firearms is rather

The beauty of gelatin is that it is the same, when done correctly, regardless of where you are or who is testing. Here, a shot gel block is being prepped for photography.

involved. To learn the process and be certified is a two-day class. That is, in part, because it takes two days to make the stuff. It has to be weighed, one part gel to nine parts water. The water has to be carefully heated and mixed. Doing it incorrectly will lead to gel that is not representative. Non-representative gel means the results using it will be off-scale and skewed, and the "knowledge" gained will be useless and misleading.

Then it has to be cooled to a specific temperature. Once cooled, it can be used. However, using it isn't easy. You have to monitor the temperature. If the temp rises too much, the gel won't be in-spec and you have to re-cool it. So, you take your gel straight from the cooler (usually a walk-in refrigerator) to the range, plop it on the shooting bench, check temp, calibrate it, and then shoot it. If you spend more than a couple of minutes in all that, your gel gets too warm, loses calibration, and your efforts have been wasted.

Calibrate? Yep. You have to shoot your gel block with an air rifle, hurling a steel BB. The BB must be traveling within a specific velocity or your calibration is not good. The BB has to penetrate a certain depth into the gel. Too much or too little, and your gel is off-spec.

A handgun block is a rectangle that is 6x6x16 inches. A rifle block is 8x8x18. A quick look and you'd say, "Okay, it's a bit bigger." Do the arithmetic, it has twice the volume. Every time I write that, I can't help myself. I pick up a calculator and do it again. Yep, twice the volume. A rifle gel block is a big, heavy, slippery thing.

Why go to all this trouble? Simple: the scientific method. The essence of science is that, if two experimenters perform the same experiment and work hard to make sure all the details are the same, they will come up with the same results. As my chemistry professor remarked when explaining this to us: "If

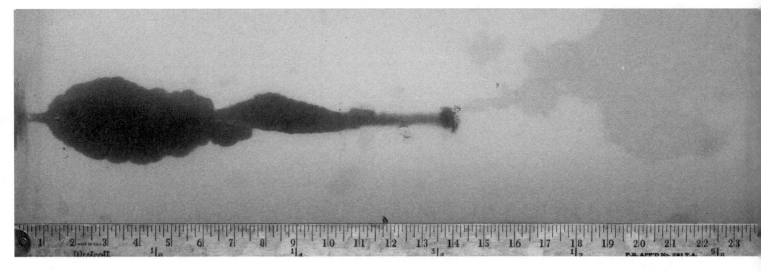

Above: The use of ballistic gelatin made it possible to test bullets in a consistent manner. It is, however, difficult to photograph, and very difficult to re-use. It remains expensive.

Below: If you are going to do this right, record the results, save the bullets, and keep them straight.

they don't, it isn't science."

So, if an experimenter in Quantico performs the test and finds that a given handgun bullet penetrates to 14 inches, expands to twice its size, and splatters gel across the range, then an experimenter for the LAPD will find the same. It doesn't matter that it is a bitterly cold (for Virginia) day in Quantico, and a balmy afternoon in L.A. If their results differ, then they can get on the phone and find out why there was a difference. Barrel length? Rifling twist? The apocryphal joke we heard in engineering class was on the test rig the U.S. Air Force built to stress-test aircraft canopies, known as the chicken gun. They developed a machine that could hurl chicken carcasses at a cockpit at takeoff speeds and see what happened. If you think this is a trivial problem or a waste of effort, let me simply point you to Captain Sullenberger and his landing in the river. His engines were destroyed by a flock of geese. Now, imagine an F/A18 taking off with a full load of ordnance, and the pilot taking a goose right through the canopy. The Royal Air Force heard about the testing, built one and did the same thing; they were horrified to see chickens blasting directly through the canopy, bulkhead and test frame, and embed themselves in the wall behind. They sent a frantic Telex (this gives you a clue as to how old the joke is) to the USAF facility. The response was a request for all test data. Soon after, the Telex reply came back: "Defrost the chicken."

Details matter, and the first thing impressed upon us in engineering lab was this: record all the data, all of it. Even the stuff that doesn't seem important. "What, you didn't record the atmospheric pressure?" "It's a tensile-strength pull test. Does that matter?" "I don't know. I may never, but if it ever does, you're screwed if you didn't record it. Write it down."

What Dr. Fackler found, once he had nailed down all the other details of the test procedure, was that what seemed to matter was the permanent wound cavity. The temporary cavity, the expansion, seemed to not matter at all.

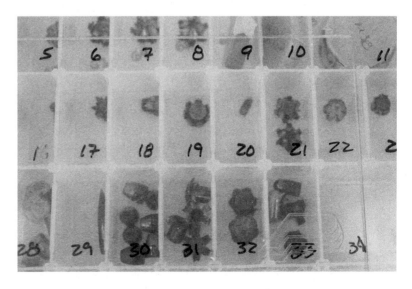

CHAPTER 6: IWBA BEGINNINGS AND HISTORY | 99

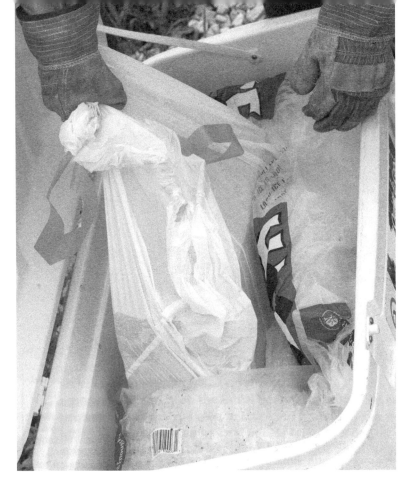

Gel has to be kept cool, almost frozen, or it does not react consistently. Here, we're digging a block out of the cooler used to haul it to the range.

In order to spread the word, he formed the International Wound Ballistics Association, the IWBA. I joined as soon as I heard of it, and found myself to be the terminal ballistics equivalent of a "plank owner." When a new naval vessel is christened, the crew members who are assigned to it from the beginning, before it has its inaugural sailing, are known as plank owners. I was just a shooter and gunsmith interested in this subject, but the late Doctor was kind enough to include me from the beginning.

WHAT IS GEL?

A ballistic gelatin block is animal gel, the same stuff of which you make your desserts. That brings with it a host of problems. First, being biological, it will attract all sorts of pests. Mold, insects and rotting are all things you have to keep in mind, and the idea of long-term storage is pretty much a non-starter. You mix gel just before (a few days or maybe a week) you will use it.

Second, it is not clear, as in not see-through. It is customary to add a drop of cinnamon oil to each gallon of gel mix, to improve clarity and reduce attractiveness to pests. A block will be a golden-brown color when new. Re-use it and it gets darker.

The mixing of the gel powder into the heated water requires a demanding temperature range (plus or minus a couple of degrees) and twenty minutes or more of pouring, stirring, pouring and stirring. This is per block, by the way. Then, the blocks have to be cooled to 39 degrees Fahrenheit. This takes a minimum of overnight, longer if you have stuffed the refrigerator full of hot blocks in their molds.

Each block is a slippery, cold, squirmy package, and it really takes two people to pick one up without damaging the block or hurting themselves.

Blocks can be re-used, but they just get worse. A melted down, re-cast and re-used block is murkier than a new one, and the third time you go to use it you probably won't be able to see the bullet in there.

The color and murk of the block makes it difficult to photograph the bullet in-place, or the wound track, unless you have specific, tested lighting to show the bullet and track. That adds cost to the equipment load and management to the testing process.

Once it is used or used up, you have to dispose of it. Animals will be attracted to it. The rotting gelatin will be a smelly nuisance if you just dump it off to the side of the range where you are testing. Hauling it to a dumpster just relocates the smell and vermin attractiveness, and once the dumpster owner figures out it is you leaving them such presents, you won't be welcome there any more.

WHAT GEL ISN'T

You cannot get more than a couple of minutes (sometimes a lot less) into a discussion about ballistic gelatin before someone says something to the effect of,

Gel is consistent, and well-made bullets are consistent in gel. Here, a set of JHPs have penetrated to the same depth, plus or minus less than an inch, and expanded very well indeed.

Gel testing is not a stopping power theory, just an observation of what bullets do to gel, and what gel does to bullets. Here a .38 Special wadcutter proves it has more than enough penetration, despite a modest velocity. Note the BB shots on the top edge of the block, for calibration.

"It's too bad we can't make a gel block with bones in it." At this point, everyone who has heard that particular discussion before, or knows even basic statistics, groans and looks for the exit.

The problems are numerous: What material? What plastic, wood, carbon fiber, nanotubedooie will closely and consistently approximate the density and strength of bone? Next, which bone? Ribs? Humerus? Femur? Skull? Then, how do we construct a statistical model for how much of that bone the bullet strikes?

Let's just take a rib simulant as a demonstration. Do we settle for five models: no strike, 25%, 50%, 75% and 100% strike? We've just multiplied the amount of work we have to do by a huge amount, and that's even before we have operational errors. Okay, we're set up for the 25% strikes. A bullet hits our bone simulant and we measure to realize it is a 33% strike. Do we count it as 25%? Or 50%? Or do we toss it and start over? And who is paying for all this?

Can we make a single layer of "rib," a sheet of it, one that will give us a reading on a rib strike? Sure, but again, how do you calibrate it? To what rib thickness, age of person, etc., etc., etc.? And, having broken the budget on the rib tests, how do we do it all again for the other bones? The FBI test is already cumbersome enough, you're talking about increasing it anywhere from 400% to 1,000% of work.

WHAT THE IWBA ISN'T, AND WHAT ITS TESTING ISN'T

The IWBA ballistic gelatin test isn't a stopping power theory. It is an assumption and a series of rational observations.

The assumption is simple: ballistic gelatin is a close-enough simulant to tissue. It may be possible at some future time to find/construct a closer approximation, a material or assembly of materials, but for now this is what we have.

The rational observations begin with penetration. Generally speaking, it takes twelve inches of penetration to be reasonably certain of getting deep enough into the human body to start hurting the important parts. Given a bell curve distribution of human body sizes, we clearly will have an excess if the victim is an anorexic five-footer. And it is entirely possible that a morbidly obese person who is markedly over six feet tall may have enough subcutaneous fat that a bullet will stop short of heart, lungs, etc.

But, this is important: generally speaking, we cannot err too much on the overpenetration side, or we will create new problems for ourselves. This was

Handgun blocks are 6x6x16 inches. Rifle blocks (to the left of this handgun block, just visible) are 8x8x18. They are cold, heavy, slimy and smelly.

one that several large city police departments faced.

When NYPD first transitioned to 9mm pistols, the orders from on-high were clear: no hollowpoints. In a very short time, they had a large number of bystanders struck by over-penetrating bullets. Not misses on bad guys, but through-and-through on bad guys, bullets which went on to strike bystanders. When in a short period of time the number of bystanders struck with pass-throughs neared twenty, the ammunition was changed to JHPs.

Detroit PD had a similar problem. They changed from their earlier policy of "use whatever handgun you can qualify with" to only allowing Glocks in .40. The city required, as had NYPD, no hollowpoints. Detroit issued ammunition loaded with 180-grain FMJ/TC bullets, perhaps the most penetrative bullet to be found. I've tested bullets that have extreme penetration for a handgun, in rifle-sized gelatin blocks. Placing two blocks end-to-end gives me 36 inches of ballistic gelatin to stop launched missiles. I have not had a standard, factory-loaded (not extra-velocity) .40 S&W 180 FMJ/TC stop within the blocks. I have to use something behind the blocks to catch exiting bullets for study.

We'll cover it in the FBI section, but the maximum limit for reasonable performance is currently taken to be 18 inches. The 18-inch maximum allows for bullets to penetrate between twelve and eighteen inches, and statistically that's a reasonable level of performance for use on human beings.

The next rational observation is that it is extremely difficult to measure the volume of the permanent wound cavity in gelatin with any precision. Instead, the approach the IWBA (and Dr. Fackler) took was to measure the performance of the bullet. That is, what the travel in gelatin did to the bullet. (It is important to keep this in mind when considering the FBI tests, and later, the FBI conclusions on 9mm vs. .40 for service use.)

Bullet penetration and expansion can be measured precisely. Bullets can (and are) saved, weighed, measured and stored for future reference.

The more a bullet expands, the more damage it has (by inference) done to the gelatin, and thus tissue. The IWBA (and Dr. Fackler) assert that the more a bullet expands, the better it performs.

A secondary rational observation is that bullets that break apart do not penetrate as deeply, or in straight lines. So, a bullet that holds together while expanding

Right: To be useful, gel has to be calibrated. So, we shoot it with a BB gun and check penetration.

Below: These are bullets extracted from bowling pins. On the left, a 230-grain wadcutter out of a .357 Magnum. On the right, a 300-grain LTC shot out of a .45 Colt Redhawk. They both blew their pins off the table with enthusiasm. Does that make them good defensive-bullet choices? Not a chance, and that is what Dr. Fackler wanted to get away from.

is preferred to one that breaks apart, or sheds its jacket from its core.

That's it. No predictions about what one will do vis-à-vis another. No ranking or estimated "one-shot stops" or anything like that. Just recorded data and the understanding that we are all rational adults, that when presented with the information we can make individual, informed choices. This is not a stopping power theory approach. It is an attempt to describe what is seen, and use it to guide further R&D and ammunition choices.

EARLY CHARTS

When Dr. Fackler got this underway, there was no digital age. Oh, there were computers, but no digital imaging. Getting the results of bullets in gelatin was difficult enough, trying to then photograph them with any consistency or clarity was next to impossible, or at least cost-prohibitive. As a result, what he depended on were line drawings. The common line drawings you might see, if you do an online search for this information, all come from the same source: the late Dr. Fackler.

So when you see a line drawing, realize you are seeing an historical artifact, the best representation that could be created, there and then, within the budget allowed.

Even today it is difficult to fully record the results in a block of gelatin or other simulants. It isn't easy to light a clear or nearly-clear gel block so the image shows the breaks and tears in the block. Even when it is done well, the results are hard to see. Standing over a block, moving around to catch the different perspectives, you can get a very good sense of what a bullet has done to a block. But

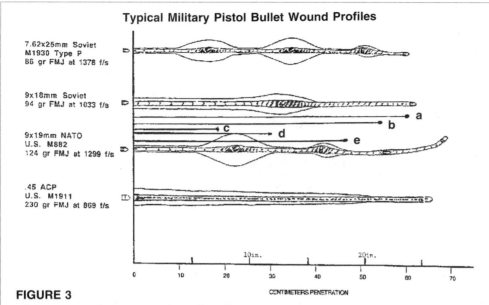

FIGURE 3
Military pistol bullet wound profiles (from presentations by Dr. M.L. Fackler) with the results of five shots by this author added as line drawings:

(a) a 105 gr. 'PM' bullet at an impact velocity (V_i) of 1025 f/s
(b) a 95 gr. 380 Auto FMJ bullet from a 380 Auto pistol, V_i=916 f/s
(c) an 85 gr. Winchester SilverTip JHP from a 380 Auto. pistol, V_i=934 f/s (bullet expanded)
(d) an 85 gr. Win. SilverTip JHP from a 'PM' pistol, V_i=667 f/s (*No* expansion)
(e) a 95 gr. 380 Auto FMJ bullet from a 'PM' pistol, V_i=740 f/s

Left: Back in the film days, it was hideously expensive to try and get good gel shot photos. So Dr. Fackler used line drawings.

Below: What you test a bullet against determines how it will perform. On the left, a bullet (Hydrashok, by the way) that performed exactly as expected in ballistic gelatin. On the right, an FMJ that impacted a soft body armor panel and went nowhere. Nor did it produce any real shock behind the vest.

there is no way to accurately and precisely record that damage. That's the stumbling block in the recent FBI discussion of 9mm vs. .40: they can't see a difference in the block, so therefore there isn't one.

False logic, but what can you do? Simple: note the difference in the bullet sizes and make the rational inference that a larger bullet, traversing a gelatin block, has to do greater damage, even if you can't see the damage done to the block.

THE END

In the winter of 2001, IWBA members received a letter from Dr. Fackler. It was both saddening and gladdening. The sad part was that the IWBA would publish no more. The last issue of the Review had gone out, there would be no more, and that was that. The reason? The IWBA had done the job so well that it was now clearly understood by all that the old methods would no longer suffice.

It had taken some time, but by 2001 law enforcement agencies were starting to adopt the exact methodology that Dr. Fackler and the IWBA had pioneered. Once they were willing to do the work, Dr. Fackler could take a break.

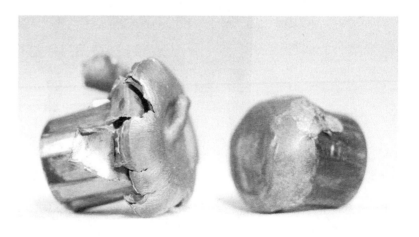

7

THE FBI ENTERS THE PICTURE

It is now more than thirty years ago. In April of 1986, in an attempt to apprehend a pair of bank robbers, FBI officers found themselves in an intense shootout in Miami. Eight agents engaged in a gunfight with two bank robbers, and when it was over the two robbers were dead, two FBI agents were dead, five were wounded and one was unharmed.

At the time, it was considered a watershed incident for bullet design and caliber selection, but the largest contributing factor to the end result was mindset. Basically, the FBI (and this is not to cast blame 30 years after the fact, only to offer an assessment of the situation) went into the fight with the peculiar American mindset I have mentioned before – handguns as primary fighting tools. They knew they were going up against bad guys who were not only willing to fight, but would start the fight, and who had demonstrated that they used long guns as primaries. Even knowing this, the FBI agents were not quick enough to go to rifles and shotguns themselves. They didn't even pack extra firearms for the rolling vehicle stakeout/search.

But, this is a book on handgun ammunition, not tactical realities of the 1980s and how they have changed since.

The mixture of handguns used by the agents was a cause for official concern. The difficulty in reloading revolvers under stress, their lack of capacity, and the poor terminal performance of the particular 9mm ammunition used were all studied, found wanting, and slated for change.

In order to change, the FBI needed both some way of quantifying what was being studied and a means of measuring improvements. To this end they convened a panel to study and report on the next step. This group was convened on Sep-

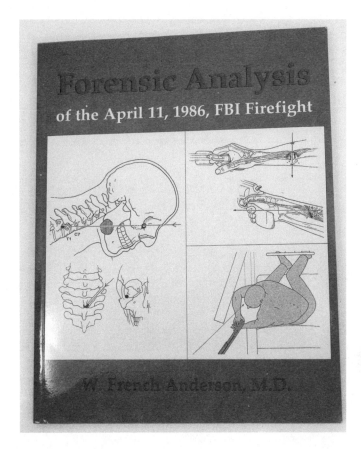

The Miami shootout was analyzed, studied, discussed, and even had the autopsy results discussed at length and turned into a book.

tember 15, 1987 and called the Wound Ballistic Workshop. The most amazing thing about it is who was there. I've gotten some complaints that I'm sometimes a bit hard on the FBI, but this was an astounding event, and I have to give them full credit for what they did. There were eight participants on the panel, and none of them were FBI agents.

The end result was that the FBI decided that the 9mm wasn't sufficient for their tasks, but they could not bring themselves to embrace the .45 ACP. They settled on the 10mm. By 1987, the 10mm was almost ready to slip into anonymity. The 10mm was developed for the Bren Ten, but that handgun never came to fruition. Colt gave the 10mm a lifeline with its Delta 1911, but the FBI brought it back to the forefront.

However, it was not to be. The problem was simple, everyone had their own ideas and the FBI had the wrong ones. First off, the FBI wanted the 10mm. As-loaded in 1987, it was a 200-grain bullet

CHOOSING HANDGUN AMMO | **107**

The FBI expects a handgun to last for the length of an agent's career, and is not interested in short-service-life options. Nor was S&W willing to make such a pistol, when the FBI wanted the 10mm. This 9mm appears on a pile of the nearly 7,000 rounds fired through it in one day.

at 1150 fps, or a 180 at 1200. That was more recoil than FBI agents could handle and shoot a passing score in the qual course. Heck, in 1987 it was more cartridge than most competition shooters wanted to shoot, so it is no slam on the FBI to say "it was too much cartridge."

To give you a handle on this, a 180-grain bullet at 1,200 fps posts a Power Factor of 216. The PF to make Major in IPSC competition at that time was 180. Even bowling pin shooters considered a 195 PF to be plenty of gun. So, having a 216 PF load as the standard issue was way over on the right-hand end of the bell curve.

Also, S&W, the company making the pistols for the FBI, refused to make any other models than all-steel pistols in 10mm. They would not make a 10mm with an aluminum frame, and they were correct to demur. The FBI themselves, in a pistol evaluation test conducted in the same timeframe as the Wound Workshop, determined that aluminum-framed pistols (as of 1987/8, remember) did not have a sufficient service-use durability to last an agent's career. The FBI estimated an alloy-framed pistol as having a service life of 10,000 rounds, where the same design or model in an all-steel version would last 100,000+ rounds. (Having shot some alloy-framed pistols past the 10,000 round point, I have to think the FBI was a bit harsh in that assessment.)

Not only would an aluminum-framed 10mm pistol have made the qual course scores worse, the guns would have had an even shorter and unhappy service life than an aluminum-framed 9mm pistol would have.

The FBI prevailed upon the ammunition companies to ease up on the throttle. 180s at 1200 became 180s at 1100, then 180s at 1050, and then 180s at 950. By the time the ammo companies got velocities down to this point, the big 10mm case had so much dead-air space in it that Winchester cleverly figured they could shorten the whole package, still deliver 180s at 950, and fit them into a 9mm pistol. Thus the .40 S&W was born.

They were right, but the pistol makers had to start all over. The great idea of "we'll just fit a .40 barrel and a heavier recoil spring" didn't pan out. While a .40 S&W (what the short 10mm was called, when unveiled in 1990) would indeed fit into a 9mm-sized pistol, it took more than just a heavy recoil spring and new barrel to make a durable, controllable .40 pistol.

We have spent twenty-five years since determining that we were all wrong. The .40 was going to be the compromise cartridge that did it all: it would have the magazine capacity and felt recoil close to a 9mm, while having the stopping power close to a .45. Unfortunately, it over-promised and under-delivered.

It ended up with capacity and felt recoil close to the .45, while not offering enough stopping power over the 9mm to be worth those costs. It also proved to be hard on guns, and hard for agents, officers and deputies to post passing scores in qual courses.

In 2016, the FBI floated the proposal (not exactly the decision, but tea-leaf-readers interpreted it as such) that the 9mm was plenty good enough and the .40 wasn't worth it. I'm not sure I agree that the .40 doesn't deliver, but if you consider the cost-benefit ratio, it doesn't do enough more than the 9mm to be worth the recoil, muzzle blast and diminished capacity.

What we did get out of it was the test procedure we now call the FBI protocols.

The FBI Workshop was not big and didn't produce a lot of literature – 51 pages in total. But it was the start of acceptance of the IWBA process, and now we are here with great bullets as a result.

(We call them the FBI Tests, Protocols, Rankings, whatever. It all came from Dr. Martin Fackler and his work with ballistic gelatin and the creation of the IWBA.)

WOUND BALLISTICS WORKSHOP

The panel was composed of eight members, none of whom were FBI agents. They were:
- Robert L Adkins, Southwestern Institute of Forensic Sciences
- Dr. Vincent DiMaio, Chief Medical Examiner, Bexar Co. Texas
- Dr. Martin Fackler, US Army Letterman Army Institute of Research
Stan Goddard, Battell Columbus labs
- Dr. Douglas Lindsey, Professor of Surgery, University of Arizona
- Sgt. Evan Marshall, Detroit Police Department

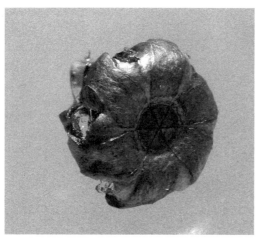

Before the FBI put their stamp of approval on testing, we were shooting bullets into gelatin. But what works, works. What is acknowledged to work might take some time to catch up, but once there is official approval, word spreads.

- Dr. Carroll Peters, University of Tennessee Space Institute
- Dr. O'Brien C. Smith, University of Tennessee Medical Center

Each of them wrote and produced a paper, detailing their research and conclusions on the subject of stopping power and the effectiveness of handguns to that end. The total page count of the workshop publication was, including all charts, appendices and notes, fifty-one pages. Not exactly an encyclopedia of stopping power, but it pointed the FBI in the right direction.

The participants differed greatly in their approach, as well as the content and quantity of material they provided. Fackler contributed a page and a half of text and a page of drawings. DiMaio three pages of text. Goddard contributed seven pages of ballistics, firearms recommendations and terminal ballistics. Lindsey contributed one page, a third of which listed his qualifications. Marshall submitted one page, eleven bullet points in all, of an outline of what in his experience worked. Adkins submitted one page, six short paragraphs, and recommended the "short block" gelatin test (15cm) which later proved to not be useful. Dr. Smith gave three and a half pages of outline, recommendations and suggestions. Dr. Peters' paper for the Workshop was twenty-one pages, with equations, charts and graphs, and reported test data, on modeling and testing of projectiles. The backgrounds and type of education each had as their history clearly influenced their contributions to the Workshop.

Looking back over the span of thirty years, it is easy to see what advice held up in the testing and reports that came after, and what was based on old knowledge or prior experience.

But the effect on the shooting public at the time, at least those paying attention, was electric. In law enforcement circles, the FBI carries a lot of weight. If the FBI looks at something, a lot of others wonder, "There must be something to it. Should we also be looking?"

If the FBI was looking at handgun effectiveness and at making pistols the default sidearm, then a lot of departments that had been sticking with revolvers, especially revolvers in .38 Special, would now be looking at the subject for themselves.

What's more, the FBI, in order to justify any changes they made, would absolutely have to come up with a standardized, repeatable, understandable test methodology, and it had to be known to all. No secret tests allowed. No FBI-only tests, no "behind closed doors" programs, no way around it, it had to be known.

Now, that's not to say that every detail is something everyone might be privy to. Let's say you have a bullet design you want the FBI to consider. They will, if

Hornady solved the problem of barriers plugging up hollow points with a simple solution: plug it ahead of time, but plug with something that still drives expansion. Here you see a cross-section of the Critical Duty bullet, flanking the excellent XTP bullet, which does not use a plug.

they have the time, budget and interest, test your ammo on their range, in their gel, and come up with a score. You will get that score, and your results. What you won't get is the identical data for all your competitors. Fair's fair, you want to know how yours did, you can submit it to the FBI. But you can't get everyone else's results, too.

The best part about this is simple; you can just buy the other companies' ammo and test it yourself. You test yours. You sent yours to the FBI and got the FBI report and data. If your results agree with the FBI's, you know you are doing the test correctly. Then, you test the other companies' ammo and see how it performs compared to yours.

Everyone does it, and everyone knows what everyone else's ammo does. That is the Scientific Method.

But, what is the test? That is covered in more detail in the next chapter. Simply put, it is the ballistic gelatin test procedure that Dr. Martin Fackler developed, with extra tests added, specific to the needs of law enforcement. That's it. And that is why, as mentioned, we all received the letter from the IWBA telling us that the "Review" would no longer be published. If the FBI was doing all the work now, the IWBA had been a success.

1993

In tracking down the information for this book I found that the FBI had convened another panel five years after the first, called the FBI Wound Ballistics Seminar. Finding a report of it has proven elusive. By 1993, the FBI test had been going on for several years, and the new information wasn't what to do, but what was doing what.

And since then, the FBI, as far as I can tell, has not had workshops or seminars on the subject, just the ongoing test and results for those who qualify to see what can be disseminated.

This makes sense. Once the program is started, the efforts should be put towards generating data, not necessarily advancing the borders. We'll see, in time, where this leads us. It may take a couple of generations to sort things out and get a sense of what really works and what doesn't.

8
THE FBI PROTOCOLS

The FBI procedure is long, thorough, detailed and once done tells you a lot about how a handgun bullet performs. Is it perfect? No, nothing is. But before we get into the nitty gritty of the test itself, you have to consider why the FBI set up the test this way, and how FBI needs may differ from the needs of other users. Specifically, the non-sworn everyday handgun carrier.

The FBI, like every other law enforcement agency, expects its agents to prevail in a fight. The agents cannot flee, however they can re-position to flank the opponent, they can back off to wait for reinforcements (sometimes, situation permitting), and they can hold their position while reinforcements come up, flank, or otherwise join the fight.

This is generally the situation any law enforcement officer faces. In New York City, a radio call or the sound of shots fired can bring dozens of officers in a minute. A sheriff's deputy in a rural county might have response time for the sole backup deputy of many minutes to an hour or more.

You, the non-sworn individual, do not have the requirement to press on and prevail in a fight. You also don't have reinforcements on the way. Flight is perfectly acceptable, and may even be financially, legally and otherwise prudent. (Even a "good shoot" incurs substantial financial costs, in legal expenses, time off of work, etc., not to mention social and psychological effects.) You cannot count on reinforcements, and when the police do arrive they don't necessarily know you are the good guy. They won't join you in the fight, but will work to get both of you to stop. (This is a consideration even when an off-duty police officer is involved in an incident. He or she may well find themselves facing the muzzles of other officers, in the moments until it gets sorted out who is the good guy and who isn't. Don't take it personally, that's just the way it is.)

Law enforcement officers, as a result, can expect to spend a lot of time with bad

The gelatin has to be melted and mixed, poured into a mold and then cooled. This is a heck of a lot of work for one shot.

guys trying to use cover, bad guys behind inadvertent barriers, and with bad guys in, on and around vehicles. As a result, the FBI tests are heavy on barriers.

The Miami shootout is both a driving force and illustrative of this. If you, a normal, everyday citizen, found yourself in a car crash, and the guy or guys in the other car got out with weapons and started shooting, getting out of there is prudent. Even if you are armed, unless there was a compelling reason to stay and fight, flight is smart. You would be praised for leaving. You would be smart to have left.

The FBI agents that day in Miami had no such option. Having found the bad guys and crashed with the bad guys, they had to fight the bad guys who would not surrender, and that meant with all the intervening barriers that might be present.

If you, an EDC non-sworn citizen, ever

Right: Gel has to be the correct temperature or it is of no use. The temperature is tested moments before it is shot, to make sure it is in spec.

Below: Gel starter, as shipped, has the consistency of sugar. And it loves water. So it comes double- and triple-sealed and in sturdy shipping containers. Otherwise, it risks arriving in a useless condition.

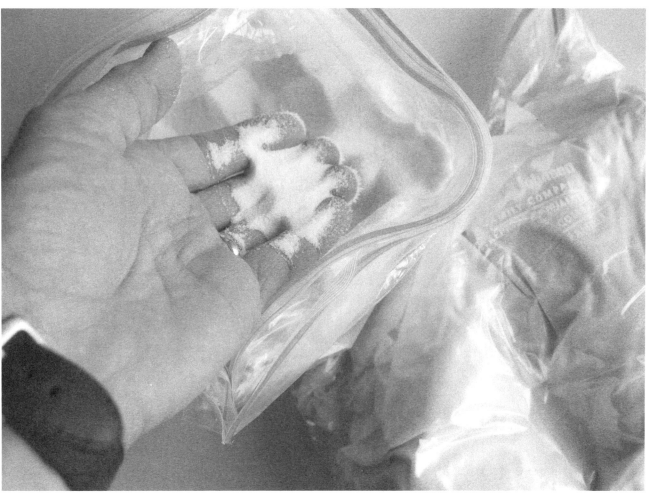

find yourself in a gunfight, it is much less likely to involve barriers through which you must shoot. As a result, you are free to consider the barrier tests as useful information, but not vital requirements of your bullet's performance. Some take the FBI barrier tests as gospel, some read them and say to themselves, "That's interesting."

FBI PROCEDURE

The full test calls for an impressive amount of equipment and materials. It consumes eight gelatin blocks per load tested. FBI soecifications for gel blocks are precise. Handgun blocks are 6x6x16 inches. Blocks used for rifle testing are 8x8x18. The blocks are created by weighing a ratio of ten percent gelatin to water, heating the water, mixing, and pouring the resulting gooey solution into molds. The filled molds are then chilled to 4 degrees Celsius, or 39.2 degrees Fahrenheit.

The gel-starting stock, as it arrives from the producer, is a powder with the consistency of sugar. It comes sealed in a plastic tub of two or two and a half gallons, with a sealed-lip lid that nearly needs a chainsaw to get off. Or, it arrives in plastic bags, with each batch of powder double-sealed. The last batch I received came not just double-sealed per mixing batch (powder in a bag, in another bag) but the half-dozen batch bags were in another, bigger plastic bag (triple-sealed) and then shipped in a cardboard carton inside of a cardboard carton. They might as well have simply slapped a shipping label on a plastic drum and let me use a power saw to get it open.

Why? It has the consistency of sugar, and it absolutely loves water. If you don't seal it, it will leak out, and when it hits humid air it turns into a gooey mess, given enough time. This is just the start of the potential mess, and the need for scrupulous cleanliness.

A handgun block is two and a half gallons of water and gelatin. As we all learned in grade school, "A pint's a pound,

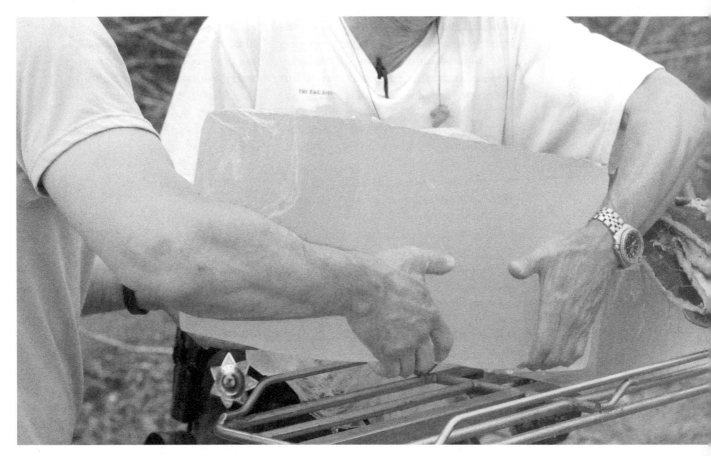

Blocks are heavy, slick and cold. You need friends to wrestle them into place properly.

Right: Bare gel makes for perfect bullets, and is the baseline against which all barrier tests are compared.

Below: Heavy cloth (the black) and light cloth (the light cloth) are used as barriers, but the light is also used to keep barrier debris off the face of the gel block, as cloth would on skin.

the world round." So that's 20 pints, and therefore a minimum of 20 pounds. (In all these years, I've never slapped a gel block onto a scale, to see how close it is to that.) A rifle block, at twice the volume, means twice the weight.

A single handgun load test, therefore, requires almost half a ton of gelatin. A rifle test requires almost a ton.

The cast blocks, once they reach test temperature, are hauled out, placed on a table and shot. The first shot is a BB, with the rifle it comes out of pumped up to produce a specific velocity, and the BB must penetrate the block to a certain depth, plus or minus. Failure on this point causes the block to be re-cooled or rejected.

Then it is shot with one round, which is centered as much as possible on the face of the block and parallel to the sides, the penetration distance is measured (to a quarter of an inch), and the bullet is extracted, measured and weighed. The FBI does this five times for each of the eight tests, one shot per block, and averages the penetration depths and expansion and weight retention of the sample bullets recovered.

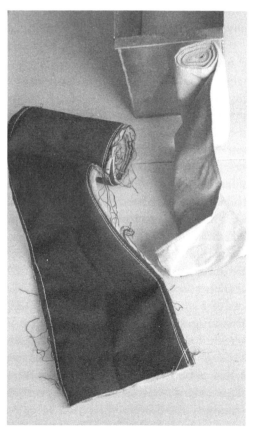

The tests are performed by firing the sample round out of a suitable duty weapon. The first six of the tests are performed with the face of the block ten

Auto glass is also tested at 20 yards, because you are not always shooting into vehicles the moment before they hit you. At least, we hope not.

feet from the muzzle of the handgun. The last two are done with the block at twenty yards.

TEST ONE: BARE GELATIN

The bare gelatin test does three things. It provides a reference for testers who only use bare gelatin, and who do not use various barriers. (Gel is expensive enough, adding the cost and extra work of barriers can be prohibitive.) It provides a test for shooting incidents where the victim might be wearing only a thin t-shirt or not wearing a shirt at all. Also, it provides a first-step check. If a bullet that is designed to expand does not perform properly or as-expected in bare gelatin, there is no point in continuing.

Consider this the "summer's day in a hot place" test.

TEST TWO: HEAVY CLOTHING

Here, the gelatin has a test sample of "heavy clothing" draped over the front face. This is a loose (not stitched or quilted) layering of four cloths: cotton t-shirt material (48 threads per inch), cotton shirt material (80 tpi), 10-ounce down comforter in a cambric shell cover (232 tpi), and 13-ounce cotton denim (50 tpi). This simulates a typical cold-weather layering, worn by someone who isn't expecting arctic conditions.

This would be the "winter work clothes" test.

TEST THREE: STEEL

Two sheets of 20-gauge, hot-rolled steel with a galvanized finish are set 3 inches apart. The steel is composed of 6-inch squares, set vertical to the face of the gelatin, facing the shooter. The gelatin sits 18 inches behind the steel, and the steel is 10 feet from the muzzle. A single layer of light clothing (the t-shirt material from Test One) is placed over the front face

CHAPTER 8: THE FBI PROTOCOLS | **117**

of the gelatin. The very-popular "light clothing" cloth is used in all the barrier tests, laid on the front face of the gelatin.

You can call this the "bad guy in a car" test.

TEST FOUR: WALLBOARD

Two 6-inch square pieces of standard half-inch gypsum wallboard are placed 3.5 inches apart and 18 inches ahead of the gelatin. The front face of the gypsum is 10 feet from the muzzle, and the gelatin is draped with the light clothing.

This is the "inside of a house" test.

TEST FIVE: PLYWOOD

One piece of AA fir plywood is used here, 6 inches square, as with the other tests. Ten feet from the muzzle, gelatin, with light clothing, 18 inches behind the plywood.

This one adds to the house test, with a standardized layer of harder-than-drywall material as the barrier. Someone might have put up a temporary section of wall, using plywood, until the rest of the remodeling is done. At the moment I write this, a neighbor down the block has part of his kitchen exterior wall as a sheet of plywood. It may not be all that common, but it is easily obtained, and a well understood barrier to test on.

TEST SIX: AUTO GLASS

One piece of A.S.I quarter-inch laminated automobile safety glass, 15x18 inches, is set at an angle of 45 degrees to the horizontal. The glass is also rotated 15 degrees laterally to the angle of the shot, to create a "compound angle" for the bullet impact. As above, glass 10 feet from the muzzle, gelatin 18 inches behind, light clothing.

This simulates the windshield of an automobile or truck. Unlike the side glass, which is called "safety glass" and will break into a thousand small pieces, the laminated glass stays intact when broken. So, this is the "bad guy in a car, trying to run you over" test.

TEST SEVEN: HEAVY CLOTHING, 20 YARDS

This one is the same as Test Two, but with the distance from muzzle to clothing 20 yards instead of 10 feet.

Bullets must be extracted to be weighed and measured. If you plan to re-use the blocks, use forceps to extract them. Otherwise, it is bowie knife time, and cut them out.

118 | GunDigest.com

TEST EIGHT: AUTO GLASS

Same as Test Six, but 20 yards instead of 10 feet. The auto glass is tipped back 45 degrees, but not laterally angled 15.

The FBI testers then (or concurrently) test velocity and accuracy. They fire 20 rounds through a test barrel for velocity, and then 20 rounds through the same service weapon used in the penetration tests. They fire two 10-shot groups through the test barrel for accuracy, and repeat that through the service weapon.

SCORING

The FBI scores the tested ammunition on a number of variables. First, it must penetrate a minimum of twelve inches or it is a failed sample. As I have said and written in the past, a bullet that penetrated eleven and a half inches and expanded to the diameter of a manhole cover fails the FBI tests. You might not consider it a failure, and you are free to select the "manhole cover man-stopper" as your ammunition of choice. Second, it cannot penetrate more than eighteen inches, or it also fails. In the defensive role, overpenetration is as bad as underpenetration, as far as the FBI is concerned. When you consider how many police shootings happen in populated areas, you have to agree. However, a deputy working a rural area, where overpenetration "endangers" the neighbors of the next farm or ranch three miles away, isn't as worried.

They measure expansion. The more, the better. But, a bullet cannot suffer a core-jacket separation, or the score suffers as a result. So, expansion while

Above: When you shoot barriers with hollowpoints, you often get a plug chipped out of the barrier by the opening. Sometimes this stays with the bullet even after it has plowed into the gelatin, and even after you extract it. This is what the CSI techs will be looking for, to prove the case.

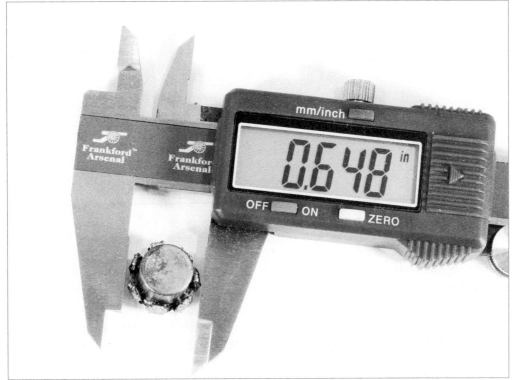

Left: When the expanded bullet is extracted, it is measured, and the expansion is the widest measurement that can be gotten. Not the average, the maximum.

It takes a pile of barriers and a ton of gel to test a bullet according to FBI specs. This takes time and costs a lot of money, which is why everyone doesn't do it.

holding together is vital. And, it has to expand even after passing through the barriers. This is known in the trade as a "barrier blind" bullet.

ANALYSIS

As you can see, a full test requires 40 blocks of gelatin, which probably takes a crew of FBI agents or technicians a full day to prepare. It takes many hours to chill, even with a walk-in freezer. If the FBI expects to get the most out of the agent's time and range time, they need a hundred molds at work, and a crew measuring, melting, pouring, chilling, etc. It is my understanding that gelatin is not re-used, but the FBI won't say one way or the other.

Barriers other than cloth are not re-used, so each load tested also consumes ten sheets of steel, ten sheets of wallboard, five pieces of plywood, and ten pieces of auto glass. (Try not to finish with "a partridge in a pear tree.")

What does all this tell us? The bare gel test is simple, it is the baseline, the yardstick. Once you know what the maximum performance of a bullet is in gel, you can then assess its changed performance in the barrier tests.

Heavy clothing is the first barrier tested. Unless the shootout is in a nudist colony, people will be wearing clothes. One of the problems we first encountered, in the beginning of the IWBA and gelatin testing, was that some hollowpoints worked well on bare gel, but when they cookie-cut a piece of cloth out of a shirt or jacket, the plugged hollowpoint failed to expand. In that instance, a JHP that had stopped and fully expanded at 14 inches of gel would, when the gelatin block was draped in cloth, sail out the back, unexpanded. Once this was known, the ammunition makers could address it by altering the design or construction of the bullets.

The steel barrier is meant to represent an

Auto glass is the hardest on bullets, with steel a close second. And yet, these bullets held together, expanded some, and still drove deeply into the gel.

automobile. Twenty-gauge is the heaviest gauge steel you'll find, and the thinnest part of a door, lacking motors, pulleys, etc. will be two sheets of steel with air in-between. If you expect to get a bullet through the other parts inside the door – the impact bars, window mechanism and motors, etc. – you had best give up all ideas of a handgun and go to rifles. And those rifles had better have calibers that start with "3". Shotguns? Buckshot can't be counted on, and even slugs might fail, depending on, of all things, how hard the lead alloy is.

The wallboard test tells what a bullet will do when fired in a frame structure. A bad guy using a doorframe as "cover" will be greatly surprised to find that it doesn't stop much, unless the shot happens to hit a stud or junction box. This is, for the homeowner, a valid test. However, do you really want something that will sail right through a wall? If you know where you family members all are, that might be just fine.

A test reported to me by a friend is illustrative. He ran a large multi-jurisdictional SWAT team, and they had a neighborhood that was going to be torn down. (I never found out why, or what would replace it.) They had an opportunity to test-fire anything they wanted, inside and through real buildings. The results, in a nutshell, were that all handgun bullets of any type exited all frame structures. Unless it hit something steel, like a pipe or junction box, or the building was sheathed in masonry, bullets left the building. They will all leave, but only some of them will expand in a felon after passing through a wall. That's what the FBI tests for.

Plywood is the test used as a general check on doors, furniture, and anything else wooden but not load-bearing. A load-bearing wooden element will stop a defensive handgun bullet. A typical load-bearing wooden element would be a 4x4. (And that would be a lightweight one, at

CHAPTER 8: THE FBI PROTOCOLS | **121**

Getting bullets to penetrate isn't hard. Getting them to expand is more difficult. Getting them to expand after going through barriers is tough. In the early days, all we had was penetration.

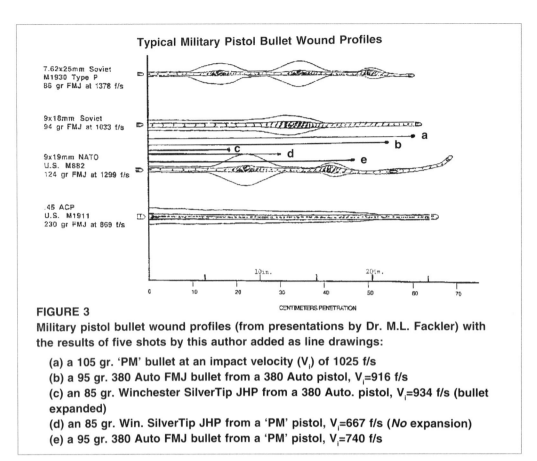

FIGURE 3
Military pistol bullet wound profiles (from presentations by Dr. M.L. Fackler) with the results of five shots by this author added as line drawings:

(a) a 105 gr. 'PM' bullet at an impact velocity (V_i) of 1025 f/s
(b) a 95 gr. 380 Auto FMJ bullet from a 380 Auto pistol, V_i=916 f/s
(c) an 85 gr. Winchester SilverTip JHP from a 380 Auto. pistol, V_i=934 f/s (bullet expanded)
(d) an 85 gr. Win. SilverTip JHP from a 'PM' pistol, V_i=667 f/s (*No expansion*)
(e) a 95 gr. 380 Auto FMJ bullet from a 'PM' pistol, V_i=740 f/s

that.) A frame wall built to hold a solid-core door is generally composed of two or three 2x4s nailed together. (Or at least it is in the frame houses I'm familiar with.)

The automobile glass is meant to represent just that, auto glass. Laminated glass has a layer of tough, clear plastic, bonded between two sheets of glass. The result is a tough barrier, one that is hard on bullets. Tipping it back is a good thing, as most windshields will be at an angle when you try to shoot through them. (If you do.) The FBI is a bit overly fussy, in my opinion, with the double angle setting.

The idea is to present the bullet with an angled impact surface on the shot, as when a car goes past an agent, or as they approach from the side and have to fire through the edge or corner of the windshield. The problem is, there is no such thing as a "compound" angle on a flat sheet. The intersection of a line (the trajectory) and a plane (the sheet of glass) simply has an angle of incidence.

A curved surface presents a compound angle, or can. But controlling for that, in a test environment, would be impossible. So they use a flat sheet of glass, and tip it back and to the side.

The auto glass in Test Eight, simply tipped back, is an easier angle to measure and set consistently.

And repeating the tests for Seven and Eight is done to see what change, if any, the loss of velocity presents to performance. Short answer: not much, if any at all. The velocity loss of a bullet, having travelled the extra 17 yards, is less than the loss of going to a shorter barrel for easier concealment.

TIME TELLS ALL

Since the FBI made it official, every ammunition manufacturer became lashed to the procrustean bed of ballistic gelatin. When a new bullet is announced, the first question is, invariably, how does it perform in the FBI tests? Even when it

Left: The FBI testing methods, which require barrier penetration, drove the bullet design efforts that lead to the Critical Duty bullet. It is mechanically bonded, and as a result, the core and jacket stay together even after traversing barriers. And it still expands in gelatin after that.

Below: The FBI tests have lead to bullets that remain intact, expand effectively and consistently, and that offer more performance than bullets ever have.

is not meant as a law enforcement load, it is held to that yardstick.

Why is this a bad thing? There are a few reasons.

One, it takes a good deal of horsepower to perform on the FBI tests. Not all calibers can do it, and some common ones fail. The exemplar here is the .38 Special. You can get many a .38 Special load to cross the twelve-inch threshold in bare gelatin. Many will even expand while doing that. But you will find it a snappy load to shoot, and it will fail the 12-inch threshold out of a snubbie. Put barriers in the way and every .38 Special load fails. They penetrate a useful distance and even expand, but they won't go twelve inches. Fail.

Big secret: some 9mm loads that pass with flying colors will also fail when fired from an ultra-compact 9mm. Why? Velocity.

The FBI tests, simply as a matter of engineering and physics, reward velocity. It takes speed or mass to penetrate. It takes speed to expand. The 9mm is rewarded in the tests, perhaps disproportionately, because it can generate speed. The .357 Magnum is in the same boat, while the real rocket here is the .357 Sig. But, put the 9mm and the .357s in an ultra-compact pistol, one that cuts into the speed, and they start to look a little more humble.

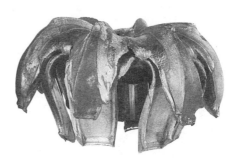

CHAPTER 8: THE FBI PROTOCOLS | **123**

The effect has also been seen in the bigger bores. The traditional man-stoppers, the .44-40, .44 Special and .45 Colt, for example, were considered to be proven performers in the olden days. They featured 200- to 255-grain lead bullets, and they thumped bad guys.

Now, if they are still loaded for defensive purposes you'll see bullets of 180 grains or 200 grains as jacketed hollow points. Why? First, because you have to give up some weight to get the velocities needed for expansion. And second, because you can't keep the weight up, create a hollow point, and fit it into the case and handgun.

So, a lead semi-wadcutter of 240 grains for a .44 Special that worked in the old days is now a 200-grain JHP, at 200 fps more velocity. The .45 Colt gets the same treatment, dropping from 255 grains to 200, adding velocity, and expanding.

THE FBI TEST ISN'T A THEORY

This should be obvious, but a lot of people still miss the point. The FBI test predicts nothing. The FBI is smart enough to avoid saying "this is better because…" and leaves it up to the end-user.

The test, properly done and considered, does not depend on the wound track in the gelatin. As mentioned, this is a very difficult thing to measure. The best I've seen to show it is done by Hornady and Black Hills. They shoot the block, then stand it on end and force red dye into the wound track to highlight what was done to the block.

This, of course, makes it impossible to re-use the block, so it is expensive. And, while it is interesting, it still is not the point.

We are considering the tests as a second-order measure of bullet effectiveness. The logic chain goes like this:

- Ballistic gelatin is a uniform and consistent product.
- It produces replicable results over time, and across distances and institutional settings.
- Ballistic gelatin is a close-enough approximation of human tissue, and bullets react to it in a manner similar to their reaction in tissue.
- We need more than a foot, but not more than eighteen inches of penetration in gelatin.
- Bullets that expand do more damage than ones that do not.
- Bullets that break apart do less damage than ones that hold together.
- The best bullet is the one that expands the most, goes as deeply as possible but not past 18 inches, holds together, and does this consistently.

That's it. No predictions that "X" is

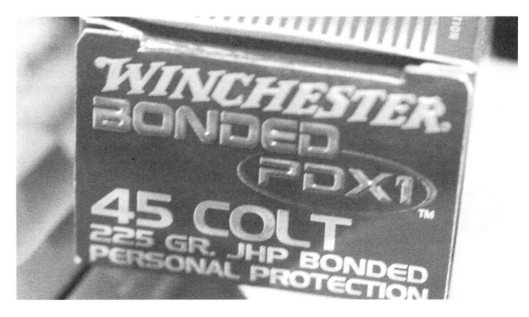

Even if we don't need FBI-compliant ammo, we end up getting it because it can be done. Making the .45 Colt pass the FBI tests is easy. After all, you're starting with a .451-inch bullet that weighs 225 grains and exits the muzzle at 900 fps, more or less. After all, we know it works well even if it doesn't expand.

such-and-such a percentage better than "Y" or "Z."

What it is, is an assumption. The assumption is that the steps in the bullet points above correlate relatively well with real-world results; that the costs to gain the benefits of those steps are worth the effort; and that people are people, bullets are bullets, and none of the situations will change much in the near future.

DO YOU NEED FBI AMMO?

That depends. There's a curious attitude out there among some who should know better. It concerns the Hornady Critical Defense line of ammunition. The naysayers look at it – the lesser velocity, lighter bullet weights, and less-than-FBI-compliant performance – and somehow come up with the idea that Hornady is perpetrating a scam. That somehow the staff and family of Hornady are sneaking into their homes at night, stealing fps out of their gun safes, and making their ammunition less-effective. They take it personally.

As I have said repeatedly and will say again: this is America. You have choices. Hornady offers ammunition with the best performance that can be extracted from a load, in loadings that will not be flinch-inducing in those who don't need, don't want, or can't take the full FBI-level performance. If the only "acceptable" ammunition is that which fully passes, even scores very high on the FBI tests, and anything else is not worthy, what do you tell someone who wants to defend themselves? What about the person who has problems of age, joint aches, or hand strength issues? Should they just "suck it up, and do it right?" Who are you to tell them what is and isn't right, in their own defense?

Hornady is in fact, quite clever. Not everyone wants or needs the noise and drama of the FBI loads. Not everyone can handle the recoil such loads generate. And some are quite happy with an accurate, soft-shooting load that lets them feel safe at night, and which they do not dread dropping the hammer on.

Some people need a four-wheel-drive ton-and-a-half pickup truck just to get to work each day. And a lot of other people just need a car that starts and gets them to the store without excessive cost, drama, insurance or stress from excessive size.

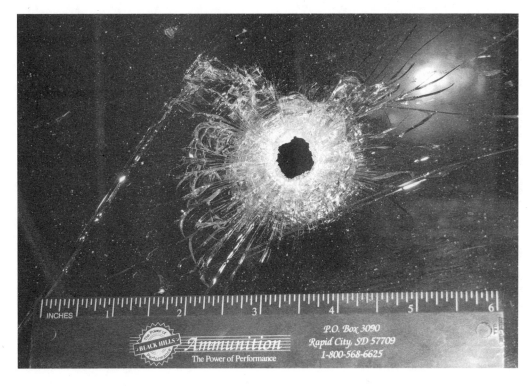

In this test of Hornady 40SW 180s on auto glass, notice that the glass holds together around the hole, despite being pulverized. Glass is very hard on bullets. Image courtesy Black Hills.

CHAPTER 8: THE FBI PROTOCOLS | **125**

9

LESS-EXPENSIVE OPTIONS

Ballistic gelatin can be injected with red dye to show the wound track. But this pretty much eliminates a second use, even while it highlights the effects.

As we saw in Chapter Six, the FBI tests cost a lot of money. To do the whole test for a single caliber bullet and load requires at least a week's worth of work for a single experimenter, nearly half a ton of ballistic gelatin, and a pickup truck of barriers, stands, chrono, gun and ammo. After all that work, you have to find a dumpster where you can shove all the gelatin (even re-used, it only lasts a few shots), and it would be good for your future use of gelatin and dumpsters if it were a dumpster where no one will complain about the smell as decomposes.

And that's for one. If you want a comparison load, you do it all over again.

Many a shooter/experimenter has thought, "There must be something that costs less." Yes, but now we're really starting to stretch the "simulant" aspect of the testing, using a simulant of a simulant. We have to be very careful about assessing the results, comparing them to ballistic gelatin, and drawing conclusions from simulant-of-a-simulant tests.

In the old days, shooters, writers and experimenters "demonstrated" the power of a particular load by shooting the weirdest things — bars of soap, for one. They were mostly used for small handgun calibers, in part because they were cheap, and a .22LR hollowpoint looked impressive when you whacked a bar of Ivory with it. The problem with soap is that it is an inelastic medium, and what it shows you is the temporary cavity in soap, frozen in time. Not much correlation to gel, tissue, or anything else for that matter.

Soda cans, aerosol cans, paint cans all looked impressive, exploding in midair and splattering their contents, if you caught them at just the right moment in a photograph. While spectacular, they prove exactly nothing, except the spectacle of exploding cans.

A lot of experimenters, especially in the Pacific Northwest, used a slurry of sawdust mixed with water. This, and water-logged newsprint, works reasonably

CHOOSING HANDGUN AMMO | **127**

If you plan to use milk jugs, rinse them out. Otherwise, the smell will be enough to make you persona non grata at the gun club for some time to come.

well for rifle calibers, testing their use on heavy-bodied or large-boned game animals. But, this approach has some particular problems, which we'll look into in a bit.

Testers looking for better, more consistent, results settled on three approaches: containers, bulk and synthetics.

CONTAINERS

The containers were flimsy objects holding water. The old choice was a half-gallon coated pasteboard box, like those that contain milk. Back before plastic took over everything, milk came in half-gallon boxes, and the boxes were made of pasteboard. It is a compressed, felt-like material of paper pulp or grindings and glue. To make it waterproof (milk-proof?) the pasteboard was coated with wax, later plastic, and finally they just changed to plastic. I'm describing them only because you rarely see them anymore, but you might be curious.

They were filled with water because milk was too expensive to shoot, and you only had to do it once to discover you were dis-invited from that range or gun club, at least until you promised to not ever shoot milk again. Gun-splattered milk and a hot summer day is a recipe for horrifying stench.

The modern replacements are one-gallon water jugs. You can buy them with water in them, or use empty milk jugs and fill them with water. Stand them in a line on a table and shoot into the fat portion of the jugs. The cost is low, the cleanup is minimal (gather the busted jugs and recycle/trash them) and there is no smell. Well, the cost can be somewhat low. If you have access to a milk-drinking family, you can score a truckload of saved, empty and rinsed milk

jugs for cheap or no cost. Then fill them with water from the tap. A gallon of water from the tap will cost you maybe a penny, unless you live someplace like Arizona or California. A gallon of water at the store costs you a couple of dollars a gallon. Five saved-bullet test shots of a handgun load can easily use up 20 gallon jugs, so a test using store-bought water would be $40 in water. From the tap, not even a quarter, so it would be very clever of you to become friendly with the neighbors who have kids.

The downsides? Many, as it turns out. First, you can only estimate penetration. There are several approaches to determining penetration, using the width of the jugs fully penetrated, and the damage done to the last jug, to calculate a gelatin penetration correction factor. That is, was the last jug one that was next in line, not penetrated, but dented on its outside? Cracked?

Was the bullet stuck between jugs? Did the bullet fail to escape the last jug it entered, but dent, or crack the back wall?

The idea is taken to a slightly finer degree of precision with a "Fackler box." This is a wooden trough, large enough to hold one-gallon Ziploc bags. Fill each bag, seal it, stand them in a row in the trough, then shoot. Measure the distance the bullet travels.

The big difference between these tests is the plastic. (And the cost of the bags, which are more expensive than free empty jugs, but much, much less than store-bought jugs of water.) The relatively tough walls of the milk jugs are a barrier that somewhat muddies the determination of penetration distance, and they act as a much more abrasive media on the bullet. While you can determine relative penetration distances, vis-à-vis ballistic gelatin, with both of these approaches, a bullet fired

Water will splash. You will get wet, and so will your guns and gear. You will also be walking in a rice paddy-like environment in short order. Dress appropriately.

CHAPTER 9: LESS-EXPENSIVE OPTIONS | **129**

We explored the use of paper in the old days. For a while it worked, but the amount of paper to be had for testing these days is much less. If you're spending more time and effort scoring paper to shoot than you are shooting, you're probably doing it wrong.

into jugs will be worked harder. A bullet that would not have a core-jacket separation in gelatin or a Fackler box might well come apart in the grabby, abrasive plastic of the jugs. In that instance, a test using gallon jugs will produce a score harsher than would one performed in bare gelatin.

But, these options are inexpensive. If you can make a Fackler box, you can buy plastic bags. If you can afford water jugs, or you feed kids the milk anyway and save the jugs, you can use those and the cost is simply the water and the work.

One detail you might want to note, if you plan to use plastic jugs: they are not sturdy. They are made of HDPE, high density polyethylene, and while it is plenty strong enough for holding milk, it isn't a long-term product. They are made by blowing a blob of HDPE into a mold, and the resulting bottle averages just about 0.02-inch thickness. It has a pretty good yield strength, which is why it is used to hold milk, water and other fluids. Dropped form a reasonable height, it won't break. But once the sheet has been "crinkled," the stress risers created will quickly cause a failure.

If you use them and store them, use the stressed ones first and store the perfect ones. Otherwise, they will age-crack and leak. This is accelerated in a cold climate. If you store your water jug supply in an unheated place, the thermal changes will not just crack them, they will split. I found this out when I first started this, and had a 50% loss rate of jugs stored in plastic bags, from the stressors I hadn't paid attention to.

One note on making a Fackler box: water is an incompressible medium. When you whack the gallon sacks in a Fackler box, the water will jet up out of the box, and back out the hole you just shot through the front plate or board. You'll get wet. And unless you make your box well, you will split, break or otherwise turn your trough into trough parts.

Dress appropriately for the task. Shooting a row of gallon water jugs with a magnum caliber on a flimsy table will damage the table. You'll soon be ankle-deep in muddy water from the jugs or box, and you and all the gear for a twenty-foot radius will also be wet or damp.

You can gain a pretty good rough estimate of a bullet's performance, for not a lot of money and just a bit of work, but not nearly as much work as ballistic gelatin would require.

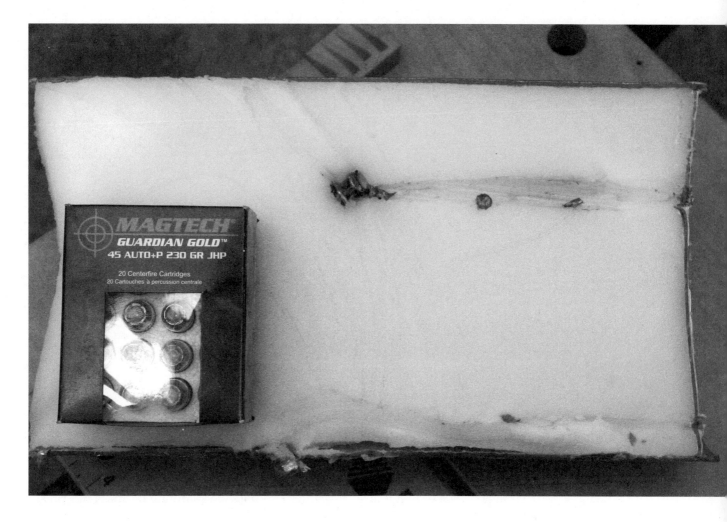

A Bullet Test Tube, shot by a 230-grain .45+P all-copper bullet. Penetration? Six inches, maybe. And expansion? The bullet fragmented, which we know is not what this bullet does in gelatin.

BULK

Bulk is waterlogged paper. You can use water-soaked phone books (although those are not as common as they used to be) or a Fackler box filled with paper pulp.

The paper approach has added problems that the water alone does not have. First of all, what kind of paper? If you save newsprint, you will find it takes months of saving to create enough paper to test a single load for a couple of shots. Newspapers are not nearly as thick or common as they used to be. When I first got interested in bullet performance (back in the second Reagan administration), I could easily cruise the neighborhood on garbage day at dawn and fill the back of my pickup truck with bundled newspaper left at the curb. Today, that simply isn't possible. When it came time to switch phone books, I could do the same thing. Back before cell phones or Internet, a phone book could be four or five inches thick. When it came time to change books (an annual event), each book was as good as a week's worth of newspaper, and easily picked up at the curb on trash day.

For those of you who think "paper is paper," I have news for you. In a previous life I used to manage a paper warehouse whose customers were the printing industry in town. Paper arrived and left our store by the literal ton. The varieties, thickness, strengths and coatings were impressive to consider. Even paper called "newsprint" was not all the same, and could make a difference were you to use it for bullet testing.

Second, how much water? And how do you keep the paper "soaking wet" long enough to stop hosing it, pick up

CHAPTER 9: LESS-EXPENSIVE OPTIONS | **131**

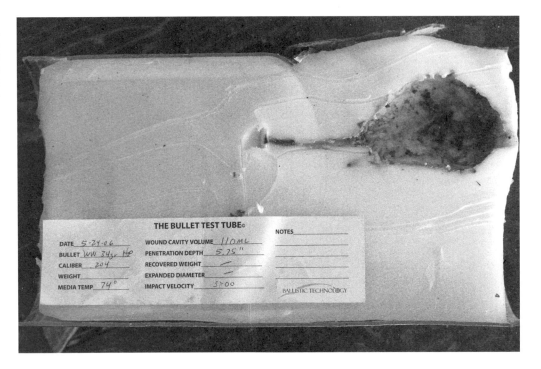

The Bullet Test Tube, whacked with a .204 Ruger varmint load. This is more like what the bullet would do, so the BTT was not useful for handgun experimenters.

your firearm, and shoot the paper? With a Fackler box it is a bit easier, as you can measure the amount. But it takes time to properly soak and make squishy a truckload of paper. So, your Fackler box had better be waterproof while you wait the half-hour, hour or two it takes to get the paper completely soggy.

A second-order problem is that paper weighs a lot. So does water. A gallon weighs about eight pounds. A carton of plain old copy paper (5,000 sheets) weighs 60 pounds. You'll need more volume than that to capture any and all handgun bullets you shoot. So, factor in two cartons of paper. A Fackler box filled with newsprint and sogged to the point of being pulpy could have twenty gallons in it. That totals 280 pounds of contents, plus the weight of the box. Are the two flimsy sawhorses you just bought at the big-box store strong enough to hold them and stay in place when they get whacked by the bullet?

The soggy box of paper is more-often seen in hunting circles, as they are interested in how rifle bullets perform on large game animals. I can't help but also notice that it is more popular in rural areas, particularly the northwest, where you might have the charge of scoring a pickup truck full of paper pulp from a mill to use in testing. As I said, saving up newspapers takes a long time, unless you are the delivery guy or a voracious reader.

Plus, determining the exact distance of penetration by a handgun bullet is tough, as you have to dig through the pulpy, wet paper to find each one. Finding fragments of the bullet? Not a chance.

GELATIN SUBSTITUTES

The problems with ballistic gelatin are not to be overlooked. It is expensive, both to acquire the gelatin pellets (it comes dehydrated, you have to mix it) and the time and effort to mix, cool, transport and work with. A block can cost you $150. It takes a working day to mix and pour blocks, and then you have to wait at least another day to use it (more unless you have a walk-in cooler the size of a garage). It is cold (4 degrees Celsius, 38 Fahrenheit), slippery, and anything that it touches will smell of gel, and later, decomposing gel.

You can re-use it, not easily, and not without a loss of precision. (Finding

Left: Clear Ballistics gel comes in cartons, easy to handle and store. It can be re-used, and it is what it says, clear, not cloudy, like animal-derived gel.

Below: Each Clear Ballistics gel block is wrapped in cellophane and can be shot with the cellophane on it. (This block has already been shot.) They come calibrated, but be sure and take off the cellophane before you melt the block to re-use it.

a bullet in a really murky, second- or third-hand block can be a trial and error process. Also, re-used blocks might not be as consistent, and there's no way of knowing if they are or not.)

If you do not fancy making gel, you can use a synthetic substitute.

Some ten years ago or more, there was a company, Ballistic Technology, that made the Bullet Test Tube. It was a cardboard tube, filled with a waxy substance, and you simply shot into the open end. Then, since the substance was not temperature-dependant, you would cut the length of the tube down the middle, and see the cavity left by the bullet. You could re-use the substance, provided you could find a suitable cardboard tube to

CHAPTER 9: LESS-EXPENSIVE OPTIONS | **133**

use, having sliced open the original one. And, you had to find a relatively clean way to melt the stuff.

The big problem with the tube was simple: the substance (I still have no idea what it was, it could well have been crystallized faerie tears for all I know) was too dense. It offered an impressive "report" on the temporary cavity, but an unrealistic dimension on penetration and bullet performance. Bullets, especially rifle bullets, basically blew up and fragmented in the stuff.

A newer one that a lot of people have suggested is Perma-Gel. I haven't used it, but it appears to do the job. You can buy it as a mix or as a gel block (obviously, shipping will be more for the block). This is not to be confused with Permagel, the solution used as a wall sealant for basements. Perma-Gel is a clear synthetic and does not have to be refrigerated. It can be re-used. It can be a bit pricey, but then anything new and useful will likely be pricey.

One I have used is Clear Ballistics gel. It and the Perma-Gel have a number of advantages over the original. First, they are synthetic, and therefore not a biological product. That means they won't rot, they won't attract insects or animals, and they can be re-used.

They are clear, enough that you can more-easily photograph the bullet in-situ and the wound track.

They do not have to be refrigerated, and they can be stored indefinitely.

Neither requires refrigeration, so you have less of a problem with calibration. When the traditional gelatin gets warmer, it becomes easier for a bullet to penetrate and the gel has less effect in creating bullet expansion. That's why the FBI/IWBA method requires a chronograph and a BB gun. If your gel warms up out of spec, you have to either re-cool it or discard it. Clear Ballistics gel, short of a blistering Caribbean afternoon, isn't going to be a problem. (And then it will be so slick, in part from your own sweat, that wrestling it into place will be not fun.)

Re-using the Clear Ballistics gel is easy. Pry out the bits and pieces of the old bullets. For most that will be easy, but everything you leave behind will make the block murkier for the next test. They recommend chopping the block into pieces, but you can just slip it back into the mold in one piece, if it is still more-or-less a unit.

Heat your oven to 250-270 degrees and, once up to temp, slide in the mold with gel in it. Be patient and wait the full, recommended four hours, or until all the bubbles are gone from the middle. Here's a tip: every time you open the door to peek and see if there are bubbles, you cool the oven and the block (and risk burning yourself) and add time to how long it will take to melt and settle. Just set a timer for four hours and call it good. Cool for twelve hours.

Now, someone is going to get the clever idea of using a water bath to cool the mold faster. Let's remember a little science, shall we? What temperature will the mold be? That's right, 250-270 F. And what is the boiling point of water? Last I checked, it was 212 Fahrenheit. So, you will be creating steam when you dunk the mold, which might, what? Yes, scald you, or cause you to drop the mold, splashing water, and perhaps tipping your melted gel into the water, and spoiling your gel for testing. Again, be patient.

What is Clear Ballistics gel made of? I downloaded the MSDS (Material Safety Data Sheet) and look a look. Hmm, the percentage of components listed as "oil" was 75-95. The percentage of "gellants" was 5 to 25. Both further described as "Trade Secret." So, rather than patent it or make it easy for competitors, Clear Ballistics just says, "It's good stuff, and good luck trying to figure out exactly what it is, so you can make a cheaper version." Which, as a college graduate with a degree in chemistry, I have to nod sagely and say to myself, "Darn straight, you figured it out, don't make it easy for competitors."

Reading through the emergency and health notifications, this stuff is about as innocuous as is possible. I'm surprised they don't have the near-obligatory, "May contain substances suspected to cause cancer by the fainting nannies of California" simply because California seems to think waking up in the morning causes cancer. Nope, no known cancer-causing agents, and to give yourself problems you apparently have to lean into the oven and breathe deeply of the vapors coming off when you re-melt it. (I joke, don't do that.)

The melting point is 198 degrees, which is why you have to heat it to 250 or so to get it to re-gel into a single block for re-use.

The point is, Clear Ballistics gel is so innocuous that your biggest risk from it is in burning yourself handling the hot mold, filled with liquid gel, on re-casting. So, be careful.

ESTIMATION

Okay, let's take another stab at this. We are using ballistic gelatin as a simulant, since we can't go shooting people at random and recording the results. We are then assuming there is a reasonable correlation between what we see in gel and what we would see in people.

Using Clear Ballistics gel or Perma-Gel is a partial but not complete step away from ballistic gelatin. As industrial products, they can be formulated to come close to what ballistic gelatin does, but neither is ballistic gelatin. (That may actually be a good thing, in the long run.)

Water in cartons, jugs or bags in a box, is a step away from ballistic gelatin. So is the use of sogged paper, pulp, sawdust, etc. The trick is to find how much they differ. I have done a lot of experimenting with water and have come to a disturbing conclusion: there is no universal correlation constant between water and gelatin.

What do I mean by that? The most common correlation factor I have read is to take the depth of water penetrated and divide by 1.55 to generate the penetration in bare gelatin. So, if a bullet goes 24 inches into water in jugs, you divide by 1.55 to determine that it would have gone 15.5 inches deep in gelatin.

Except, I have found that some bullets (and there is no clear way to sort one from another) require a different correlation factor. I've had some bullets that required a 2.15 divisor to get their water depth number to correspond to their ballistic gelatin penetration depth.

This is like the confusing-to-some change that the ammunition companies and loading data publishers made, when they switched from copper crusher measurements to transducers. Both were measured in PSI. And yet, it was not possible to apply a uniform corrective factor from the copper measurement PSI numbers to the transducer measurements.

And so it is with water jugs. Some bullets will compliantly penetrate in water jugs, the same adjusted depths they would have in gelatin. Others will not, penetrating deeper in water jugs (with the standard 1.55 correction factor) than they would in gelatin. And there's no way to predict which it will be.

As a last note to keep things in the correct frame of reference, the water jug test will also be harder on the bullet itself than bare gel would be. A bullet that will not show jacket-core separation in bare gel will show separation in water jugs. Water jugs are more abrasive in that variable than bare gel, but less-so than the FBI barriers would be.

Use the water jug test to see expansion, don't hang too much weight on penetration until you can do a cross-check with ballistic gelatin, and keep in mind that you are working the bullet harder than bare gel, but not as hard as barriers.

10 TESTING

Left: Chronographs are cheap now. If you are planning to actually test bullets, you must have a chronograph or no one will take your data seriously.

Below: The first two of many numbered bullet boxes, each with a particular tested bullet or bullets in it. Keep them safe, keep them separate, or someday you'll look at a pile of bullets and ask, "Which one is which?"

I've been testing bullets for a couple of decades now and have experienced almost all of the available methods, with a host of calibers. Some of this has been in law enforcement seminars and ammunition manufacturer visits. I've done testing in LE classes, where we demonstrate how bullets work and dispel some of the greater urban myths. I started before digital photography, so the first half of that work was done with film. (For those who have worked their entire lives so far with digital, you cannot imagine the hassle and cost of doing everything with film. It was just awful.)

I did not set out to re-do all that work for this book. It would have been impossible. Instead, I gathered all my notes, photos, etc., and used those as the starting point. I also used manufacturers' information with regard to bullet performance. Fortunately, thanks to the work of Dr. Fackler and the FBI to ensure uniformity in testing, if a test done with bullet "A" by the maker is done properly then I can reasonably compare it to bullet "B" by that maker.

In fact, use of IWBA/FBI tests is now comparable to the widespread availability of chronographs. We can all now check the velocity of a given load for ourselves, in our own handguns, and be certain of the numbers. If there is a variance between performance from one report to another, it is due to atmospheric conditions or the variables of chamber

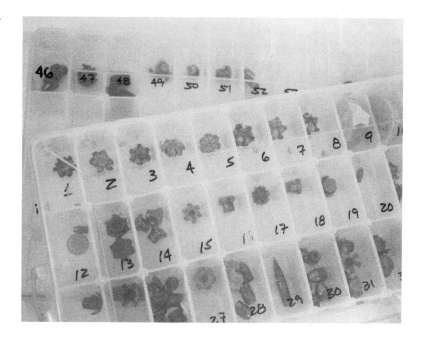

CHOOSING HANDGUN AMMO | **137**

Right: Ballistic testing can be elaborate and involve specialty equipment. This gel bench allows for portable testing, provided you can arrange for the gel to be there. The gel is heavy part.

Below: If you are trying to be non-messy, you use big hemostats to pluck the bullet out of the gelatin. Otherwise, you just slice in with a big, sharp knife and get the bullet out. After all, you are using the gel once, right? Right? In case of a fragmenting bullet, you might melt the gel and run the remains through a filter, to get all the fragments. In any case, it is a lot of work.

and bore size, not a PR attempt to prove one is better than another.

The difference remains, however, that a chronograph is relatively inexpensive now, but ballistic gelatin still comes at a staggering cost.

So, the images in this publication are not uniform. They've come from a variety of sources, over a span of time, relatively speaking. And yes, a lot of them are from the manufacturers. That's life.

HOW TO DO THIS

It is fun and games, testing bullets and saving samples, but if you expect to have a body of knowledge at some time in the future, you have to do some work along with the fun.

First of all, write everything down. Day and date. Weather. Firearm used, distance, material shot into, results, impressions. Don't forget the brand, caliber and bullet weight of the ammunition, and it wouldn't hurt to write down the lot number as well. That can be found on the inside of one of the flaps of the box the ammo came in.

When you save the bullets, find some way to keep them separate, numbered and identified.

Why go to all this trouble? Simple, no one has a memory good enough to keep it all straight. And if you do, you have more important things to do with such a fabulous memory than keep assorted bullets correctly identified. If you have one or two to remember, no problem. But once it gets past a dozen, which is which?

The gun writers I know who hunt for a living keep notes. (We all shoot ammo for a living, I just shoot gel, cardboard

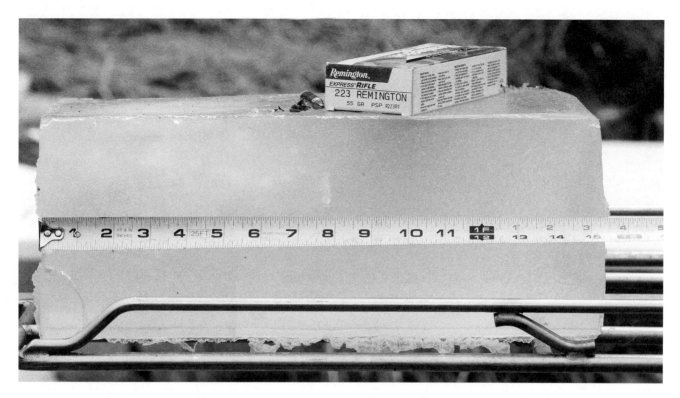

and steel. They shoot critters.) Loose-leaf after loose-leaf notebook, with pages and pages. Day and date, location, caliber, bullet, distance, animal reaction, they log it all. I had an occasion one day at an industry gathering to casually ask Craig Boddington, "Craig, have you been to Africa 100 times?" I was just joking around. To my amazement, he stopped, thought about it for a moment, and then replied, "Well, if I haven't, I'm awfully close, and will be there soon."

You may well remember your one-and-only whitetail hunt in Wisconsin, where you bagged a ten-pointer and saved the bullet. That bullet won't be forgotten. But when you test bullets in gelatin or water and end up collecting a dozen or more? You won't keep that all straight.

In LE classes (which are primarily devoted to rifles, but we do shoot gel with some handgun calibers, mostly to demonstrate the difference in performance), we write up each round and glue the recovered bullet to a big sheet of cardboard. That way each student can see the results, the details are right there with the bullet, and the bullets don't get lost, pocketed or mixed up.

The ammunition companies that do this take detailed photos, record measurements, and then print and save everything in large loose-leaf binders. The last time I visited a pressure and ballistics lab, the shelving with the loose-leaf binders stretched over twelve feet long. The bullets were in compartmentalized boxes, in the cabinets under the bookshelves.

You also keep the bullets separated so you don't ding them up. If they were tossed into a coffee can, edges would get knocked off, and they'd be dinged,

Above: The beauty of ballistic gelatin is that it is consistent. It works for handguns, rifles and shotguns, and across the continent. You just have to use it properly.

Below: Testing is target-specific. This is what happens if you shoot a steel plate with a very low velocity full-metal-jacket bullet. Would it penetrate gelatin? Oh, yes. But this "test" might lead you to a wrong conclusion. Be careful what you test for.

Above: Bullet boards from LE classes allow students to note which bullet did what, with all the data right there, and the bullets don't disappear into pockets. (Not that police officers are light-fingered, but if it "walks off" it is lost for future data.)

Right: You don't have to do barrier tests, but if you do, make sure you do them properly. Distances, angles, materials – it all matters, and must be recorded.

dented and otherwise shopworn. You don't want that to happen to your sample bullets. You worked hard to create and recover them, don't damage them.

It doesn't cost that much to get your hands on a decent digital calipers. (A quick check showed an embarrassingly large assortment of them, from $20 to $40. If that breaks the bank, you really ought to find another hobby.) As part of the detailed note-taking, measure the diameter of the expanded bullet. It is customary to record only the largest single distance, not the average of largest and smallest.

Also weigh the bullet. If you reload, you have a digital scale, use that. If not, you can acquire one. Scales come in two types, the beam scale and digital scale. Beam scales are the ones with a moving weight and a pan. They can be had from $25 to $100. Digital scales run from $25 to $75.

The process is simple, depending on your test medium. If it is ballistic gelatin or one of the clear gels, follow the FBI protocol as closely as you can and record everything. If you are using water jugs, make sure you pack a towel

Above: Measure expanded diameter. Digital calipers are inexpensive and they work like a charm. Just be sure to stock up on batteries, because you know if you have only one battery, it will die when you need it most.

Left: A digital scale is inexpensive, and you need it to record weights of recovered bullets.

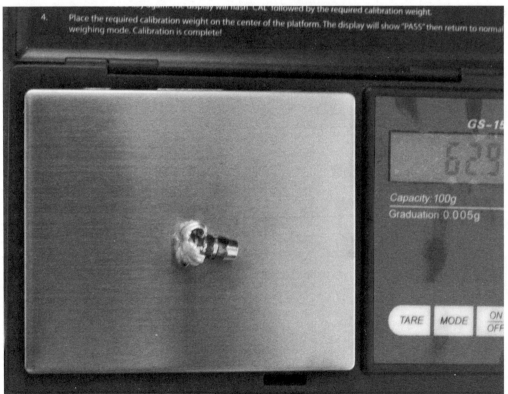

CHAPTER 10: TESTING | **141**

Right: When you set out to test bullets, you never know what you'll be testing, sometimes handguns, sometimes rifles, occasionally shotguns. They all splash gelatin.

Below: You can "test" a cartridge or bullet with just about any metric. If you make sure you keep data straight, your test is useful. What clears these bowling pins off of the tables may or may not be a suitable handgun load. But it will be proper for bowling pins.

and waterproof boots (for the mud) and clean up after yourself. Again, record everything, including detailed notes on how many jugs, and what the ending point of the bullet was like. Was the last jug surface that was struck dented, cracked, broken through or perforated?

Once you get started, you'll find more things to note and record. The more detailed and thorough you are from the start, the more useful the body of information you create will be.

Have fun.

Left: This is what happens to a full metal jacket bullet in ballistic gelatin at standard velocity (.45 ACP, 230, at 811 fps, by the way). It penetrates more than 36 inches of gelatin, does not expand, and could be loaded again.

Below: You can do more elaborate testing, and if you need the info, that's great. But, everyone measures by the FBI tests, so make sure you do those before you go exploring other avenues. Without the barriers, this is a good example of a Fackler box.

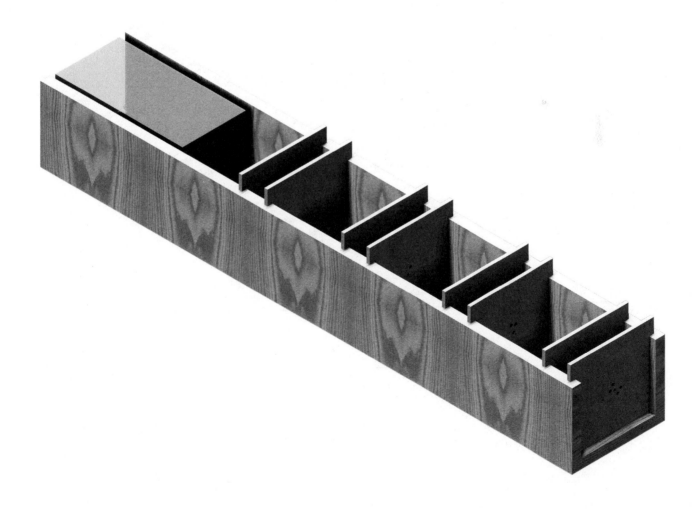

MICRO GUNS

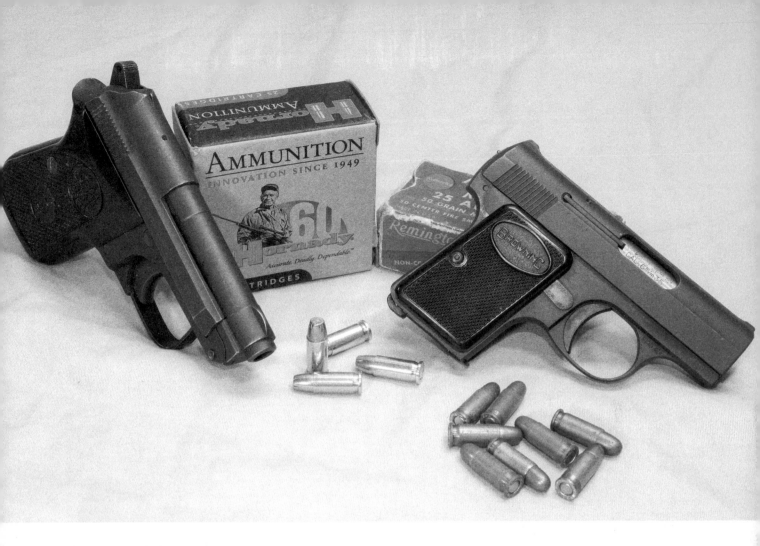

The subject of a .22, .22 magnum or .25 Auto for defense is controversial. They are not stoppers, period, end of story. However, they are still lethal weapons. The reason they exist is twofold: compactness and low recoil. The smallest handgun to be had is an ultra-compact .22LR, or a .25 Auto. The lowest-recoiling handgun you can shoot is a standard-sized pistol chambered in .22LR, like one of the smaller-sized Ruger Mk I, II, III or IV.

The .25 ACP/auto is not much different from the .22LR, with the exception that the bullet, almost always a full metal jacket, can be counted on to feed more reliably than the lead-bullet .22LR. But, that can also be a matter of maintenance (a lint-choked pistol isn't going to feed anything reliably) and handling.

.25 ACP

I will just pass right over the .25. Despite the compactness of some of the pistols that use it, it offers nothing the .22LR doesn't, ballistically, and does so at greater cost, less availability, and fewer options for pistol choices.

.22LR

The standard .22LR offers only a straight, bullet-diameter permanent wound, with a depth of 14-15 inches. There may be some expansion with hollowpoint bullets, but that comes at the expense of a couple of inches of penetration. Also, some bullets may yaw and end up stopping base-first in the wound track. When traveling sideways, it does create a marginally larger permanent wound than a simple cylinder, but hardly something to boast about.

The .22LR is not a big stick when it

The .25 ACP is ultra compact, but also ultra-unpowerful. Yes, it can kill, and no, I wouldn't want to be shot with one. But that doesn't make it a good choice for a defensive caliber.

CHOOSING HANDGUN AMMO | **145**

Above: The .22LR bullet, compared to a .32 and a .380 JHP. This is not the Hammer of Thor, so don't expect miracles.

Right: The .22LR will sometimes expand, and sometimes not. The bullet on the left is a hollow point, and you can see how much (not) it expanded. The middle one is a regular round–nose, and the loaded cartridge is to the right. The big advantage is the low cost.

comes to defense, but it is better than a knife or a club. Especially for someone who can't handle heavier recoil.

The trick to its use in defense is to realize two points. First, you will have to depend on more than one shot. In fact, the standard response when shooting in defense with a .22LR should be to empty the magazine and immediately reload. Second, placement matters. The hits have to be high center of mass or else the effort is wasted.

This combination of needs does not make the .22LR a high-percentage option,

146 | GunDigest.com

You can see the loaded .22LR, scaled up to the size of a mortar round (left). The priming compound in a .22LR is in the rim. This makes it inexpensive to manufacture, but complicates magazine design for feeding (right).

even in the handgun realm. But, for those with no other choice, there is no other choice.

.22 MAGNUM

Stepping up, you have the .22 Magnum, which is a longer case than the .22LR and designed to contain the bullet inside the case. The jacketed bullet offers the promise of expansion, but not always the realization. You see, a .22 Magnum out of a rifle generates plenty of velocity. Out of a handgun, it is often no faster (or not enough faster to matter) than a .22LR.

The expansion of any of these bullets is not a reliable outcome. Even if they do expand, the degree is not great. An expanding .22LR, all 40 grains of it, could bump up to .27-inch in diameter.

Hornady has lead the way here, offering a defensive-use .22 Magnum loading, with a bullet designed to expand at velocities the .22 Magnum can deliver. Called their Critical Defense, it gives 9-10 inches of penetration in ballistic gelatin out of a handgun.

Speer also makes their Gold Dot line of ammunition in the .22 Magnum. If you want as much performance as you can get, in a pistol that isn't going to kick much, then the .22 Magnum can be a good choice.

Combined with a handgun such as the Kel-Tec PMR-30, someone who can't handle a larger caliber can reasonably expect a good outcome. Part of that is the improved performance of the .22 Magnum over the .22LR, and the other is capacity. A standard .22LR pistol has a 10-round magazine. The PMR-30 magazine holds 30 rounds.

Nine to ten inches isn't FBI-passing performance, but it also doesn't offer anything like the recoil of an FBI-compliant load. This is part of the compromise.

5.7X28 FN

The outlier here is the FN 5.7x28 cartridge. This centerfire cartridge uses a jacketed bullet, longer than a .22LR or

CHAPTER 11: MICRO GUNS | **147**

.22 Magnum. Out of the firearms for which it was intended it works reasonably well. That is, out of an SMG-sized firearm like the P90, with a 10.4-inch barrel, it can generate enough velocity to work. The PS90, with its 16.1-inch barrel, really delivers the goods, but that isn't a handgun. Put into a handgun, it comes in a bit ahead of the .22 Magnum in velocity.

There is not a lot of data for the 5.7. It has been adopted by some law enforcement agencies, and has been used in shootings by them. Getting information out of those sources is difficult. The only one we have that offers a reasonable data set is the shooting at Fort Hood. There, Major Nidal Hasan fatally shot 13 people and wounded 32 more. He used an FN FiveseveN pistol and two ammo types:

Right: The .22 Magnum offers a better bullet at higher velocity, but at more cost and noise. (Recoil is still pretty minimal.)

Below: Gel, water, critters, the .22 Magnum is more likely to expand than any .22LR (left). This .22 Magnum bullet started at .221 inch and expanded to .30. Not bad (right).

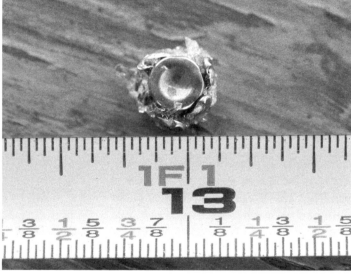

the FN SS192 and SS197SR. The SS192 is (or was, FN stopped making it in 2004) a jacketed hollowpoint with an aluminum core. Not much expansion, and not armor-piercing. The SS197SR is loaded with the Hornady V-max bullet, using a blue polymer tip to indicate a slightly higher velocity than the SS196SR.

The ability of the rounds to stop fights was out of proportion from what one would expect with such a small cartridge. Three of the victims valiantly charged the shooter, attempting to stop him. They were shot for their efforts, were stopped and subsequently died. They charged from close range (the incident happened indoors, so there were not long distances to cover) and yet failed to close the distance due to the gunshot received.

Those wounded with hits to the extremities were unable, in many instances,

Above: The Kel-Tec PMR-30 may not look like the Hammer of Thor, but it is soft in recoil, it holds 30 rounds of .22 WMR, and a spare magazine gives you another 30 in a couple of seconds. 30 or 60 rounds of .22 WMR is very comforting, for those who find recoil hard to deal with.

Left: The 5.7, next to a .22 Magnum, and on the left, a .22LR.

CHAPTER 11: MICRO GUNS | **149**

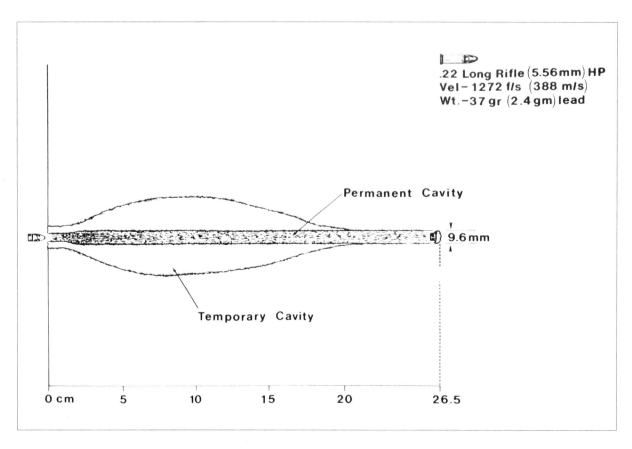

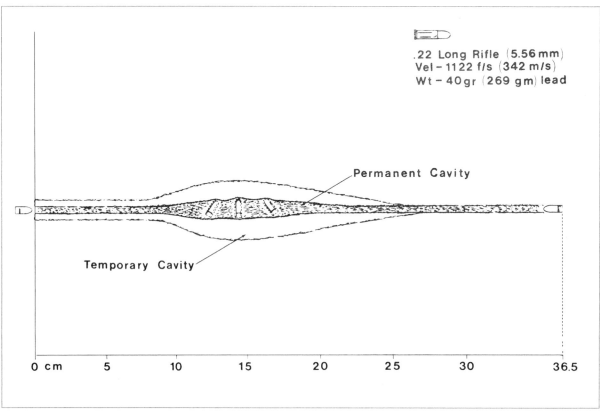

Top: The .22LR in a high-speed hollowpoint sometimes expands. It did for Dr. Fackler, back when he tested one. Image courtesy the late Dr. Martin Fackler. Bottom: The more likely result is a bullet that does not expand or deform, maybe yaws, and penetrates full depth. Image courtesy the late Dr. Martin Fackler.

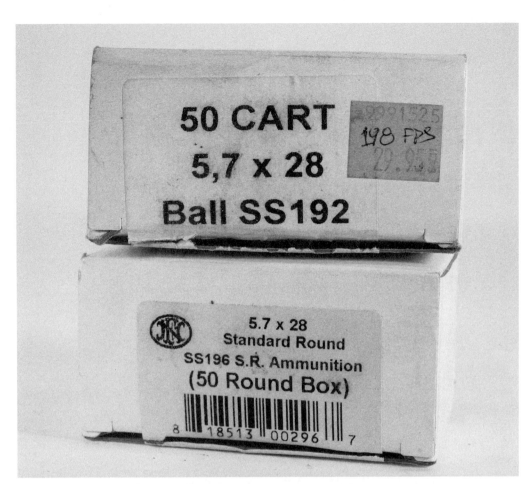

Left: There are a lot of loadings for the 5.7x28, and you want to make sure which you have, and that it is indeed what you want, so you are using the right ammo.

Below: The FN FiveseveN pistol holds 20 (or 30) rounds of 5.7 ammunition. It is a bit larger in the grip than .22LR and .22 Magnum pistols would be, so if that matters, be sure and test before you buy.

CHAPTER 11: MICRO GUNS | **151**

Given the choice of something in .22, I'd opt for the 5.7 with FMJ ammo and lots and lots of practice.

to flee or fight, due to broken bones. When a "mere" .22 handgun cartridge can break a femur, there's something going on that must be explained. That shot was received by one of the first responders, an in-base civilian security person. She took a hit to her wrist which made that arm unable to function, and a hit to the upper leg that broke her femur.

The drawback to the FiveseveN approach to low-recoil defense is cost. A FiveseveN lists for around $1,180, compared to the Kel-Tec PMR-30 at $455. The FN pistol holds 20 rounds (optional extensions make it a 30-round magazine) compared to the Kel-Tec at 30 rounds standard. An FN magazine is $35, with the extension costing another $18-20, while the Kel-Tec is $31.

5.7x28 ammunition costs (at the moment) $28 per box of 50 rounds, while .22 Magnum can be had for as little as $10 per box of 50 practice FMJs, up to $15 for a box of Hornady Critical Defense.

The last hurdle for the 5.7 is size. The grip is a bit larger than that of the Kel-Tec, and even if the recoil is mild, if you (or the person you are coaching in this situation) can't get a hand or hands around it, it isn't a good choice.

RECOMMENDATIONS

If you already have a .22LR pistol and need it for defense, then use the most accurate, readily available .22LR ammunition to be found. Practice getting as many hits out of a full magazine, on a playing-card-sized target at 7 yards, as quickly as you can. Volume and accuracy need to be your focus here.

A better choice would be either Hornady Critical Defense or Speer Gold Dot in .22 Magnum in the Kel-Tec. The PMR-30 isn't going to cost much, if anything, more than a good .22LR pistol. Use whichever of these two loads

shoots reliably and accurately out of your Kel-Tec. As with the .22LR, practice hitting a playing card at 7 yards, as quickly as possible, and train yourself to keep shooting on the target until it (he, she, they) goes down.

If you have the hands and the budget, but not the recoil resistance, for something bigger in caliber, then go for the FN FiveseveN in 5.7x28, the 40-grain FMJ. The V-Max is accurate, but is designed as a varmint-level bullet. I'd be much more confident with an FMJ in this situation, than with a readily-expanding bullet of only 40 grains.

While the effect is likely to be better than the .22LR or the .22 Magnum, the process should be the same: playing card accuracy, 7 yards, continuous fire until the bad guy goes down.

CAVEATS

There will be those who want to throw me under the bus for recommending the various .22s for defense. I have attempted to be clear: a rimfire is better than anything not a firearm; and for those who cannot handle more recoil, this is perhaps the only choice. I would rather someone who needs a firearm for defense has a weak one than none at all, as long as they realize the limitations of the tool they are using.

There are no .25s I can recommend. For the cost, you can easily acquire .22LR or .22 Magnum ammo that will perform better. And since you have to depend on volume and speed of fire, the ultra-compact .25s are poor choices, as clever as some of the designs might be.

No, this is not the pistol to be carrying daily, concealed. But, if it's the only pistol you have and you are at home, this will be your tool. Learn to shoot, learn the law, and learn to stay calm. The police are coming, but you have to deal with your problem until they arrive.

CHAPTER 11: MICRO GUNS | **153**

AMMO PERFORMANCE CHART: RIMFIRES AND .25 ACP

BRAND, BULLET	VELOCITY	PENETRATION*	EXPANSION
.22LR			
Gemtech subsonic 42 gr	1017	14"	.222"
Winchester Expert 36 gr	1107	--	--
Remington GB 40 gr	1117	--	--
Aguila Super Extra 40 gr	895	--	--
Winchester Super Silhouette 42 gr	969	--	--
.22 Magnum			
Speer GDHP-SB 40 gr	1242	10"	.297"
Hornady FTX 45 gr	1024	11"	.312"
5.7x28			
SS195 LF 28 gr	1936	--	--
Training T194 28 gr	1871	--	--
American Eagle FMJ 40 gr	1638	--	--
SS 197 SR V-Max 40 gr	1686	--	--
.25 ACP			
Hornady XTP 35 gr	843	--	--
Winchester Xp-Pt 45 gr	776	--	--

*Bare gelatin for penetration and expansion, unless otherwise indicated

12

.32 & .380

Not everyone can handle a full-sized pistol in a "manly" caliber. If you can't use one of these in a comfortable and efficient manner, don't let someone talk you into them. Using a handgun because "the police carry it" or "you can't use something too big" is false logic. Use what you can handle, and learn to use it competently.

There was a time when a .32 or a .380 pistol for protection was not seen as an inconsequential option. Gentlemen (and some men who were not so gentlemanly, as well as a few ladies) would slip a pocket pistol someplace convenient and head out the door, secure in the knowledge that it was enough for the job.

Today, using something that small will likely get you sneered at. And yet, they can get the job done.

.32 AUTO

As cute as it is, and as classic (designed by John Moses Browning himself), the .32 Auto is really not much more than a .22LR or .22 Magnum. It's offered in hollowpoint bullets, but the velocity it can generate really isn't enough for reliable expansion. The best approach is to use the most accurate ammunition in your pistol and, even if it is a JHP, treat it as if it were an FMJ. A .32 Auto FMJ *does* have enough penetration to reach the vitals.

A .32 classic combo is the Colt M1903. You can see it, or one in .380, in the movie "The Maltese Falcon." In fact, you can see it in a lot of movies from the classic era (including "Kiss me Kate," where Keenan Wynn presents one in the theater dressing room to threaten Kathryn Grayson) in part because it was a sleek, stylish and good-looking pistol.

CHOOSING HANDGUN AMMO | **157**

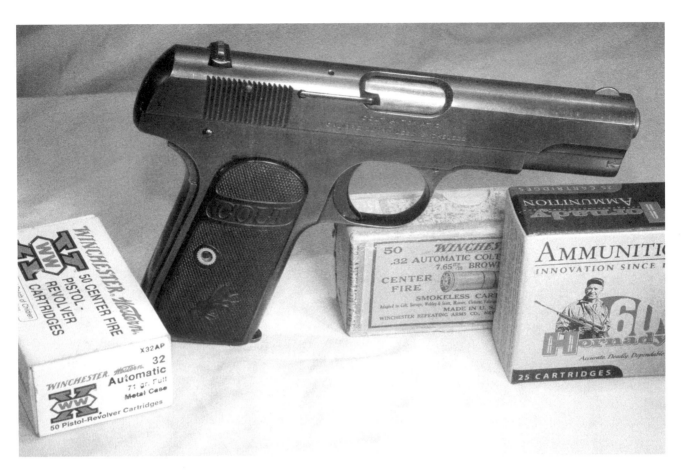

For decades the Colt Pocket Model was the classic small defensive pistol. It still would be, if collectors hadn't priced them out of reach.

A determined defender, obviously prepared and knowledgeable about firearms, even armed "only" with a .32 can pose enough of a problem to a would-be attacker that it serves as a good-enough tool.

As a ballistic solution, it is as marginal as they come.

.380 AUTO

The .380 offers more in performance. It can be had in JHPs that actually expand, at least in ballistic gelatin. While expanding, they also penetrate to a useful depth. Rounds such as the Hornady Critical Defense, 90 grains of JHP, can expand to half an inch. The Federal Premium HST has expanded to almost .6 inch in testing, and they do this while penetrating to almost a foot.

In an interesting development, the LAPD, which allows .380 pistols as backup and off-duty pistols, requires officers load their .380s with FMJ. They are worried that the JHPs will not have sufficient penetration, deeming 10-12 inches as not enough penetration for their needs. An FMJ in the .380 weighs 95-100 grains, and can be counted on to go 16 – 25 inches in ballistic gelatin.

What is clear in testing the .380 is that the velocity of the cartridge is right at the borderline for creating expansion and/or penetration. The 9mm Parabellum typically has a greater mass (even at "only" 115 grains) and more velocity. The added 20-25 grains the 9mm brings, and the extra 150 or so fps, allows the 9mm to both expand and penetrate. The .380 can do one or the other. A 90-grain FMJ that penetrates 20+ inches, in the same weight but expanding, will do half that, only 10 inches.

In comparison, a 115 FMJ in 9mm will penetrate 25-30 inches, perhaps even exit the back of the two blocks stood end-to-end. But, when allowed to expand, the half the distance penetration is still well within the FBI requirement of not less

Little guns can be hard to shoot. Compact means easy to carry and conceal, but can also mean "doesn't shoot small groups." Learn how well your combo works for you.

Top: Not all defensive guns have to be brand-new and state of the art. Here we have a Hungarian Femaru and a Beholla .32. One is a product of the 1940s and the other of the 1920s, and they both served their previous owners well as defensive handguns. Bottom: The trigger pull and fit of a handgun can matter. This is a little pistol in .380, but it shoots well in part because the trigger pull is single-action.

Top: Okay, it is a .32 revolver. And it is a common-enough handgun. But, the ammunition is rare, there are no hollow-points available, and you will find no speedloaders for it. Still, if all you have is this Nagant, then it is better than a lot of other choices. Bottom: Lasers on handguns are a good thing in the less-lit times and areas of our lives. But you must make sure everything works, and that you can work them, or you will not be happy. It is a tool, not a magic talisman.

LAPD insists that its officers who carry a .380 (as a backup or off-duty) load it with FMJ ammo, as they do not wish to give up penetration.

On a good day a .380 bullet like this Hornady will both expand and penetrate. But it will still only reach a foot of depth, maybe.

This Federal HST expanded like there was no tomorrow. If this is what you want, and you're willing to put up with decreased penetration, then go for it.

than 12 inches, but not more than 18.

It is this performance that has caused a large number of shooters, and many firearms makers, to try and design a 9mm pistol that is no larger than most .380 pistols. However, a 9mm that is the size of a .380, firing full-power 9mm ammunition, is a handful in recoil. It can be work, and it can cause the unwary to learn a flinch.

That is the main reason the .380 is still around and the subject of much R&D for performance-enhancing design. It is a soft-enough recoiling cartridge in an ultra-compact pistol for daily carry. The 9mm, the next step up, either has to be in a larger pistol to make it comfortable to shoot or, if compact, becomes real work to shoot even if it's a joy to carry.

RECOMMENDATIONS

First, carefully consider the choice of firearms. Use the biggest compact .380 you can carry comfortably. This will give you the best control and accuracy, and the most ammunition.

Next, the choice is clear and yours to make: do you depend on JHPs and expansion, or do you side with the LAPD and opt for FMJs and ensure penetration?

If you go with JHPs, then the Gold Dot or Hydra Shok will serve well. If you want the most accuracy (not a bad thing in a .380) then you'll likely find that the Hornady offerings are real tackdrivers.

If you opt for the FMJs, the choice is easy: practice with everything you can get, find what your particular handgun shoots most accurately (and hits to the sights) and use it exclusively.

Top: Kel-Tec makes compact, inexpensive, easy-to-carry pistols, and they can be had in useful calibers. Here is a P-3AT .380 that also can be had with an extended magazine. Bottom: There was a time when the .32 and .380 pistols were not seen as "marginal" choices. Makers such as Colt and Savage made all-steel pistols that have lasted now for decades. They still work.

CHAPTER 12: .32 & .380 | **163**

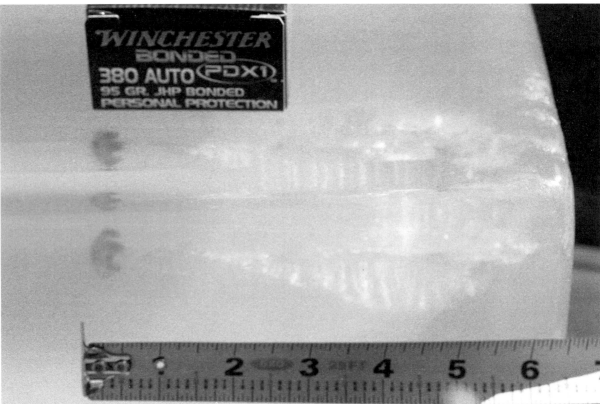

Top: Sccy makes modern pistols that are inexpensive, reliable and easy to use. On your belt or in your home, you are well-armed. Bottom: Winchester PDX1 .380 ammo expanded well, but it only penetrated 6.5 inches. That's a bit short in most people's estimation, but if you want expansion, this is good.

AMMO PERFORMANCE CHART: .32 & .380 AUTO

BRAND, BULLET	VELOCITY	PENETRATION*	EXPANSION
.32 ACP			
Winchester FMJ 72 gr	826	14"	.312"
Corbon 60 gr	1051	9"	.499"
Winchester Silvertip 60 gr	939	--	--
Remington UMC 71 gr FMJ	923	--	--
Hornady XTP 60 gr	930	8"	.349"
.380 Auto			
Black Hills X-PT 95 gr	831	--	--
CCI Blazer FMJ 95 gr	811	14"	.355"
Corbon DPX 80 gr	969	13"	.650"
Corbon DPX 80 gr**	980	15"	.450"
Federal HST 99 gr	884	--	--
Hornady FTX 90	908	--	--
Hornady Critical Defense 90 gr	969	10.5"	.521"
Hornady XTP 90 gr	1001	12"	.474"
Polycase ARX 56 gr	1199	15.5"	.355"
Remington Golden Saber 90 gr	911	10"	.579"
Sig V-Crown, 90 gr	897	8.2"	.545"
Speer GDHP 90 gr	1011	10"	.495"
Winchester Defend 95 gr	901	10.5"	.624"

*Bare gelatin expansion and penetration, unless otherwise indicated
**Windshield test

13

.32 REVOLVERS

The hottest round around, for any handgun short of a cannon, the .327 is perhaps too hot for some of the ultra-compact revolvers that are chambered for it.

The .32 used to be a popular revolver cartridge. The .32-20 was the Winchester design from 1882 for their lever-action rifles. Colt chambered it in the SAA, the Peacemaker, and interestingly enough, the .32-20 was the third most popular chambering for the Colt, behind only the .45 Colt and the .44-40. Apparently a lot of cowboys thought the .32-20 was plenty-enough gun.

While there was a high-speed loading of the .32-20 a century-plus ago, it and the other .32 revolver chamberings did not get the improvements that the larger cartridges did.

The bottom end included the .32 S&W Short and the .32 S&W, then the .32 S&W Long. All had lead, round-nosed bullets of 86 grains, and propelled those bullets at 800 fps or less. Sometimes much less.

In 1984, H&R tried to update it with the .32 H&R Magnum, which was limited by the action strength (or lack thereof) of their top-break revolvers. The .32 H&R did not equal the .38 Special of the time, which then was being savaged for being "inadequate" as a defensive cartridge.

The latest is the .327 Federal Magnum, which corrects all of those shortcomings, perhaps too well. Where the older cartridges have MAPs in the 12,000 to 14,000 PSI range, and the .32 H&R has an MAP of 21,000, the .327 has an MAP of 45,000 PSI.

Yes, it exceeds the ceiling of the 9mm+P loadings, and it delivers true .38 Special+P performance, out of a .32 revolver. This is not without cost.

In a compact, lightweight snubbie, it is simply punishing to shoot. In a larger revolver it is manageable, but the only advantage it offers is that it can add a round to the cylinder. This, of course, assumes the manufacturer makes it that way. That is, a five-shot snubbie in .38 Special can be a six-shot snubbie in .327. A six-shot medium-frame revolver, in .38 Special, could be a seven-shot .327, but I'm not

CHOOSING HANDGUN AMMO | **167**

Above: Left to right: .32 Short, .32 Long, .32 H&R lead bullet, .32 H&R JHP, .327 Federal Magnum.

Right: The .327 Federal Magnum performs, but it does not come without a cost.

sure anyone makes such a beast. I'd love for S&W, for example, to make their M15, a .38 Special revolver, in .327 Federal Magnum and make it a seven-shot revolver. They made such a revolver, the M-16, back when the .32 H&R was new, but it was a six-shot and they only made them for a few years.

Existing revolvers can't be reamed out to accept the .327. Well, physically they could be, but it would be an imprudent gunsmith who did it, considering the pressure difference between the original cartridge and the .327.

The .32 revolvers sit in a ballistic Bermuda triangle, in too-big a gun to warrant the power, or too small a gun to handle the power. They don't offer capacity advantages and the ammunition is not inexpensive.

But if you have one, you can do just fine with it.

RECOMMENDATIONS

If you have a revolver chambered in the lesser .32s, you really ought to get something better. Anything will be better than a century-old top-break revolver in .32 S&W Long. If you happen to have a revolver chambered in .32 H&R, then you can practice and learn with the various cowboy loadings and get good with it. For defense, you'd best be using either the Federal Personal Defense 85 grain JHP or the Hornady Critical Defense 80 grain FTX loads.

And if you have a revolver chambered in .327 Federal Magnum, you can use either of the above loads (the difference, besides chamber pressure, is only the length of the case), or .327 Federal Magnum from Federal at 85 grains, or the Speer Gold Dot 115-grain ammunition. Fair warning: it will have sharp recoil, and you likely won't find it a whole lot of fun.

If you want the most punch out of the smallest revolver, it is hard to criticize the .327 Federal Magnum. Charter Arms makes snubbies in the .327, and you will find it a handful.

CHAPTER 13: .32 REVOLVERS | **169**

Right: There was a time when packing a .32 meant you were well armed. Cowboys bought more SAAs in .32-20 than all but two other calibers. Police officers before WWII felt that an S&W in .32-20 was plenty for the job.

Below: The Ruger SP-101 in .327 is a stout little pistol and it shoots well. You just have to be prepared to hang on.

170 | GunDigest.com

AMMO PERFORMANCE CHART: .32 REVOLVERS

BRAND, BULLET	VELOCITY	PENETRATION*	EXPANSION
.32 S&W			
Winchester LRN 85 gr	597	--	--
.32 S&W Long			
Magtech LRN 98 gr	532	--	--
.32 H&R Magnum			
Black Hills FPL 90 gr	663		
Hornady FTX 80 gr	1079	12.5"	.365"
Hornady LFP 90 gr	687		
.327 Federal Magnum			
Federal Hydra-Shok 85 gr	1342	13.5"	.405"
Am Eagle Softpoint 100 gr	1410	16.5"	.374"
Speer GDHP 115 gr	1316	14.5"	.417"
Buffalo Bore JHP 100 gr	1233	--	--
Buffalo Bore L-SWC 130 gr	1136	--	--

*Bare gelatin for penetration and expansion, unless otherwise indicated

14

9MM PARABELLUM

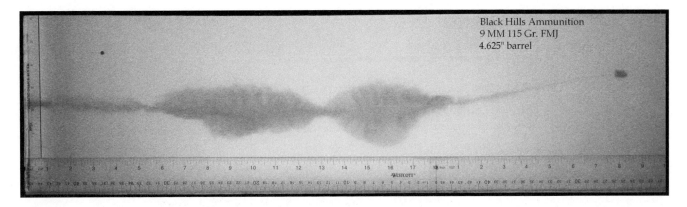

Invented in 1904, the 9mm Parabellum came about because the German army couldn't bring themselves to adopt a .32 pistol – the 7.65x21 Luger. So, Georg Luger opened up the bottle-necked case of that 7.65 as much as he could and, viola', the 9mm Parabellum came about.

It is a hot number, with an MAP of 36,000 PSI. The standard bullet weights range from 115 to 147 grains, with velocities from just under 1,200 for the 115s and just under 1,000 for the 147s.

As a compact cartridge, the 9mm has an advantage that larger or longer cartridges cannot offer: a high-capacity magazine, with a double stack of cartridges, does not become too large a magazine and grip for the average shooter to handle. This offers a significant increase in capacity. Where a 1911 pistol in .45 offers eight rounds in a magazine, a 9mm magazine in the same-size pistol doubles that. And, the higher operating pressure means it can generate enough velocity to expand bullets.

These two advantages caused the 9mm to be the main focus of bullet improvements. Some might say, "Sure, because it needed it," but I see it as ballistic advantage waiting to be reaped. As a result, you will find more hi-tech bullets in 9mm, from more makers, than any other cartridge. Even in the hottest loadings, in a not-ultra-compact pistol, it is manageable for the average shooter, and this is another advantage. If it is manageable, people will learn to manage it. If it can be fun they'll find the fun.

With the 9mm, the convergence of all the advantages created a product that now is going to re-set the law enforcement landscape, moving many agencies back from the .40 to the 9mm.

The big problem in selecting the best 9mm ammunition is determining what platform you will be using it in.

For instance, the +P and +P+ loads are best performers when launched out of a full-sized gun. So, using a Glock 17 or 34, a full-sized Government Model or similar other big 9mm, you get all the benefits of the velocity. Using the same ammo in an ultra-compact Kel-Tec is simply making excessive noise, beating up your hands and not getting the velocity you thought you were. Oh, you'll get more than the standard ammo would deliver, but not so much more that it's worth all the drama, noise, flash and recoil.

The 9mm Parabellum seems to be the cartridge the FBI tests were made for. It has enough velocity to punch through the various barriers and still have speed enough to expand on the other side. The 147-grain bullet is so long (it barely fits in the case, with room for powder) that you could expand it to double its diameter, and it still has enough lenght of bullet cylinder left to support the expanded bullet.

It is soft in the lighter loads and manageable in the hottest loads, so it is accurate. It used to not be accurate. When the U.S. Army and Air Force began testing in the early 1980s, to replace the "worn

FMJ bullets do not expand, they penetrate, tumble, and stop eventually. NYPD found them sometimes stopping in bystanders. This was seen as a not-good outcome.

CHOOSING HANDGUN AMMO | **173**

Above: The Browning Hi Power (this is a Novak Custom) was for a long time the only hi-cap 9mm. Now they are common, but the BHP is still a valid choice for those who want a single-action system pistol.

Right: The days of non-expanding bullets are over. Fired out of a compact 9mm, this 9mm 150-grain HST expanded as shown.

out" 1911s with something new, something 9mm, they found that the 9mm ammunition of the time wasn't as accurate in new pistols as the then-current .45 ammo in the "worn out" 1911s. This temporarily stopped the pistol program, and initiated a crash program to develop match-grade 9mm ammo, then started the tests again.

Now, we have accurate 9mm because it is all accurate.

Old habits and old customs die hard. Old attitudes die hardest of all. The attitude of "real cartridges start with the numeral 4" do not take into account the fact that a lot of people just don't want to deal with, or can't handle, the size of a "4" pistol and the recoil it brings with it. For them, the 9mm is plenty good enough.

The trick is finding the firearm that works for you, and then (and only then) selecting the load that works in it. Picking a load and making it fit a "suitable" handgun is going about it backwards and asking for trouble. Not to pick on Kel-Tec (they make fine compact psiotls), but starting with a +P or +P+ load and then trying to manage it in an ultra-compact pistol is just doomed to failure.

To that end, the 9mm can be divided into three areas.

The Barnes Tac-XP all-copper bullet is soft to shoot but performs like a champ.

LIGHT LOADS

These would be the Hornady Critical Defense loads and similar low-recoil loads, such as Federal HST offerings, the Barnes TAC-XP (all-copper bullets don't need as much velocity to perform) and others. They offer as much performance as can be had, without going to the full FBI performance and recoil that the other end of the spectrum entails. Why would you use such a load? As explained, because you are loading it into an ultra-compact pistol and you don't want the extra recoil, for no gain, that hotter ammo would provide.

MEDIUM POWER

The middle ground would be standard-weight ammunition in normal velocities, such as a 124-grain JHP at the normal 9mm velocity of 1095 fps. One reason to select such a load would be simply that your ultra-compact pistol does not run reliably with a "softy" 115-grain or a heavy but slow load.

One of the advantages of the 9mm is the huge variety of pistols and ammunition to be found. That is also one of the disadvantages, as the more combinations you have, the more you can find that don't work.

This is the firearms variation of the old "Doctor, doctor" joke.

"Doctor, doctor, it hurts when I move my arm like this."

"Then don't move your arm like that."

If your desired carry pistol does not shoot well or is unreliable with a particular load, move on to some other load. There are plenty of good ones, don't get hung up on "there can be only one." Select something else, something that works.

CHAPTER 14: 9MM PARABELLUM | **175**

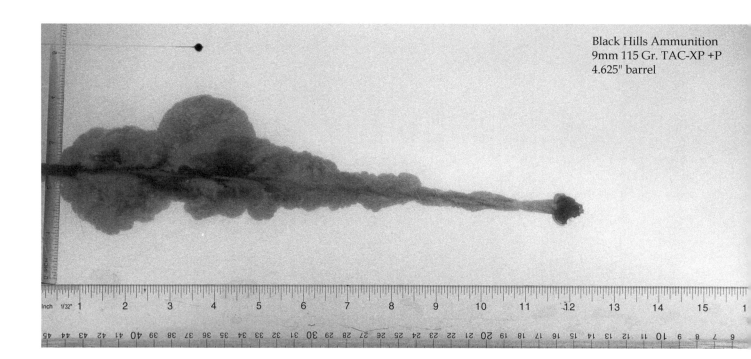

Black Hills Ammunition
9mm 115 Gr. TAC-XP +P
4.625" barrel

Top: You can see what the Tac-XP does in gelatin. It expands and penetrates, all with mild recoil. Bottom: Black Hills makes a medium-power 9mm 124 JHP that is brilliantly accurate, is easy to shoot and performs well in tests.

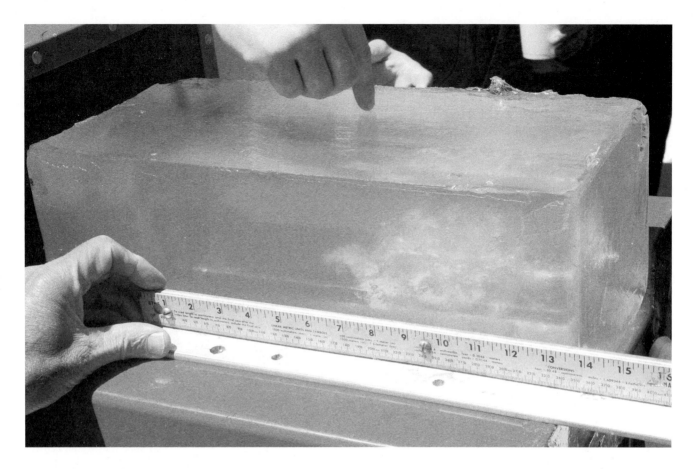

SUPERSONICS AND HEAVYWEIGHTS

Last are the full-out, pull-out-all-the-stops loads that fully comply with and even crush the FBI scoring method. Here, we have two options.

One is the lightweight bullet at the absolute screaming velocity the case can muster. For that, you're looking at something like the Winchester Kinetic or the new, resurrected Super Vel. This will push 90- to 115-grain bullets at supersonic velocities.

A soft-shooting but lightweight bullet is the Federal Guard Dog. At only 105 grains it isn't the lightest load, but for those who don't want or can't use hollowpoints, the expanding metal jacket bullet is just the answer.

The other options here are the heavies, the 147-grain JHPs that manufacturers push to just under 1,000 fps. They are both subsonic and expansionist.

What do you pick? Pick what you like, and what your pistol likes.

An example of the heavies is the Winchester PDX1, in 9mm it is 147 grains. I first encountered it while doing my TV show, and we got a carton of ammo fresh off the loading line. The range had a test car nearby, so I loaded 9mm and tried a round through the windshield. It went through the windshield, through the cardboard target in the driver's seat, the

Above: It is hard to fault a 9mm bullet that travels 14 inches into gelatin, expands, and does so on a straight line. No, it isn't a .45, but it isn't nothing, either.

Below: Long for weight (the polymer core does that), the Guard Dog expands even though it is built to be a full metal jacket bullet.

CHAPTER 14: 9MM PARABELLUM | **177**

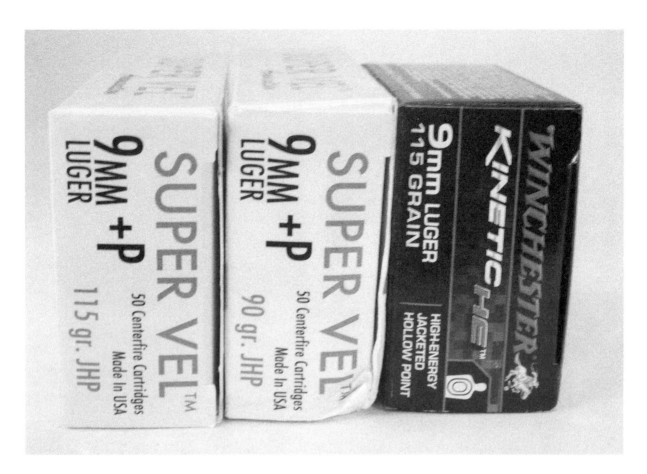

Top: You want high velocity? Ammo makers make ammo for you. Lightweights like the 90-grain Super Vel, and the standard weight Kinetic, are plenty supersonic. Bottom: The car I shot with Winchester PDX1 9mm. Someone behind the car would have been subject to hits.

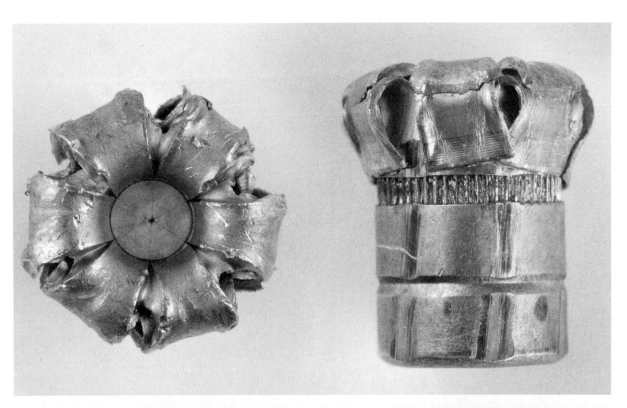
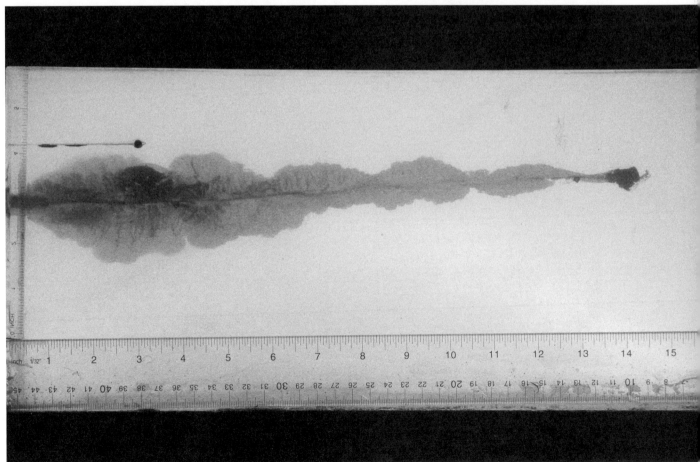

Top: This is what a Hornady Critical Duty does, pretty much with any barrier or no barrier.
Bottom: Here is the Critical Duty load in gelatin. Nothing to complain about.

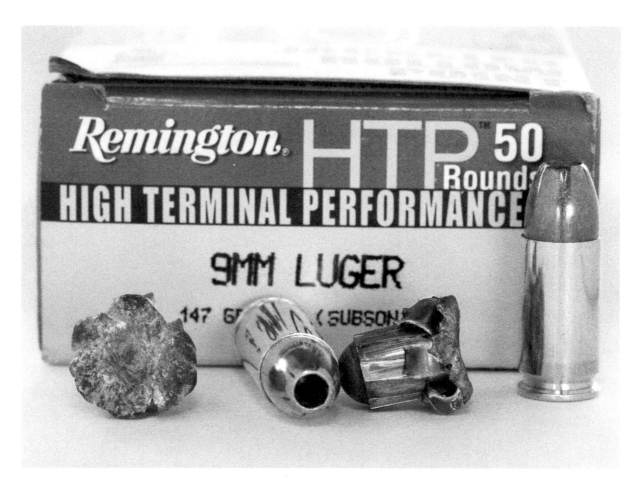

Top: The Remington HTP is a well-performing bullet, and if it shoots accurately in your pistol, it could be your first choice. Try it and find out. Bottom: This is what extra pressure and velocity can do for you. Just chrono, and be sure you're getting the extra velocity.

Top: Be sure and use a chronograph when you decide to buy, use and carry +P or +P+ ammo. If you aren't getting any real extra velocity, why do it? Bottom: Not all 9mm pistols must be duty-sized pistols. This Kel-Tec PF-9 is compact, but you can also add rounds with an extended magazine. The extended magazine not only gives you extra shots, but more of a grip to hold onto.

CHAPTER 14: 9MM PARABELLUM | **181**

A name-brand handgun lasts. This Ruger SR-9 fired 6,800 rounds in one afternoon. It fired 15,000+ rounds in testing and still has plenty of life left. That's a lot of practicing, at 50 rounds a week.

headrest, and caromed off the back shelf and out the back window, taking window trim with it.

Hornady delivers much the same performance with their Critical Duty load, a 135-grain bullet that is +P and stout to shoot, for a 9mm.

That's the kind of performance that the modern, bonded bullet in a 9mm can deliver. And it is why I am not giving a list of recommended rounds or options in the 9mm chapter or many of the subsequent chapters.

All bonded bullets in the modern choices will perform in a similar fashion. That is why they are expensive, and why they have stiff recoil.

The trick is to pick the one that you are comfortable with, that shoots accurately in your handgun, and that feeds reliably. Because they are all so good, the work of picking one over the other is just not worth it for the great bunch of us. For a police department, willing to go through the herculean labors of picking one (or more likely, four or five potential, good-enough-the-best) rounds, fine.

Me, I can't be bothered, and I do this for a living. I'll pack whatever the gun I'm packing shoots well, and be happy.

HONEY BADGER

The idea of a non-expanding bullet that stops and does not over-penetrate is new. One of these is the Honey Badger, a fluted all-copper bullet. It does not care about barriers, because the shape is not changed by punching through a barrier. It does this at amazingly mild recoil levels. It is new, and it will likely be the thing of the future for bullets. Time and testing will see.

9mm 125 gr honeybadger: In a gelatin test of the Honey Badger, it penetrates the full 18 inches and does so at a subsonic velocity, with a 125-grain bullet. Wow!

+P & +P+

Should you, or shouldn't you? That depends. Do you want the extra performance it will deliver? Because either will give you more. But, are you willing to pay the cost in extra noise, blast, flash and recoil? Because even if they don't deliver more performance, they will deliver more of the costs.

The choice is yours, and keep in mind: if you do not pack a full-sized pistol, you won't get the extra performance, but you will get an extra dollop of the costs.

Modern, striker-fired pistols can be had from full-size, holding 18 rounds, to medium-sized, holding ten or so. Use what works for you, is comfortable, and you can shoot well. Don't pick something "because SEALs use it."

CHAPTER 14: 9MM PARABELLUM | **183**

The Hornady Critical duty bullets performed so well, and so similarly, that I had to mark the bases of each to keep straight what test they had been subjected to.

AMMO PERFORMANCE CHART: 9MM

BRAND, BULLET	VELOCITY	PENETRATION*	EXPANSION
Ruger Polycase ARX 80 gr	1461	16"	.355"
Barnes TAC-XPD 115 gr	14.1"	.692"	--
Black Hills TAC-XPD 115 gr	1163	14"	.693"
Black Hills Honey Badger 115 gr	1025	18.5'	.355"
Federal HST Micro 147 gr	1021	16.25"	.695"
Federal Guard Dog 105 gr	1254	13.5'	.602"
Black Hills XTP 124 gr	1146	17"	.547"
Hornady FTX 115 gr	1060	15"	.520
Hornady XTP, 124 gr	1150	13.5"	.611"
Hornady Critical Duty 135 gr	1121	14.5"	.575"
Remington HTP 147 gr	927	14.5"	.615"

Sig V-Crown, 115 gr	1149	14.75"	.501"
Sig V-Crown, 124 gr	1163	15"	.519"
Sig V-Crown, 147 gr	979	15.5"	.529"
Super Vel 90 gr	1463	--	--
Super Vel 115 gr	1352		
Winchester Ranger T 147 gr	16"	.711"	--
Winchester Ranger 127 +P+	1257	12"	.709"
Winchester Defend 124 gr +P	1196	12"	.626"
Winchester Defend 147 gr	995	14.25"	.591"
Winchester Nato 124 FMJ**	1180	26.5"	.355"
Winchester Forged 115 FMJ**	1105	27"	.355"
Winchester Kinetic 115 gr	1315	--	--

*Bare gelatin for penetration and expansion, unless otherwise indicated
**This is not unusual, FMJ is expected to penetrate fully, and then some. It is meant for military use.

15

.38 SPECIAL

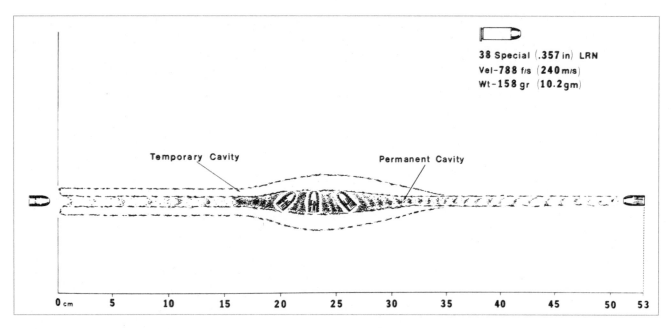

The .38 was invented in the late 19th century, given up for dead in the latter half of the 20th, and resurrected by the time the 21st rolled around. It is now a viable choice for those who feel a compact carry gun is more important than shooting through cars.

The original load, a lead round-nose 158-grain bullet, was marginal as a stopper. It was earth-shattering in 1898, when invented, but even before WWII we knew better.

It just took a long time to develop something better and get it out where it could be tested.

One aspect of a .38 Special revolver that people might have forgotten is accuracy. Revolvers can be amazingly accurate, and a quality DA revolver delivers all of that.

You do, however have a few choices to make, choices that will determine your path in life.

First, snubbie or medium-sized revolver?

SNUBBIELAND

Short-barreled revolvers are harder to shoot, kick more and deliver less performance than those that are bigger. The smallest have diminished capacity, five shots vs. six. So, you have to determine how much recoil, blast and difficulty in shooting you are willing to put up with to get the performance you desire. Snubbies are easier to carry, but they extract a cost in velocity. As a starting point, knock 100 fps off of the book value of a load if you are using a snubbie. More if it is lightweight bullet.

Medium-sized revolvers, the six-shot wheelguns and those with 3- or 4-inch barrels, are a lot easier to shoot and deliver the ballistics you want.

AMMO CHOICES

This breaks down in a three-axis decision making tree. Light weight bullets or

Above: If it wasn't for the yaw, there'd be not much of a wound track at all. The old lead .38, the great perforator.

Below: The .38 Special is one of the most versatile cartridges to be found, and you can get bullets from 77 to 158 grains.

CHOOSING HANDGUN AMMO | **187**

Top: Two inches, single action, 25 yards, with Critical Defense 110-grain FTX bullets. Any complaints? I thought not. Bottom: A snub-nosed revolver is a joy to carry. It can, however, be a beast to shoot well. The smaller and lighter it is, the harder it is to shoot well, and the less fun it will be to shoot. Keep that in mind when picking a defensive handgun.

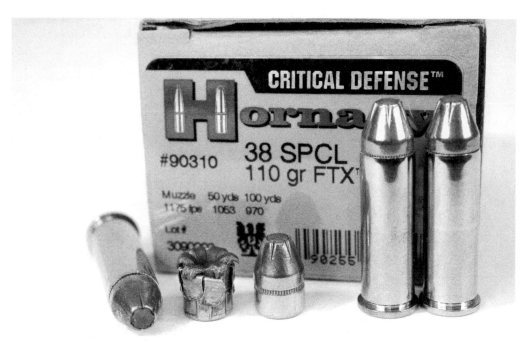

Left: The Hornady Critical Defense line is meant to offer good performance without beating up the shooter. Don't fault it for that.

Below: This is what extreme velocity does for you, expansion from a 90-grain bullet that practically turns it inside-out.

heavy? Jacketed bullets or lead? Standard pressure or +P?

In lightweight bullets, you have high speed and normal. A high speed would be something like the Super Vel Super Snubbie load, which features a 90-grain bullet at over 1,200 real fps out of a snubbie, and recoil to go with it.

A lightweight load that won't punish you would be the Hornady Critical Defense, or Critical Defense Lite. These are 110-grain bullets and they do not get to 1,000 fps out of a 2-inch barrel. They are easy to shoot, but they will not deliver performance like the stouter loads. You get what you pay for, and you pay for what you get.

There are some loads that feature weights less than full but not all the way to light. Generally around 125 to 130 grains, they are compromise loads. They offer more mass for more penetration, but you have to either give up velocity or accept a bit more recoil.

The heavyweights top out at the normal for .38 Special weight, 158 grains. You can have jacketed hollow points, all-lead or lead hollow points.

Pressure is all. The standard pressure limits for the .38 Special are just fine for the snubbies and make for a soft life for the medium-sized revolvers. If you want more you can have it, but you will pay for it. in particular, a +P load in a five-shot snubbie becomes work, or even painful, to shoot. Unless you absolutely need that level of performance (and I can't imagine how to require it, and not move up in gun size), then live with it.

But, if you want the benefits of extra pressure you need extra barrel length. This makes for EDC problems. A 6-inch .38 revolver might be entirely suitable

CHAPTER 15: .38 SPECIAL | **189**

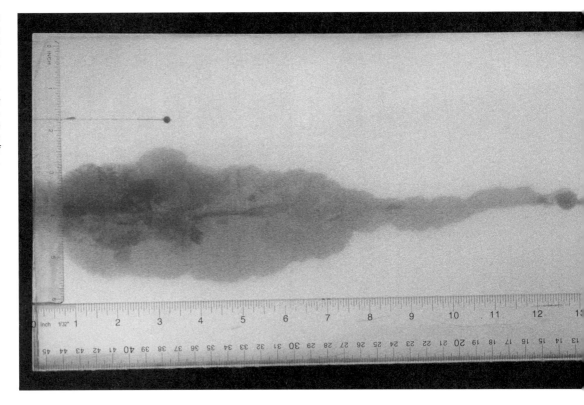

Right: This is what extra pressure and a 6-inch barrel will get you. You will not get this out of a 2-inch barrel.

Below: The combination of a bit more weight and a bit more velocity nets you a lot more performance, but also a noticeable amount of extra recoil.

for a home defense gun. But for Every Day Carry it would be bulky. You need the barrel length to get all the velocity the extra pressure promises.

POLYCASE ARX

This is a new approach, and we see it working in the .38 Special. It offers barrier perforation, but doesn't have to expand to stop in the FBI distance. It is super-soft to shoot, but the extra velocity can cause it to hit low, below your usual point of aim, due to barrel lift timing differences.

OLD-SCHOOL

Wadcutters are an anomaly. They offer a full-diameter cutting shoulder, and yet they penetrate as well as anything else out there. A super-soft load to shoot, if you were arming someone who was really recoil sensitive, using wadcutters might be a viable approach. Just be sure they understand they must make use of the tack-driving accuracy that wadcutters offer.

FBI CLASSIC

The FBI load in .38 Special, 158-grain, lead semi-wadcutter, at +P pressures, worked then and works now. It just doesn't perform well in barrier testing. If you do not anticipate barriers, then you will be happy.

190 | GunDigest.com

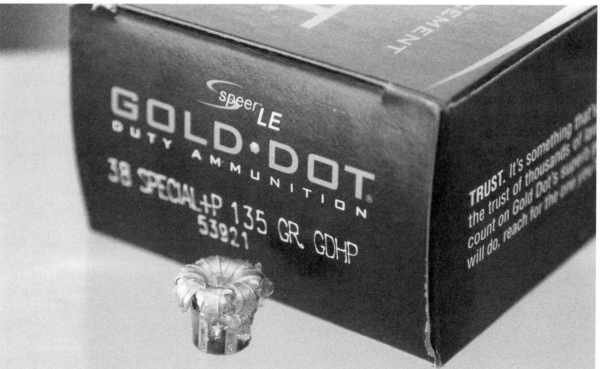

Top: The Gold Dot snubbie load is even better out of a full-sized .38 with a 4-inch barrel. Bottom: If you want this expansion along with penetration you can get it, but you have to pay for it. The Gold Dot 1235 grain +P load will thump your hands pretty hard.

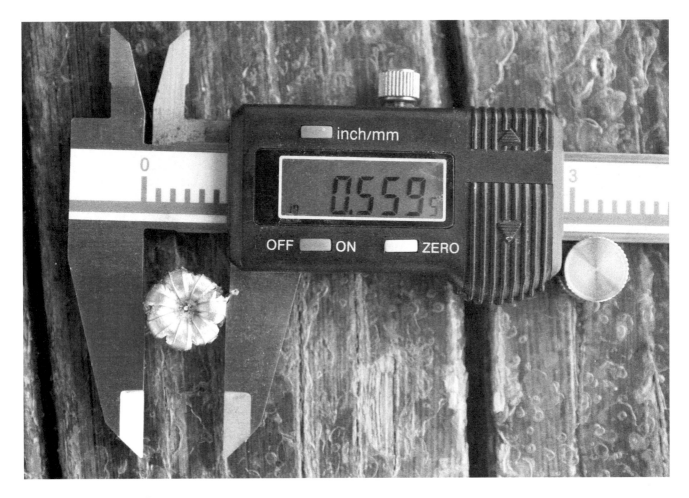

Above: Here it is, full expansion from a .38. Your hands will be sore, practicing with this, so brace yourself.

Right: Polycase thought outside the box and this is the result. A sintered, epoxied, fluted bullet that does not need expansion to deliver.

FEDERAL HST .38 SPECIAL

Federal took a different approach. They took the old reversed hollow-base wadcutter, put a jacket on it, tuned the jacket for consistent expansion, and then loaded it to normal .38 Special performance, not wadcutter performance. As a result, it delivers every bit of the power a .38 can muster and expands well while doing so.

HONEY BADGER

The performance of the Honey Badger, a solid copper, fluted bullet at less than robust recoil, seems to have been made for the .38 Special. Even if it does not work out in pistols, I suspect that the Honey Badger load for a backup or snubbie may just be the perfect load of the future.

Top: Wadcutters are old-school, but some things continue to work even in the digital age. These will penetrate, drive straight, and do it even through barriers. They won't expand, but c'mon. Bottom: No expansion, but for the soft recoil and target accuracy, this is great out of a 2-inch snub.

CHAPTER 15: .38 SPECIAL | **193**

Top: The FBI load is full weight, +P and all-lead. But for expansion like this, you are good. Just don't expect barrier-blind performance, because lead can't do that. Bottom: You will get smoke, because a lead bullet does that. But you get great performance..

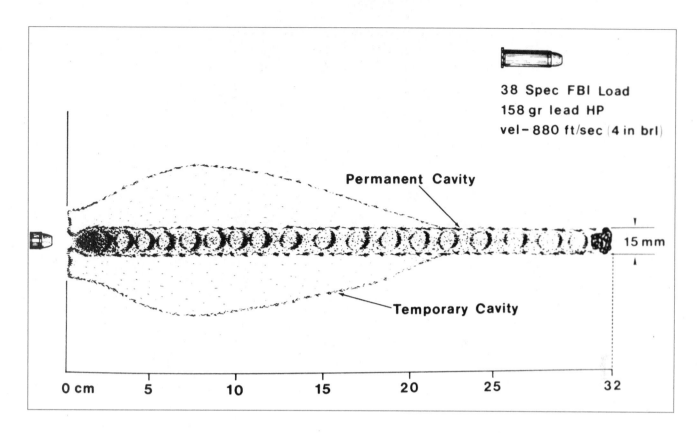

HOW TO PICK?

What is your carry need? How compact/concealed must you be? Is this a main gun or a backup? How resistant to recoil are you? Be honest with yourself on this one, because no one else is going to take the recoil hit for you.

Then, pack the largest .38 revolver you can comfortably carry and conceal, and use the stoutest load in it that you can comfortably shoot. I know, it sounds like the most basic common-sense advice you've ever heard. It surprised even me.

Above: Even back in the old days, we knew how good the FBI load was. Image courtesy the late Dr. Martin Fackler.

Left: Federal makes the HST a full wadcutter hollowpoint. It is jacketed and in the case. You have 100% loading density. This is fabulous.

CHAPTER 15: .38 SPECIAL | **195**

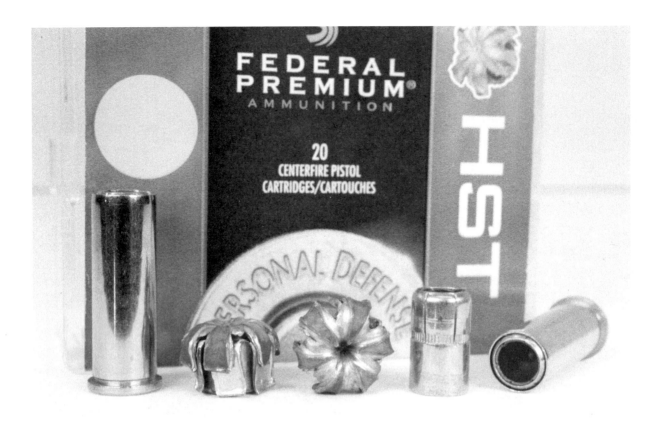

Top: Federal re-thought the .38 Special and came up with the HST. Bottom: A bigger revolver, here a six-shot, is easier to shoot than a snubbie. Here we have the results of 10-yard double action shooting.

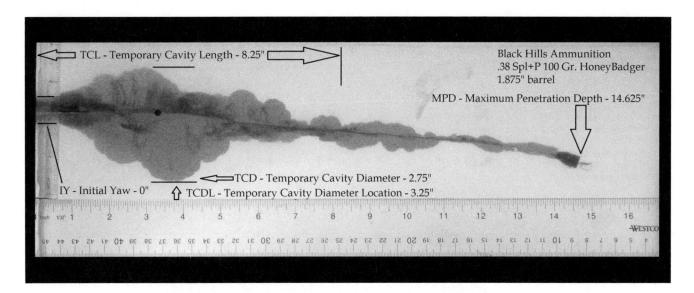

Above: Hard to believe that a soft-shooting load can perform like this, but there it is.

Left: Barrel length matters in the .38 Special universe. Longer is better, as it gives you more velocity. Just remember that a longer barrel is also a better lever for the bad guy who wants to take it away from you. Don't let him get that close.

CHAPTER 15: .38 SPECIAL | **197**

There is a subset of collectors who collect police-marked revolvers. If you have one of these, you can probably sell it to such a collector for enough to buy a new, hi-cap 9mm, if that is what you want. If you don't want to sell, a revolver such as this will continue to work as a defensive tool for another century, at least.

AMMO PERFORMANCE CHART: .38 SPECIAL & .38 SPECIAL +P

BRAND, BULLET	VELOCITY	PENETRATION*	EXPANSION
Black Hills Honey Badger 100 gr	982	14.6"	.355"
Black Hills Sierra +P 110 gr	945	9.75"	.583"
Black Hills Sierra 125 gr +P	873	13.6"	.529"
Remington golden Saber 125 +P	767	--	--
Black Hills 148 gr WC	689	15.5"	.428"
Federal HST 130 gr	834	14"	.486"
Hornady FTX Lite 90 gr	1129	8.5"	.467"
Hornady FTX 110 gr	833	13"	.440"
Hornady FTX+P 110 gr	1031	12"	.501"
Hornady 125 gr XTP +P	807	16"	.437"
Polycase ARX 77 gr	1059	14.5"	.358"
Speer GDHP 135 gr	840	13'	.565"

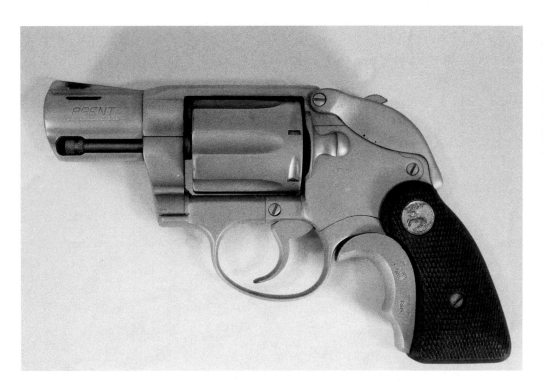

Here we have a Colt Agent, a lightweight little beast that is great to carry, a handful to shoot, and an impossible repair if it should go toes-up. Do not depend on something that might break and cannot be fixed, unless it is all you have, and can afford.

Super Vel 90 gr	1278	11.5"	.574"
Winchester Defend 130 gr +P	939	11.5"	.617"
Winchester FBI 158 gr L-SWC+P	799	13"	.521"
Hornady XTP 158 gr	758	15"	.472"
Corbon FMJ 147 gr	773	27"	.357"
CCI Blaser LRN 158 gr	815	25"	.358"
Black Hills CNL 158 gr	725	--	--
Winchester FMJ RN 130 gr	765	28"	.358"
Remington HBWC 148 gr	655	30"	.358"
Oregon Trails 148 DEWC 2.7 gr Bullseye	657	36"	.358"

*Bare gelatin for expansion and penetration, unless otherwise indicated.

CHAPTER 15: .38 SPECIAL | **199**

Small revolvers come in various sizes, materials and weights. There is no "one size fits all" choice. And, if you carry, be sure to use a good holster, also.

CHAPTER 15: .38 SPECIAL | **201**

16

THE .357s

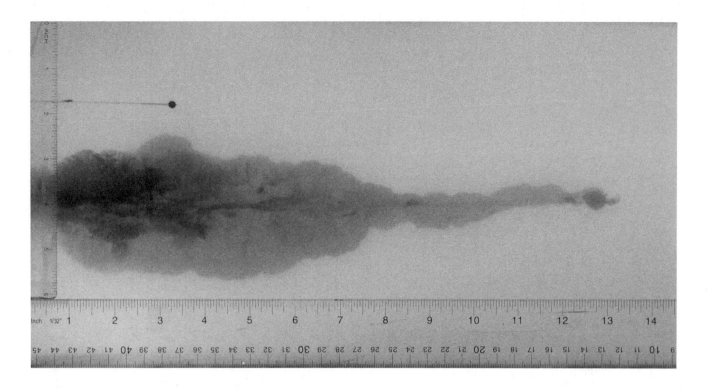

This is the performance the lightweight bullets can deliver, but you need a long barrel to do it. This 110-grain Super Vel bullet came out of a 6-inch barrel to deliver this wound track. Image courtesy Black Hills.

The .357s are the start of the revolver cartridges that have enough horsepower to easily pass the FBI tests. This is both good and bad. It's good in that you can count on any of the modern bullet designs to get the job done. No new bullet, in either .357 Magnum or .357 Sig, will fail the tests. They will all, in any weight (the .357 Sig doesn't offer many choices there, but that's not a big deal) penetrate well past the minimum depth, expand, and do so even after passing through barriers.

No, the problem is blast and recoil.

A .357 Magnum load in particular was the focus of stopping power inquiry a few decades ago. The 125-grain JHP was seen, even by those who were not fans of the "smaller" calibers, as having a sterling reputation as a stopper. As well it should have. The projected velocity of the 125 JHP was 1,450 fps. That was not the real velocity, of course, but that was what everyone used as their goal, their aspirational speed, if you will.

It came close out of a 6-inch barrel, doing high 1,300s, but out of the more-common carry gun it was between 1,250 and 1,300 fps. Which was plenty to get the job done.

Where in the 9mm the research was to produce a bullet that would expand at the velocities that could be generated, in the .357 the task was to design a bullet that would hold together at the velocities already existing.

.357 SIG

The Sig was designed to deliver the ballistics of the .357 Magnum out of an autoloading pistol. The case is essentially (but not as a practical, handloading matter) the .40 S&W necked down to 9mm. It has a capacity close to that of the .357 Magnum, and therefore can generate the same velocities as the longer revolver cartridge.

But, and this is important to understand, it is limited in the same way the .357 Magnum is: it needs barrel length to deliver. If you expect to get the full .357 Sig ballistics out of a 4-inch barrel, you are kidding yourself. If you go for a compact .357 Sig, you are basically doing the 9mm+P+ dance, but only with more noise and blast.

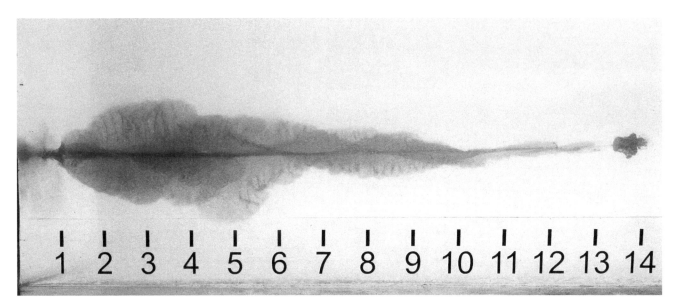

Above: If you want power and performance in an autoloading pistol, then the Hornady Critical Duty .357 Sig delivers. Just don't expect this out of a compact pistol. Short barrels and the Sig are not a happy combo. Image courtesy Black Hills.

Right: If you want compact, then this FNP does that. But chambered in .357 Sig, you are hobbling it with the shorter barrel. Better to have gone for the FN in 9mm and gained a lot more in magazine capacity. Still, it is hard to fault the accuracy.

So, if you want the full .357 Sig power, you have to be willing to pack a full-sized handgun. If you are not willing to pack the biggest one, then save yourself the hassle and step back to a 9mm, since that is about all the velocity you will be getting anyway.

.357 MAGNUM AND .38S

One of the big advantages of the .357 Magnum is that revolvers chambered in it can also readily fire .38 Special ammunition. This is good, as it allows for less-strenuous practice. This is bad if you use .38s for practice and then load up with .357s for EDC. This was supposedly one of the problems encountered in the Newhall incident. At the time, the California Highway patrol and many other law enforcement agencies felt it entirely appropriate to practice with .38s (sometimes even soft-recoiling .38 wadcutter ammo) and then carry .357s on duty.

One problem is that the shorter .38

cases cause lead and powder residue buildup in the chambers. The bigger problem is that the practice isn't similar enough to be useful.

If you want to use .38s in a .357 because you don't want the recoil, and want a stronger, longer-lasting revolver, go right ahead. Just don't think that practicing with .38s is going to fully prepare you for use with .357s.

LIGHT BULLETS

The lightest carry revolvers often have a warning to not use the lightest bullets. This is for good reason: the bullets will "jump the crimp" due to inertia and recoil. While it is rare for a round to pull longer (the revolver moves back, the bullet "attempts" to stay in place) enough that it will tie up a revolver in only four or five shots, you should not risk it.

If you want to test, fair warning: the recoil is beyond stout, it is sharp enough to be painful, and you can easily work yourself into a flinch. In fact, you probably shouldn't use full-power .357 Magnum ammunition in the lightest-available carry revolvers. It's just no fun and you can't really practice, just learn what your pain threshold is.

CHOOSING AMMO

The problem is not picking what works, they all work. The problem is in picking something you can live with. In addition to the advice with other calibers (use what is reliable, use what is accurate), you can add use what you can stand to shoot.

In a certain sense, you could call me a professional shooter. I shoot more ammo on an annual basis than most people walk by at the big-box store when they go to buy ammo for a day at the range. I have shot, and continue to shoot, every handgun caliber made. Several times a week I'm at the range, and several times a year I spend a week at a class, range, seminar or other industry function. I shoot a lot.

I don't find any full-power .357 Magnum ammo to be fun in any revolver below the medium-frame all-steel ones. One of my favorites is an old S&W M-65, 3-inch, in .357. That I'll shoot a lot, but not all day. If I'm shooting all

Left: Given the choice between an all-steel .357 revolver and an all-steel pistol in .357 Sig, I'd opt for the Sig, just on the speed of reloads alone. But if you like revolvers, they are a viable option, for sure.

Right: The barrel of lightweight revolvers gives you a clue about limits. Pay attention so you don't get in trouble, and know your own limits, too.

This is what a full-sized pistol and Critical Duty gets you.

day with .357s, then they go through the M-27. The lightweights? Unless it is for an article or a test, I will only put .38s, and not a lot of .38+Ps, through them. It's just no fun, it's too painful and I don't want to learn a flinch.

This will take some work and range time. That's good, because there is no such thing as too much, and certainly there is such a thing as too little. The bad news is that this may be work, could be annoyingly painful and will take time.

Now, in the .357 Sig I have one top choice, and that is the Hornady Critical Duty. Of course, I'll only pack it in a full-sized pistol, but boy, what performance you get.

AMMO PERFORMANCE CHART: .357 SIG AND .357 MAGNUM

BRAND, BULLET	VELOCITY	PENETRATION*	EXPANSION
.357 Sig			
Sig V-Crown, 125 gr	1298	11.5"	.676"
Winchester Defend 125 gr	1311	12.75"	.581"
Fiocchi FMJTC 124 gr	1366	31"	.355"
Corbon JHP 125 gr	1470	13.5"	.614"

Georgia Arms FMJ 125 gr	1449	29"	.355"
Hornady FTX 115 gr	1199	14.5"	.568"
Hornady XTP 124 gr	1394	15"	.549"
Hornady XTP 147 gr	1241	16.5"	.504"
Hornady Critical Duty 135 gr	1206	14"	.605"
Speer Gold Dot 125 gr	1329	15.5"	.599"
Michigan Ammo FMJ 125 gr	1324	32"	.355"
Sig Sauer V-Crown 125 gr	1332	14"	.710"
.357 Magnum			
Super Vel 110 gr	1339	11.75"	.546"
Black Hills XTP 125 gr""	1083	16.75"	.525"
Black Hills XTP 125 gr***	1340	14"	.589"
Hornady FTX 125 gr	1257	13"	.575"
Sig V-Crown 125 gr	1394	--	--
Hornady Critical Duty 135 gr	1241	14.5"	.604"
Aguila JSP 158 gr	1183	--	--
Federal Premium 158 gr	1172	--	--
Hornady XTP 158 gr**	1199	18"	.567"
Black Hills XTP 158 gr***	1222	19.25"	.553"
Remington L-SWC 158 gr	1201	--	--

* Bare gelatin for penetration and expansion, unless otherwise indicated
** 4" barrel
*** 6" barrel

In any revolver caliber, a longer barrel gets you more velocity. It is a trade-off between handiness and speed.

208 | GunDigest.com

17

THE .40 S&W:
ONCE KING, NOW FRIENDLESS

The world is spinning backwards on its axis; the FBI is going to drop the .40 S&W. Well, maybe. And maybe not, we'll see. But what happened?

Simple, we were wrong. The plan was simple: as the in-between cartridge, the .40 S&W was going to deliver near-.45 performance at near-9mm recoil with enough capacity to make it worthwhile.

Alas, Sir Isaac Newton and his laws are not so forgiving. What we found was that, by the time you got the .40 up to near .45 levels, it was delivering near-.45 recoil. If you eased up on the throttle and made it kick more like a 9mm, then, gee whiz, it performed like a 9mm.

All the while, the 3-D geometric problem of fitting enough of them into a magazine was an obstacle. The first .40s, the Glock aside, had 9mm magazine tubes, and as a result they held 10 or 11 rounds of .40 ammo. Going from eight of the .45 to ten of the .40 was not enough to make it worthwhile.

It took re-designed guns and re-proportioned magazines to get capacity up to 15 rounds.

The first loads featured only 180-grain bullets, and a lot of those were FMJs. But we demanded more, so Federal designed their Hydra Shok in the .40 at 180 grains, and it performed quite well. It still does.

PROGRESS?

Then someone had the bright idea that, since the .40 was limited in bullet weight with an absolute ceiling of 180 grains (there's just no more room for more weight), the way to get more performance was to go lighter and faster.

Bullet weight went down, down, down. From 180 to 165 to 150 and then to 135 grains. Pain ensued. I ran into Robbie Leatham a decade ago at an industry function. I had just tested the Springfield EMP, a compact little pistol,

Above: These are recovered .40 bullets, WW PDX1, that have been into gel, and some after barriers. This is impressive, but it is also near .45 in recoil.

Below: In this cross-section of the Hydra Shok .40 round, you can see the post in the middle of the hollow point, and you can also see that there is no room left in the case for any more bullet weight.

Top: If you want near-.45 performance like this, you have to be willing to put up with near-.45 recoil. Nothing in life is free. Bottom: If you want performance, and you want to have fun, and you want your pistol to last a good long time, then load it with 180-grain bullets. These Remington Golden Sabers performed like champs.

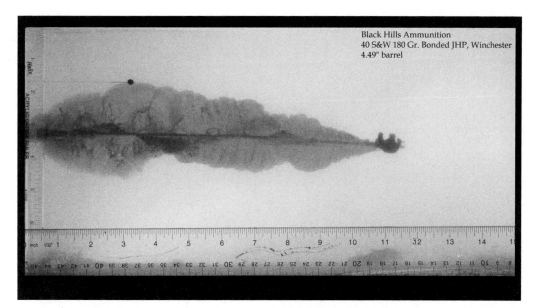

Left: This is what a full-weight bonded bullet (a WW PDX1) does in gelatin, even out of a compact pistol.

Below: Not all 135s are painful to shoot. This Guard Dog went through the wallboard barrier and still did this, and penetrated to the FBI depth in gel.

a 1911 re-proportioned to take a 9mm-only magazine, and as a result a very comfortable little pistol. I mentioned that I had tested the .40 version of it. He was curious. "What did you think?" "Great, I even tested it with the 135s and 150s."

He winced. "Those things hurt."

When a professional shooter comments on a particular loading of a cartridge with "those things hurt," you know it has sharp recoil.

And the guns showed it, too. Fed a diet of the lightweights, they did not last as long as they would with the standard-weight bullets.

So why is the FBI thinking of going back to the 9mm from the .40? Partly to increase the service life of the pistols, and partly the need to actually get people to shoot well enough to pass the qualification course. This is not a slam on the people involved. If you can defend yourself well with a 9mm and will shoot poorly with a .40, then it is just accepting reality that you should not be using a .40.

That's the lesson here for the rest of us. Do not let your ego talk you into jumping up to a bigger caliber than you can handle, simply because "Real Men shoot calibers starting in 4."

If you can handle it, use it. If you can't, don't.

CAPACITY REDUX

Where the .40 really costs is when you get to the compact and ultra-compact pistols. There, you have a double whammy. Not only are you giving up capacity (as in a magazine with five or six or seven shots, at best), but you're also using a pistol with a much smaller grip, and this with a cartridge that kicks hard. A hard-kicking, ultra-compact 9mm is bad enough, but when you force

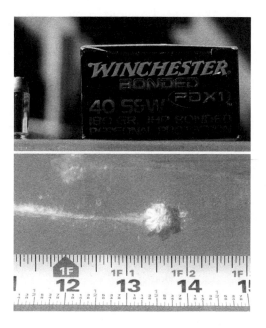

Here is an early PDX1 .40 load tested in gelatin. Even out of a compact pistol it penetrates past the FBI threshold and expands.

CHAPTER 17: THE .40 S&W: ONCE KING, NOW FRIENDLESS | **213**

Right: Here is the target, behind the windshield, on which the PDX1 .40 load demonstrated its worth. After seeing these go the length of the car, I was set on 180 grains being the best weight for the .40.

Below: The Guard Dog .40 still offers enough bullet weight, with the bullets of 135 grains, and not the snappy recoil most 135s create in the .40. And they perform like this, always a good thing.

a .40 into the same package it becomes just too much gun.

AMMO SELECTION

Here the choices diverge. If you are going with a bonded bullet, then you go full weight and you use whatever your pistol shoots well or most-accurately. Pick from the 180-grain offerings and you can't go wrong. When I tested the 9mm PDX1, I also shot the car in question with the .40. I angled the shots a bit differently and found that .40s outperformed the 9mms. The .40s not only punched through the windshield, the target, the seatback, the rear seat and trunk divider, but half of them exited the trunk lid. The other half put big dents on the sheet metal of the trunk lid.

Those were 180-grain weight, and I see no reason to change weights when using a bonded bullet.

However, the new solid copper bullets, like the Honey Badger, offer a lot of promise. If they can do the job as it appears they can, at reduced recoil, then they will be a future choice. Right now, they are in the testing phase.

GUARD DOG

If you are unable to use a hollowpoint or a softpoint and must use FMJ, then the Guard Dog is your option. And while the 9mm Guard Dog is clever, I, personally, would only go as small as the .40 for the choice here. But then, I'm willing to pack a larger gun than a lot of EDC shooters, and then the capacity limits of the .40 are not so bad.

214 | GunDigest.com

Practice ammo should not be defensive ammo, unless you have no other choice. This is great for practice, but will greatly over-penetrate in a defensive situation. Unless you live in New Jersey, don't use this for defense.

AMMO PERFORMANCE CHART: .40 S&W

BRAND, BULLET	VELOCITY	PENETRATION*	EXPANSION
Black Hills TAC-XP 140 gr	1131	12.75"	.763"
Corbon JHP 135	1390	--	--
Corbon DPX 140 gr	1163	--	--
Federal HST 155 gr	1171	14.5"	.637"
Federal HST 180 gr	--	14.5"	.777"

CHAPTER 17: THE .40 S&W: ONCE KING, NOW FRIENDLESS | **215**

Federal Guard Dog 135 gr	1242	14.5"	.629"
Hornady XTP 155 gr	1123	13.2"	.649"
Hornady FTX 165 gr	1047	16"	.647"
Hornady Critical Duty 175 gr	1005	14"	.581"
Black Hills Nosler 180 gr	1005	12"	.739"
Black Hills Berry plates 180 gr	961	9.5"	.851"
Hornady XTP 180 gr	1037	14.5"	.697"
Polycase ARX 104 gr	1367	16.5'	.401"
Sig V-Crown, 180 gr	1011	14.75"	.625"
Speer GDHP short barrel 180 gr	907***	14.5"	.611"
	949****	14"	.633"
	1013*****	13.5"	.649"
Winchester Defend 180 gr	931	13.1"	.701"
Winchester JHP 180 gr**	1036	14.25"	.647"
Winchester PDX1 180 gr	1023	15.5"	.763"

*Bare gelatin for penetration and expansion, unless otherwise indicated
** Windshield test
*** 3" barrel
**** 4" barrel
***** 4.25" barrel

What is great for competition isn't always great for defense. This old S&W 4046 is a better choice for home defense than this highly refined hi-cap 40, complete with a spare upper for use in a competition division no longer recognized.

CHAPTER 17: THE .40 S&W: ONCE KING, NOW FRIENDLESS | **217**

18

10MM & CHOICES

The 10mm is much-loved in some circles and elicits a yawn in others. I think it is perhaps the best handgun cartridge design of the 20th century, perhaps only surpassed by the .44 Magnum, but that's just me.

It is also the shortest chapter in this book. The reason is simple: it is the Dr. Jekyll and Mr. Hyde of handgun cartridges.

You have to decide what you will be using it for. If you are going to use it for personal defense against people, then simply use the information from the .40 S&W chapter. You opt for a moderate-velocity (for the 10mm) 180-grain bullet, and a bonded bullet at that. You will be using this in a full-sized pistol or revolver simply because the number of compact 10mms is vanishingly small. Recoil will not be a problem, it will be fun to shoot, and you'll have a grand time of practice.

The other choice will be as a hunting or animal defense cartridge. There, you follow the advice of hunting experts, and ballisticians like Max Prasac in his book *Hunting Revolvers*.

You will most likely be using heavier 200- or 220-grain bullets, hard-cast, with big meplats, and hurling them as fast as your hands can stand. Life will be work, and you will not be having as much fun, but you will be prepared

Above: You'll find most 10mm handguns to be all-steel, full-sized, and easy to control in .40-power-level loads. Even in full-power loads, it isn't a big deal.

Below: The 10mm (center) requires a .45-sized handgun, unlike the .40 S&W (left) which was made to fit into a 9mm-sized handgun.

CHOOSING HANDGUN AMMO | **219**

The 10mm, like all other handgun cartridges, benefits from a longer barrel. However, unless you are using it for hunting, there's not much point in a long-slide 10mm pistol.

CHAPTER 18: 10MM AND CHOICES | 221

The .38-40 was the original .400/.401-inch-bullet handgun, and it's now seeing more use in Cowboy Action Shooting, in part because there are many bullet choices to be had.

when someone nasty tries to bite/claw/stomp you.

The 10mm is not the first .400-inch-bore handgun. That title belongs to the .38-40 revolver cartridge. When trying to develop a cartridge in-between the 9mm and the .45, experimenters used the bullets made for the .38-40, and built/modified cases to use them. That led to the 10mm, which lead to the .40 S&W, and in a case of going full circle, the availability of .401-inch lead bullets for 04/10mm practice caused an upsurge in interest in .38-40 revolvers for Cowboy Action Shooting.

Sometimes life is just strange.

A hard-cast bullet penetrates like you wouldn't' believe. Take these 200-grain lead truncated cone bullets, load them hot in a 10mm, and you will shoot through a lot of animal. Not so good for people, however, unless you really need the ability to shoot through 4-5 feet of ballistic gelatin.

AMMO PERFORMANCE CHART: 10MM

BRAND, BULLET	VELOCITY	PENETRATION*	EXPANSION
Hornady FTX 165 gr	1264	--	--
Hornady XTP 180 gr	1141	--	--
Hornady XTP 200 gr	1127	17.5"	.564"
Hornady Critical Duty 175 gr	1178	16.5"	.611"
Wilson Combat XTP 180 gr	1319	--	--
HPR JHP 180 gr	1226	--	--
ProGrade JHP 180 gr	1206	--	--
Doubletap Nosler JHP 200 gr	1198	--	--
CCI Blazer TMJ 200 gr	988	36"+**	.400"
Remington JHP 180 gr	1080	--	--
Federal Trophy Bonded 180 gr	1181	24"***	.601"
Civil Defense JHP 60 gr	2468	--	--

*Bare gelatin for penetration and expansion, unless otherwise indicated
**Exited the back of two blocks, not unusual for this or other big-bore cartridges.
*** This is a tough, hunting-focused bullet, for deer, not people.

19

THE .44s

The .44s pose the same sort of dilemma as the 10mm, but even more so. You can acquire ammunition for them (the .44 Special can be fired in a .44 Magnum revolver, just like a .38 Special in a .357) in a wide power range. Power from a soft-recoiling .44 Special for cowboy shooting, a 200-grain lead bullet at 650 fps, up to a T-Rex hunting load of a 320-grain hard-cast flat-nose at 1,200 fps.

Just to make it even more confusing, Hornady makes a special bullet for use in lever-action rifles. The bullet has a pointed nose, but the point is a soft polymer, one that will not detonate the primer of a cartridge in front of it, under recoil.

This is meant for rifle use, and it will do great on four-legged critters. It will be too much, in recoil and performance, for people, although if that's all you've got, get to work saving yourself and don't mind me.

So, we have two choices: .44 Special or lightweight bullets in .44 Magnum. What you don't want to do is use traditional all-lead bullets for defense. The .44 Special loads are loaded for use in Cowboy Action matches. That means a 200- or 220-grain bullet at under 700fps that is soft to shoot and fast in competition, but not anything anyone has wanted to use since before Kaiser Wilhelm was

You'll be using your .44 ammo in a full-sized gun. Even a lightweight N-frame is a big piece of ordnance.

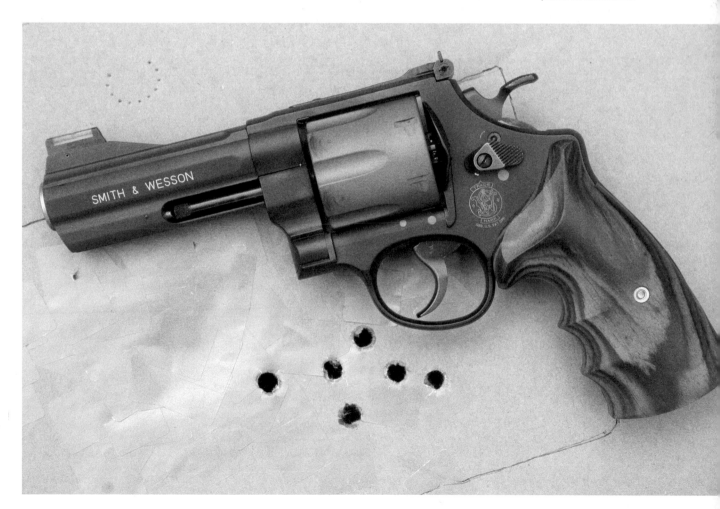

CHOOSING HANDGUN AMMO | 225

Top: The Hornady .44 Leverevolution is meant for use in lever-action rifles. This is more than your handgun needs, although it is safe for use. Your hands might object, however. Bottom: Rifle-oriented loads will deliver rifle-like performance. Yes, 22 inches of gelatin penetration can be useful at times, but you will pay for it in recoil.

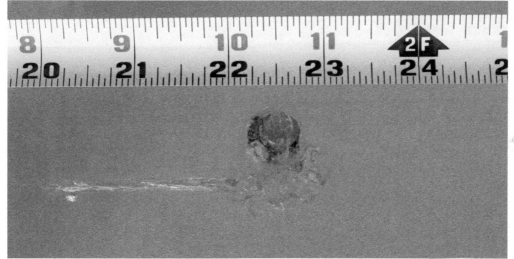

Above: Expansion? Yes, the .44s deliver that. Just be sure you are comfortable with the level of recoil they can generate.

Left: For animal defense, you may not even want this level of expansion. For personal defense, you certainly don't need this level of penetration.

alive and complaining about the weather in Serbia.

You'll be using these in a full-sized handgun, an S&W N-frame in .44 Special or .44 Magnum, so it will be a full two pounds or more. In one of those, you'll find something like the Sig V-crown load to be a pleasure to shoot.

If you opt for a lightweight bullet loading in .44 Magnum, be aware; they are not doing it for low recoil, they are loading it for maximum velocity. Where the Sig load will be fun, the 180-grain .44 Magnum load will not be.

All bullets will pass the FBI test, and the newer bullet designs will post maximum scores. Both of these cartridges have mass and speed in their favor, and so you need to find what your revolver likes, what you can shoot, and what is available in your area.

Using a .44 of any type for defense is a pretty specialized area. The vast bulk of shooters use something in 9mm, .40 or .45 ACP.

AMMO PERFORMANCE CHART: .44s

BRAND, BULLET	VELOCITY	PENETRATION*	EXPANSION
.44 Magnum			
Hornady FTX 225 gr	1319	16.5"	.851"
.44 Special			
Black Hills LFN 210 gr	623	--	--
Black Hills JHP 200 gr	797	--	--
Hornady FTX 165 gr	817	10.5"	.617"
Hornady XTP 180 gr	798	--	--
Remington LRN 246 gr	623	--	--
Sig V-Crown 200 gr	699	--	--
Winchester Silvertip 200 gr	727	--	--

*Bare gelatin for penetration and expansion, unless otherwise indicated

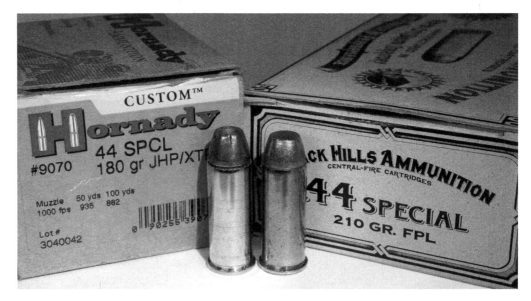

Do not use the various cowboy loads for defense. They are meant to be soft-recoiling loads, with lighter than normal bullets at modest velocities. Great practice, learning or teaching, and competition loads, but not what you want when you are defending yourself.

20

THE .45s

The obvious topic for discussion here is the .45 ACP. But, let us not forget the .45 Colt, which has been seeing some resurgence. First, the .45 ACP.

When the FBI was trying to find something better after the Miami shootout, there were those counseling the .45. However, there was a lot of resistance to jumping up to it and it alone. A lot of agents simply wouldn't be able to handle a .45 ACP, especially since the two choices were the 1911 and the S&W 645. Both big guns, they would have been too big for the smaller agents, and the recoil would have been too much for even those who weren't small.

The FBI had just settled a case where the training program, as it existed at that time (the early 1980s), flunked female candidates, candidates who would have passed the FBI qual course had they been given the qual course and not the academy course. The FBI was sensitive about disparate impact.

So, they selected the 10mm, and wrangled and fought and changed plans. They could have avoided all that, and the subsequent 25 years of wandering in the wilderness with .40s, if they had simply opted for the .45 (the 10mm had to be in a .45-sized pistol anyway), figured out how to build guns for female and small-handed agents, and taught them how to shoot.

All the R&D and bullet technology that improved the 9mm and .40 translated perfectly to the .45, and as a result, it is even better now than it was back in the 1980s.

The problem with the .45 ACP isn't the cartridge, but the pistols it is in. It is a big cartridge and requires a big pistol. Even the most compact .45s are still kind of big, and the smallest are harder to shoot as a result.

So here, your choices are easy in ammo and hard in pistol.

Any modern bullet in .45 ACP will easily pass the FBI test. The .45 is also amenable to the adoption of the new hollowpoint all-copper bullets. There, you can get impressive, even eye-popping expansion out of bullets – with petals expanding to over three-quarters of an inch.

Where the old wound tracks of FMJ, also known as hardball, were simply .45 diameter tunnels, the new bullets expand and create impressive wound tracks.

The .45 is also a very efficient cartridge. The bullet is mostly inside the case, and the case capacity is well-suited for the bullet. (That was a point considered in the first decade of the 20th century, when the .45 ACP was developed.)

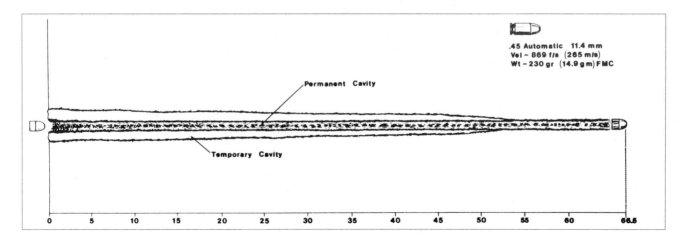

The wound track of 230 FMJ, what we had back in the old days. Not impressive by today's standards, but it did good work before we had better. Image courtesy the late Dr. Martin Fackler.

Right: The 185s do not have to take a back seat to the 230s. Here a Hornady XTP 185 performs like the king of the hill.

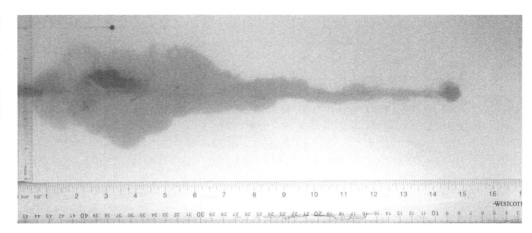

Below: You want expansion? Then you want all-copper bullets, and here is the champion: Silverback 230 .45 ACP. Look at those petals.

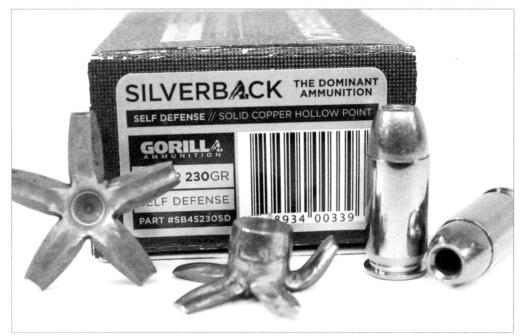

It doesn't take a lot of powder to get its bullet up to speed, and as it does its work through mass and frontal area, even if they didn't expand much, they'd still be great. That they do is a grand bonus.

GUARD DOG

Even more so than the .40, the Guard Dog in .45 is a great choice. If you are limited to FMJ, this delivers 165 grains of soft-recoiling .45 bullet, and the expanding full metal jacket is a bonus.

.45 ACP+P?

Do you need the extra boost of +P? Maybe. If you can handle it, if it doesn't cause a decrease in your shooting and you want the extra performance, then go for it. You probably don't need it, but some want it, so there it is.

.45 COLT

The .45 Colt dates back to 1873 and the Colt Single Action Army. It has an MAP of only 14,000 PSI, but that's plenty. Given a .45 bullet of full weight, the .45 Colt smacks the FBI tests with authority, and delivers plenty of expansion. And since the pressure is so low, you can get a lifetime of shooting out of one revolver, as it simply isn't worked that hard by the recoil or pressure. You just have to be willing to put up with a full-sized revolver, is all.

Left: Big bore, soft recoil, and if it expands (they do so, consistently) then you get even more. This from a bullet that can rightly be pointed to as a full metal jacket design. The Guard Dog really works in .45 ACP.

Below: The .45 and 9mm are both unusually efficient cartridges. It doesn't take a lot of powder to generate the velocities they deliver. Here is a cutaway of the Syntech, showing the 100% loading density many loads benefit from.

Back when Detroit PD allowed personal sidearms in calibers officers could shoot a passing score with, we saw bunches of S&Ws in .45 Colt on the street. Back before the FBI tests, a flat-nosed 255-grain lead bullet was well thought-of, and it should still be so today.

FUTURE

If something works in 9mm, it works better in .40, right? Then it obviously should work better still in .45 ACP, because we have it all – mass, frontal area, and we aren't giving up velocity. I speak of the Honey Badger, which does not expand, stops in gel like bonded bullets, and ignores barriers. This just may be what all bullets are in the future.

SELECTION

As with the other big-bore choices, you do not have to obsess about weight. 185s work as well as 230s, and if your handgun (or your hands) prefer the 185s over the 230, then go for it. Don't get hung up on bullet weight, go with accurate and easy to shoot.

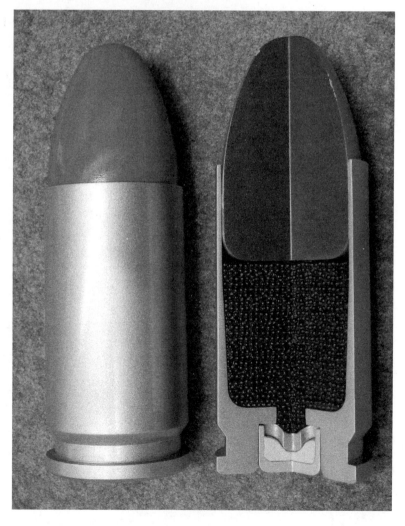

The .45 has a hollow point so big you can see the results in this .45 Colt bullet. That's a plug of cloth from the heavy cloth barrier test, in the open petals of the PDX1 bullet. It cut the cloth out, still expanded, and tracked so straight the cloth stayed in place.

CHAPTER 20: THE .45S | 235

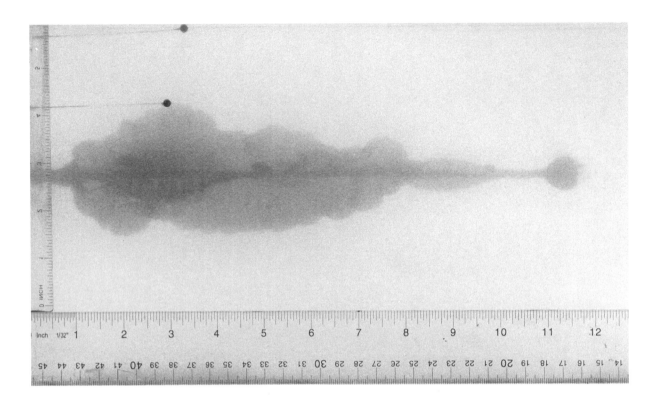

Top: Sometimes more is not more. This +P load causes the bullet to expand more, and stops right at the FBI limit. Of course, if this is what you want, then mission accomplished. Image courtesy Black Hills. Bottom: The .45 Colt can be amazingly accurate. Twenty-five yards, offhand, with full power PDX1 ammo.

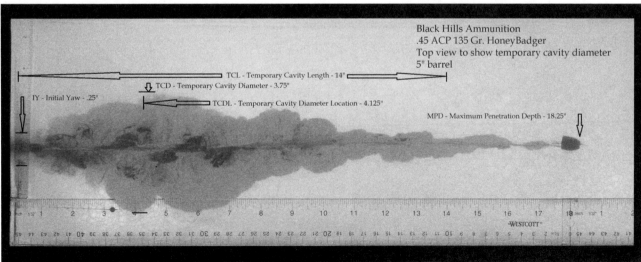

Top: Hollow point, gaping hollow point, or big flat point on a lead bullet, the .45 Colt is not to be trifled with. Bottom: Eighteen inches of penetration from a non-expanding bullet, and a wound track that looks like that? Where do I get some? Image courtesy Black Hills.

The Hornady 220-grain Critical Duty bullet.

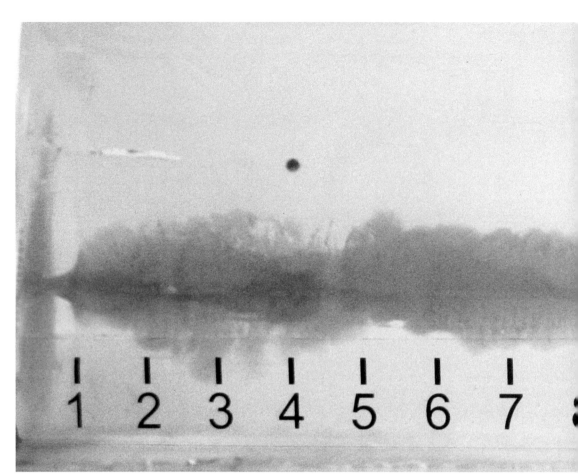

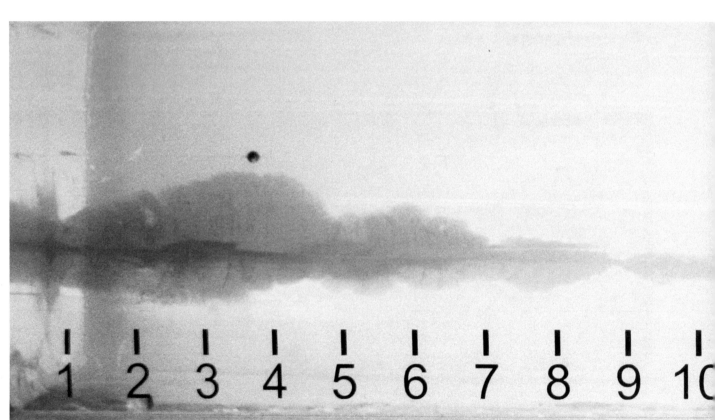

238 | GunDigest.com

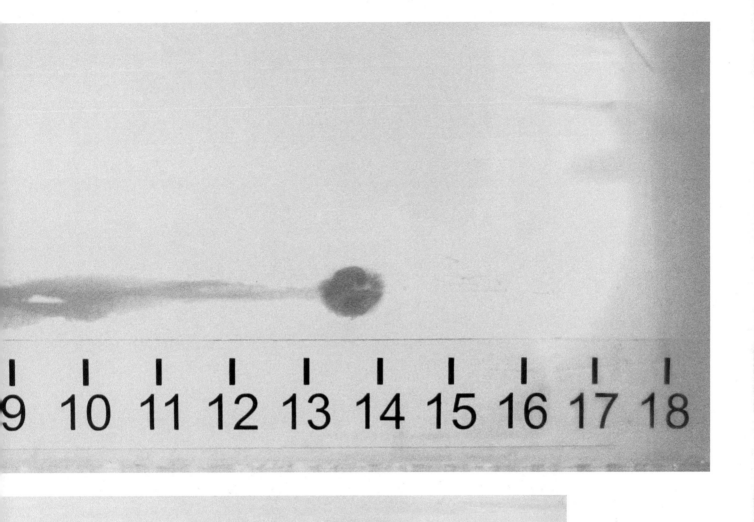

Even after going through the steel barrier, the Flexlock bullet expands and stops at the 18-inch mark.

Top: The Black Hills Honey Badger load in .45 ACP uses a bullet that weighs only 135 grains. It is all copper, and machined with flutes, and it does not expand. It doesn't care. Bottom: One of the details that we constantly learn and re-learn is that revolvers work, but you have to reload. Six shots may be enough, but more is always better. So, practice, practice, practice.

The .45 Colt has been dealing with bad guys for almost 150 years now, and the plain lead bullet works well. Yes, there are loads that work better, but not without cost in recoil.

AMMO PERFORMANCE CHART: .45s

BRAND, BULLET	VELOCITY	PENETRATION*	EXPANSION
.45 ACP			
Asym Bonded 230 gr	819	15.5"	.712"
Black Hills Honey Badger 135 gr	1311	18.25"	.452"
Black Hills TAC-XPD 185 gr	1012	12.1"	.819"
Federal HST 230 gr	866	15.5"	.699"
Federal Guard Dog 165 gr	1048	13.5'	.657"
Hornady XTP 185 gr**	998	16.5"	.565"
Hornady XTP 185 gr***	1057	15.25	.605"
Hornady XTP 185 gr****	1051	12"	.636"
Hornady FTX 185 gr**	846 fps	16"	.660"
Hornady FTX 185 gr***	933 fps	14.5"	.710"

Black Hills XTP+P 230 gr	895	13.75"	.737"
Black Hills Berry plated 230 gr	930	13.2"	.581"
Hornady XTP 230 gr**	786	13.8"	.700"
Hornady XTP 230 gr***	802	14.25"	.707"
Hornady Critical Duty 220 gr	946	14"	.708"
Polycase ARX 114 gr	1216	16"	.452"
Remington HTP 230 gr	811	16"	.799"
Sig V-Crown 230 gr	874	14.5"	.695"
Speer GDHP 230 gr		14.2"	.719"
Winchester Defend 230 gr	899	13.5"	.812"
Winchester PDX1 230 gr	937	14"	.729"
.45 Colt			
Black Hills LFN 250 gr	803		
Hornady FTX 185 gr	871	12"	.689"
Hornady LFN 255 gr	723	--	--
Magtech FP 250 FP	610	18"	.462"
Winchester Silvertip 225 gr	752	13.5"	.598"
Winchester PDX1 225 gr	824	15"	.629"
Winchester LRN 255 gr	618	--	--
Corbon JHP 200	1123	14"	.671"

*Bare gelatin for penetration and expansion, unless otherwise indicated
** 4" barrel
*** 5" barrel
**** 5" barrel, windshield test

21

HUNTING

The problem isn't whether it will do the job, but can you hit with it? The harder-kicking it is, the more you need to practice to be accurate.

Full disclosure here: I can't give you extensive advice on hunting with handguns, as I have not done much of it. Oh, I've had my fun and games with whitetails and broadheads, decades ago, but not with handguns. So, I have to go with what makes sense to me, and that comes down to this: whitetails are more or less people-sized. You would do well to go with the upper limit of what you can shoot well, that works on people. In that vein, I'd suggest you start at the .357 Magnum, with bonded bullets, and move up from there.

The biggest problem is a shooting problem. You will be less engaged in a shootout, a defensive encounter, and more in an ambush, sniping as it were. What is the maximum distance at which you can reliably place your shots into the lethal zone of the deer standing in front of you? 25 yards? 50? 75? You'd better find out, and practice to get better.

Once you exceed the .357 Magnum threshold, the biggest obstacle is accuracy. It depends on both the handgun and you. Yes, a .44 Magnum is a more effective cartridge, but if you can't hit as well (due to recoil) then it isn't necessarily a better choice. Rein in your ego and pick the one you can hit with.

For bigger animals, I must defer to a fellow writer Max Prasac. In *Gun Digest Book of Hunting Revolvers*, he covers all the angles, calibers and animal sizes. A quick summary would be thus: use the biggest caliber you can handle, with the heaviest, hard-cast bullet with a big wide flat on the front end. If you can't handle a caliber big enough to deal with the animal you are contemplating hunting, then don't go.

To put it crudely, a 20mm Bofors isn't enough to do the job, if you shoot a moose in the hind end.

Follow the advice of Harry Callahan: Know your limitations.

CHOOSING HANDGUN AMMO | 245

Whitetails are more or less people-sized, so what works on people (and is DNR-approved) will work in deer.

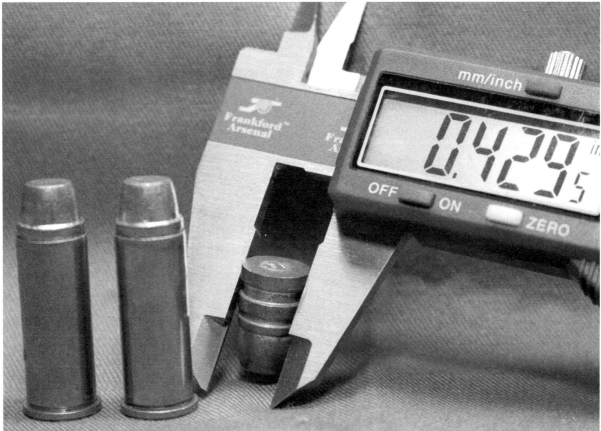

Top: Bullet weights in the .44 Magnum alone can range from 240 to 320 grains. Bigger bores add even more mass. Bottom: The big bores have exacting requirements for bullet diameter, weight, powder, and the handguns they will work in. Know this before you go loading "perfect" hunting ammo.

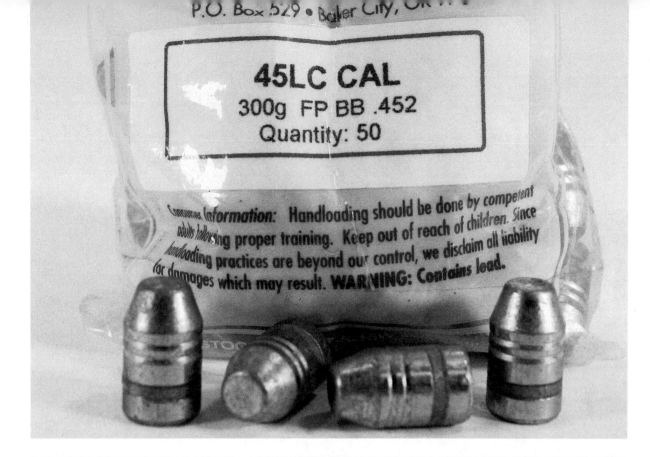

Top: If you are loading your own hunting ammo, and you have a really strong revolver, like a Ruger, and you want the utmost in performance, then you can load 300-grain truncated cone bullets. At 1,000 fps or a bit more, they will shoot through a moose. They will also throw your S&W N frame out of time and break your Colt SAA, so keep this ammo separate. Bottom: The 300-grain .45 bullets have two crimp grooves, not so you can crimp them twice, but so you can use them in either .45 Colt cases or .454 Casull cases.

Top: And, as always, test before you depend on your ammo. Bottom: A Freedom Arms single action, in .500 Wyoming Express. If what you are hunting doesn't weigh a ton or more, you have more gun than you need. But still, when you want impact like a ton of bricks, here you go.

Top: S&W topped everyone with the .500 S&W Magnum. There are a lot of rifles that do not have the terminal ballistics that this cartridge produces. And, curiously enough, my test-fire volunteers stand in line to shoot it. Bottom: This is a custom gun, a Ruger Redhawk that has been rebuilt by Hamilton Bowen into a bear-gun snubbie. Chambered in .500 Linebaugh, it hurls a 500-grain bullet at a thousand feet per second. Shooting it is an…..experience.

22 IN SUMMARY

After all this, what have we learned, and what should you do to have the most effective ammunition? Well, one thing we've learned is that there is more than one way to skin a cat. The choices come down to bullet diameter or caliber, mass or speed, or some combination of two or all three. The tricky part is finding a balance that you can manage, since this is to a certain extent a zero-sum game.

We've all heard the phrase "zero-sum game," but what does it mean? Simple: someone gains, and that gain comes at the expense of someone losing. A poker game is a zero-sum game, as you win by taking money from the other gamblers.

You can have a mixed-sum game. Blackjack would be one. Your winning or losing is a zero-sum game with the House, but not with the player next to you. Your winnings to not necessarily come at his expense, and he does not directly benefit from your losses.

So what does this have to do with selecting a defensive caliber and load? Simple, you must give up something to gain something. This is not just a matter of game theory, but of thermodynamics. There are limits, and a big part of that is you. It may be glib, but no matter how good your attorney is, you cannot escape the three laws of thermodynamics.

One: When a system gains or loses energy, its state or internal energy changes.

Two: The sum of the entropies of the interacting systems increases.

Three: Entropy approaches a constant, as the temperature approaches absolute zero.

What do these laws mean? My chemical thermodynamics professor summed it up this way: "Rule one, you can't win. Rule two, you can't break even. Rule three, you can't get out of the game."

The first law simply tells us that we get what we pay for, but that we pay for what

Record results, however you do it. Know what your ammo does before you go and select the "perfect" ammo. Choose based on knowledge, not advertising or the wishful thinking of the local gun shop expert.

CHOOSING HANDGUN AMMO | 253

we get. Want more performance out of your ammo? You will have to pay in recoil, muzzle blast and flash, and extra weight or bulk. You cannot get something for nothing, and you cannot gain something without added cost. That cost may have secondary effects. Move up in caliber, and you not only have more recoil, but less ammunition capacity for any given size pistol.

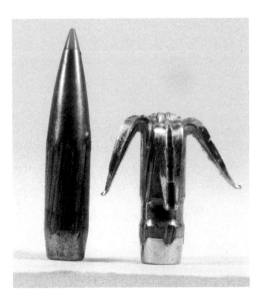

Above: Besides being way too blasty, this "handgun" is not at all concealable. No matter how much power it produces, it just won't work.

Right: AR handguns chambered in .300 Blackout are becoming quite popular. If you expect your subsonic ammo to expand, you have to select the bullets correctly. The 208-grain bullet on the left, designed to be shot out of a .308 Winchester, does not expand in ballistic gelatin. The all-copper one on the right does.

The second law tells us that any change will not only be paid for, but the cost will increase faster than the change. I recently finished testing an ultra-lightweight snub-nose revolver (all of 14 ounces, empty) using .357 Magnum ammunition. The recoil was beyond stout or even sharp. It was pain-inducing. No mortal could shoot a full box of 50 rounds in one session and live to tell the tale. (Well, they'd live, but they wouldn't be shaking hands for a week or more afterwards.) You can have light weight, but you pay for it in recoil. You can have leading-edge performance, but you'll pay for it. If you want both, you'll pay for it in spades.

The third law tells us that everything has a cost. Practice costs in the ammo expenses, but also in the service life of the firearm as it is consumed, and in the time spent, and the wear and tear on your body. Everything costs, and everything fades. The skills you built in practice will fade with time. As you practice, you use up ammunition and the service life

Accuracy counts. Can you have too much? Here, I'm shooting on a 50-to-300-meter rifle course, with a handgun. I got 14 of the 20 targets. That's accurate enough.

of the firearm you are practicing with. To maintain a given skill level requires a certain amount of time, ammunition, and used-up service life of the handgun you are practicing with. There's no getting around it.

And it all comes back to you being the limiting factor.

The ideal carry gun? It would have the size and weight of an aluminum-framed Walther PPK. Such a beast exists. I found one, and before I realized what it was I sold it to my brother. It is called the PPK-L, and it's a rare and lightweight little gem. This ideal EDC firearm would use ammunition no more expensive than .22LR, it would have terminal effectiveness comparable to a .44 Magnum, and it would have built-in target acquisition so every shot was delivered as precisely as possible. It doesn't take much thought to find the shortcomings in all that, and the realization that we're stuck with the choices we have. So, here goes.

RULE ONE, HAVE A GUN

For your "ideal" ammunition to be effective, you must carry the firearm that uses it.

It may seem trite, but if you don't have it with you when you need it, it matters not how effective your chosen handgun is, as far as defensive use is concerned. For those armed as a service to society, i.e., law enforcement, there isn't much choice. You use the sidearm that is issued, or one from the short list of approved, and you do what you must to make it a comfortable fit. The rest of us have a lot more options.

It has to be light enough to wear all day, but heavy enough to not be painful

Above: Something that doesn't work is obviously a poor choice. Don't depend on unreliable in your gun ammo.

Below: Use ammo that works and that you can practice with. If you have one box of otherwise unobtainable ammo, that's not what you carry.

to shoot. It is entirely possible to have a handgun that is too light, and as a result, shoot it poorly.

It has to be compact enough that you can keep it hidden under clothing, clothing appropriate for the location and climate. "Not hidden" is viewed in a lot of jurisdictions as "brandishing," which is a legal way of saying "threatened with a weapon."

It has to use a cartridge powerful enough to be useful, and to give you confidence. There may be times when you have to compromise greatly here, as something that can remain hidden may be so small and less-powerful that you're really giving up a lot of potential effectiveness. That's a social and tactical decision you have to make, none of us can do that for you.

It has to hold a useful amount of ammunition. How much is a "useful amount" is not within your control. If you find yourself holding the entryway against a would-be mall shooter and you're using only a five-shot snubbie, you'll wish for more rounds. Then again, you may only need one or two, and he could move on to the next store. (Bad luck for them, but there's only so much you can do in that, or any, situation.) The classic description of your "typical" shootout, of 2.3 rounds fired, in a second and a half, at an average of three yards distance? That's fine, if you believe it. But, if we went with the odds, we would not be carrying a gun.

So, a five-shot snubbie is the absolute bare minimum, and you'd be wise to have spare ammo, and not just as loose rounds in your pocket.

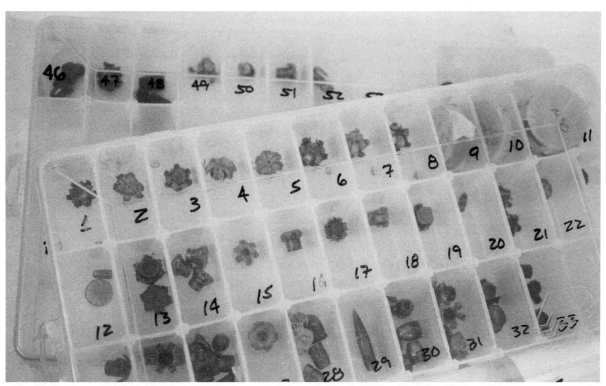

Top: You can now get ammunition that is matched. This is Federal (Winchester started it) ammo, practice ammo in the same weight and velocity as the carry ammo, all in one box. Bottom: If you test, save. Knowledge is a fragile thing, and years from now will you really remember which bullet, in a jumbled box of them, is the one you want to examine?

RULE TWO, USE WHAT WORKS

Use what works; not necessarily what works in a theoretical defensive encounter, but what works in the firearm you have selected. If the world's greatest, most-effective defensive ammunition choice runs unreliably in your handgun or is inaccurate, then it isn't much use to you, is it? There are plenty of good options to choose from. Find the load that shoots with 100% reliability in your firearm. As a side note, if you have a firearm with fixed sights, then select ammunition that hits to the sights.

A load that shoots one-hole groups, but inches to the side and up or down from your sights isn't what you want. Under stress, will you be able to apply Kentucky windage? Probably not.

So, choose what hits to the sights and is accurate.

RULE THREE, USE WHAT YOU CAN PRACTICE WITH

Use what you can practice with. Not necessarily carry ammo as practice ammo, but you must be able to practice with something that comes close. The closer, the better. I was once handed a box of ammo, pocketed from an FBI class, that had a previously unknown stock number on it. "This is some new secret ammo the FBI is using." I actually looked around to see if anyone was wearing a trench coat, it was so much like the stereotypical "hot watches on the street corner" transaction, except I wasn't paying for it, it was being offered for information.

So, I called up my rep for the ammo company and asked, "What's up?" The answer was simple; this was an otherwise identical load, with the same weight bullet and velocity as the duty load, but loaded with the least-expensive bullet of the same weight the ammo company could make. It was practice ammo. The practice load, because it did not use the hand-made bonded bullet, cost half or less of what the duty load did. For the same money, the FBI could get in twice as much practice. Smart of them.

Why was it secret? No secret, the FBI just wasn't in the business of touting the new ammo, or in crowing about how much money they had saved.

So, if you find that for your chosen defensive caliber the bullet is (just to pick a number) 57 grains, and the big-box sporting goods store only stocks bulk ammo in that caliber that weighs 110 grains, how realistic do you think it will be to practice with the 110-grain ammo? "Not very" is the answer you were looking for. The two loads may not even hit the the same point of impact, and there goes your practice and using the sights.

Back to the real world. If you carry a 9mm and you find that your selected defensive ammunition uses bullet of 115 or 124 or 147 grains, you will have no problem finding practice ammo or loading it yourself. You will even be able to find a load, factory or handload, that has the same velocity, felt recoil, point of impact and muzzle blast/flash.

Which leads us to the next point.

RULE FOUR, NO EDC HANDLOADS

No EDC handloads. I'm with my friend Mas Ayoob on this, carry factory ammunition. I haven't heard of a case where someone was given extra problems in court because they used reloads, but why hand the prosecution that club? Use factory ammo, and make sure it is something you can point to a police department using, and you won't have any problems there.

I can see one instance where you might use reloads. You've spent the day practicing at the range. You clean your handgun, go to load up for the drive home and realize that you have inadvertently shot up all your carry ammo. You only have practice reloads left. Given the choice between driving home "naked" or driving home with your EDC handgun packed with reloads, I'd opt for the reloads and change as soon as I got home. But don't make a habit of it.

PROCESS

So, how do we do this? Start with the handgun. Which one will you be carrying? That will determine the caliber ammunition you choose. Next, pick the combination of factors you are comfortable with: bullet weight, velocity, type. Keep in mind that you may have to actually shoot this load in your defense, so don't pick an ultra lightweight snubbie "because it is easy to pack" and then stuff it with .357 Magnum ammo "because it is effective." Remember, sooner or later, you'll have to actually fire this combination.

This is what the FBI had in mind when they issued the memorandum on caliber selection. This is the now-famous (at least, in firearms circles) "Executive Summary of Justification for Law Enforcement Partners" of 2014. For those who missed it, here it is:

MAY 6, 2014

FBI TRAINING DIVISION: FBI ACADEMY, QUANTICO, VA

EXECUTIVE SUMMARY OF JUSTIFICATION FOR LAW ENFORCEMENT PARTNERS

- Caliber debates have existed in law enforcement for decades.

- Most of what is "common knowledge" with ammunition and its effects on the human target are rooted in myth and folklore.

- Projectiles are what ultimately wound our adversaries and the projectile needs to be the basis for the discussion on what "caliber" is best.

- In all the major law enforcement calibers there exist projectiles which have a high likelihood of failing LEOs in a shooting incident and there are projectiles which have a high likelihood of succeeding for LEOs in a shooting incident.

- Handgun stopping power is simply a myth.

- The single most important factor in effectively wounding a human target is to have penetration to a scientifically valid depth (FBI uses 12-18 inches).

- LEOs miss between 70 and 80 percent of the shots fired during a shooting incident.

- Contemporary projectiles (since 2007) have dramatically increased the terminal effectiveness of many premium line law enforcement projectiles (emphasis on the 9mm Luger offerings).

- 9mm Luger now offers select projectiles which are, under identical testing conditions, outperforming most of the premium line .40 S&W and .45 Auto projectiles tested by the FBI.

- 9mm Luger offers higher magazine

capacities, less recoil, lower cost (both in ammunition and wear on the weapons) and higher functional reliability rates (in FBI weapons).

- The majority of FBI shooters are both FASTER in shot strings fired and more ACCURATE with shooting a 9mm Luger vs. shooting a .40 S&W (similar sized weapons).

- There is little to no noticeable difference in the wound tracks between premium line law enforcement projectiles from 9mm Luger through the .45 Auto.

- Given contemporary bullet construction, LEOs can field (with proper bullet selection) 9mm Lugers with all of the terminal performance potential of any other law enforcement pistol caliber with none of the disadvantages present with the "larger" calibers.

JUSTIFICATION FOR LAW ENFORCEMENT PARTNERS

Rarely in law enforcement does a topic stir a more passionate debate than the choice of handgun caliber made by a law enforcement organization. Many voice their opinions by repeating the old adage "bigger is better" while others have "heard of this one time" where a smaller caliber failed and a larger caliber "would have performed much better." Some even subscribe to the belief that a caliber exists which will provide a "one shot stop." It has been stated, "Decisions on ammunition selection are particularly difficult because many of the pertinent issues related to handguns and ammunition are firmly rooted in myth and folklore." This still holds as true today as it did when originally stated 20 years ago.

Caliber, when considered alone, brings about a unique set of factors to consider such as magazine capacity for a given weapon size, ammunition availability, felt recoil, weight and cost. What is rarely discussed, but most relevant to the caliber debate is what projectile is being considered for use and its terminal performance potential.

One should never debate on a gun make or caliber alone. The projectile is what wounds and ultimately this is where the debate/discussion should focus. In each of the three most common law enforcement handgun calibers (9mm Luger, .40 Smith & Wesson and .45 AUTO) there are projectiles which have a high likelihood of failing law enforcement officers and in each of these three calibers there are projectiles which have a high likelihood of succeeding for law enforcement officers during a shooting incident. The choice of a service projectile must undergo intense scrutiny and scientific evaluation in order to select the best available option.

UNDERSTANDING HANDGUN CALIBER TERMINAL BALLISTIC REALITIES

Many so-called "studies" have been performed and many analyses of statistical data have been undertaken regarding this issue. Studies simply involving shooting deaths are irrelevant since the goal of law enforcement is to stop a threat during a deadly force encounter as quickly as possible. Whether or not death occurs is of no consequence as long as the threat of death or serious injury to law enforcement personnel and innocent third parties is eliminated.

"The concept of immediate incapacitation is the only goal of any law enforcement shooting and is the underlying rationale for decisions regarding weapons, ammunition, calibers and training."1

Studies of "stopping power" are irrelevant because no one has ever been able to define how much power, force, or kinetic energy, in and of itself, is required to effectively stop a violent and determined adversary quickly, and even the largest of handgun calibers are not capable of delivering such force. Handgun stopping power is simply a myth. Studies of so-called "one shot stops" being used as a tool to define the effectiveness of one handgun cartridge, as opposed to another, are irrelevant due to the inability to account for psychological influences and due to the lack of reporting specific shot placement. In short, extensive studies have been done over the years to "prove" a certain cartridge is better than another by using grossly flawed methodology and or bias as a precursor to manipulating statistics. In order to have a meaningful understanding of handgun terminal ballistics, one must only deal with facts that are not in dispute within the medical community, i.e. medical realities, and those which are also generally accepted within law enforcement, i.e. tactical realities.

MEDICAL REALITIES

Shots to the Central Nervous System (CNS) at the level of the cervical spine (neck) or above, are the only means to reliably cause immediate incapacitation. In this case, any of the calibers commonly used in law enforcement, regardless of expansion, would suffice for obvious reasons. Other than shots to the CNS, the most reliable means for affecting rapid incapacitation is by placing shots to large vital organs thus causing rapid blood loss. Simply stated, shot placement is the most critical component to achieving either method of incapacitation.

Wounding factors between rifle and handgun projectiles differ greatly due to the dramatic differences in velocity, which will be discussed in more detail herein. The wounding factors, in order of importance, are as follows:

A. PENETRATION

A projectile must penetrate deeply enough into the body to reach the large vital organs, namely heart, lungs, aorta, vena cava and to a lesser extent liver and spleen, in order to cause rapid blood loss. It has long been established by expert medical professionals, experienced in evaluating gunshot wounds, that this equates to a range of penetration of 12?18 inches, depending on the size of the individual and the angle of the bullet path (e.g., through arm, shoulder, etc.). With modern properly designed, expanding handgun bullets, this objective is realized, albeit more consistently with some law enforcement projectiles than others. 1 Handgun Wounding Factors and Effectiveness: Firearms Training Unit, Ballistic Research Facility, 1989.

B. PERMANENT CAVITY

The extent to which a projectile expands determines the diameter of the permanent cavity which, simply put, is that tissue which is in direct contact with the projectile and is therefore destroyed. Coupled with the distance of the path of the projectile (penetration), the total permanent cavity is realized. Due to the elastic nature of most human tissue and the low velocity of handgun projectiles relative to rifle projectiles, it has long been established by medical professionals, experienced in evaluating gunshot wounds, that the damage along a wound path visible at autopsy or during surgery cannot be distinguished between the common handgun calibers used in law enforcement. That is to say an operating room surgeon or Medical Examiner cannot distinguish the difference between wounds caused by .35 to .45 caliber projectiles.

C. TEMPORARY CAVITY

The temporary cavity is caused by tissue being stretched away from the permanent cavity. If the temporary cavity is produced rapidly enough in elastic tissues, the tensile strength of the tissue can be exceeded resulting in tearing of the tissue. This effect is seen with very high velocity projectiles such as in rifle calibers, but is not seen with handgun calibers. For the temporary cavity of most handgun projectiles to have an effect on wounding, the velocity of the projectile needs to exceed roughly 2,000 fps. At the lower velocities of handgun rounds, the temporary cavity is not produced with sufficient velocity to have any wounding effect; therefore any difference in temporary cavity noted between handgun calibers is irrelevant. "In order to cause significant injuries to a structure, a pistol bullet must strike that structure directly."2 2 DiMaio, V.J.M.: Gunshot Wounds, Elsevier Science Publishing Company, New York, NY, 1987, page 42.

D. FRAGMENTATION

Fragmentation can be defined as "projectile pieces or secondary fragments of bone which are impelled outward from the permanent cavity and may sever muscle tissues, blood vessels, etc., apart from the permanent cavity"3. Fragmentation does not reliably occur in soft tissue handgun wounds due to the low velocities of handgun bullets. When fragmentation does occur, fragments are usually found within one centimeter (.39") of the permanent cavity.4 Due to the fact that most modern premium law enforcement ammunition now commonly uses bonded projectiles (copper jacket bonded to lead core), the likelihood of fragmentation is very low. For these reasons, wounding effects secondary to any handgun caliber bullet fragmentation are considered inconsequential. 3 Fackler, M.L., Malinowski, J.A.: "The Wound Profile: A Visual Method for Quantifying Gunshot Wound Components", Journal of Trauma 25: 522?529, 1958. 4 Handgun Wounding Factors and Effectiveness: Firearms Training Unit, Ballistic Research Facility, 1989.

PSYCHOLOGY

Any discussion of stopping armed adversaries with a handgun has to include the psychological state of the adversary. Psychological factors are probably the most important relative to achieving rapid incapacitation from a gunshot wound to the torso.5 First and foremost, the psychological effects of being shot can never be counted on to stop an individual from continuing conscious voluntary action. Those who do stop commonly do so because they decide to, not because they have to. The effects of pain are often delayed due to survival patterns secondary to "fight or flight" reactions within the body, drug/alcohol influences and in the case of extreme anger or aggression, pain can simply be ignored. Those subjects who decide to stop immediately after being shot in the torso do so commonly because they know they have been shot and are afraid of injury or death, regardless of caliber, velocity, or bullet design. It should also be noted that psychological factors can be a leading cause of incapacitation failures and as such, proper shot placement, adequate penetration, and multiple shots on target cannot be over emphasized. 5 Ibid.

TACTICAL REALITIES

Shot placement is paramount and law enforcement officers on average strike an adversary with only 20 – 30 percent of the shots fired during a shooting incident. Given the reality that shot placement is paramount (and difficult to achieve given the myriad of variables present in a deadly force encounter) in obtaining effective incapacitation, the caliber used must maximize the likelihood of hitting vital organs. Typical law enforcement shootings result in only one or two solid torso hits on the adversary. This requires that any projectile which strikes the torso has as high a probability as possible of penetrating deeply enough to disrupt a vital organ.

The Ballistic Research Facility has conducted a test which compares similar sized Glock pistols in both .40 S&W and 9mm calibers, to determine if more accurate and faster hits are achievable with one versus the other. To date, the majority of the study participants have shot more quickly and more accurately with 9mm caliber Glock pistols. The 9mm provides struggling shooters the best chance of success while improving the speed and accuracy of the most skilled shooters.

CONCLUSION

While some law enforcement agencies have transitioned to larger calibers from the 9mm Luger in recent years, they do so at the expense of reduced magazine capacity, more felt recoil, and given adequate projectile selection, no discernible increase in terminal performance.

Other law enforcement organizations seem to be making the move back to 9mm Luger taking advantage of the new technologies which are being applied to 9mm Luger projectiles. These organizations are providing their armed personnel the best chance of surviving a deadly force encounter since they can expect faster and more accurate shot strings, higher magazine capacities (similar sized weapons) and all of the terminal performance which can be expected from any law enforcement caliber projectile.

Given the above realities and the fact that numerous ammunition manufacturers now make 9mm Luger service ammunition with outstanding premium line law enforcement projectiles, the move to 9mm Luger can now be viewed as a decided advantage for our armed law enforcement personnel.

DID THEY GET IT RIGHT?

Those of you who have been paying attention will note that the FBI has, in their Justification, basically only summed up what we have spent the last three or four decades learning. This is not a slam against them, there's no need to keep re-inventing the wheel. There are areas where I agree, and areas where I think they missed the point. (But I also wonder if they "missed the point" so as to get on with things and not get bogged down in pointless arguing with those who will not otherwise accept change.)

FIRST, AGREEMENT

9mm vs. .40? A done deal. For law enforcement, the .40 turns out to have not been what was promised. In fact, the .40 over-promised and under-delivered.

The promise was that it would deliver near-.45 terminal ballistics, with near-9mm recoil, and maintain 9mm magazine capacity.

While the .40 can deliver near-.45 terminal ballistics, it does so with near-.45 recoil. The vanilla-plain .40 load level, a 180-grain bullet at 900 fps, is so close to the .45 ACP non+P load (a 185 at 900 fps), how anyone could shoot a .40 and exclaim, "It shoots softer," is beyond me.

This was something of a minor grumble in certain quarters, including the USPSA competition Single Stack division. This is devoted to single-stack 1911 pistols, and the top competitors were winning the division with 1911s built as .40 S&W pistols, not .45 ACP. Complaints arose that the .40 was somehow softer in recoil, because it was a .40, and that there should be some change to account for this.

I asked some of the top shooters why they went with .40, was it the recoil? One answer pretty much summed it up, "I have a reloading press devoted to .40 for my Limited gun. I've shot Limited for years, I'm not even sure I can find my .45 components. It was easier just to build a single stack in .40 than to switch the press over, find the components, and begin loading."

The .40, to deliver .45 power, has .45 recoil. To make it kick like a 9mm, you'd have to load it down to 9mm power, which is pointless.

Law enforcement agencies do not staff their patrol units with gunfighters. You'd be surprised at how little practice most get, and how low the qualification standards are set.

If switching to an effective 9mm load enabled all your people to qualify and many to become actually competent, why would you (for the same cost and effort) use pistols in .40 and have the worst barely qualify and almost none truly competent (because of recoil)?

Departments have budgets. Part of the qualification budget is ammo, part is instructor time, and part is lost patrol time from officers/deputies on the range. Anything that keeps officers on the range longer, instructors on the range longer, and shooting more ammo is not good.

From that viewpoint 9mm makes sense. And since we do have 9mm ammunition that works well, it is prudent for a department to opt for 9mm.

The same holds true for you.

You want to be competent (or at least, I hope you do) so you can effectively defend yourself when the time comes. If a .40 is more work than a 9mm and costs more, and you'll practice less, and have lesser skills, then have you really made an advantageous choice, in going with the .40? If you have not, swallow your pride, step "back" to the 9mm, and get good with it.

VOLUME OF FIRE

It should be obvious that given the same level of skill, a shooter will be able to get more and faster hits with a 9mm than with a .40. That it has to be stated, or even experimented to be proven, says more about the inertia of acquisition and use, than the ability to choose from available options. Many departments are locked into what they have until the next acquisition cycle, and it is somewhat alarming that it takes a statement from on high (the FBI) that the 9mm is acceptable for departments to change. But again, departments are not staffed with gunfighters. The handgun is a tool, like any other, and those in charge no more obsess over calibers than they do selection of radios or vehicles.

And since they do use radios and vehicles every day, they might well be more informed about those, and the choice of sidearms and calibers is more at the level of which copy paper to use in the department printers. And I say that not to insult, but to make clear the competing imperatives that departments have for them, budget, maintenance and training.

WOUND TRACK ANALYSIS

I think the FBI goes astray when they declare that there is no apparent difference between wound tracks, in ballistic gelatin, between the different calibers. Well, duh. We have not yet found an effective way to measure or record the volume of the permanent wound track in ballistic gelatin. Eyeballing it just won't do. I find it curious that surgeons have reported that they cannot tell the difference in people, not just between calibers (except in the grossest differences, like distinguishing a .22LR wound from a .44 magnum, for instance), but also that they are unable to distinguish between FMJ, JHP, any of the hollow points, etc.

FBI agents are not surgeons. If they had simply stated, "We are unable to distinguish a difference between the wound tracks in gelatin between the various calibers," then I'd be happy. But saying there is no difference implies that they could see one, were there one.

OUTPERFORMING?

The last is a flat rejection of the FBI conclusion that "9mm Luger now offers select projectiles which are, under identical testing conditions, outperforming most of the premium line .40 S&W and .45 Auto projectiles tested by the FBI"

Excuse me?

Expanding bullets expand. A 9mm can only expand so much, and then it is done. A .40 or a .45 can start out larger than a 9mm and expand to a greater diameter. Simply due to the laws of physics, a larger-diameter bullet, of greater mass, has to be creating a larger wound track. To steal a quote from Ronald Reagan, "A rising tide lifts all boats."

One might argue that the larger wound track of the .40 and .45 comes at a disproportionate cost, in recoil, muzzle flash, capacity and slower shooting speeds, but it is silly to argue that the 9mm out-performs the larger calibers.

But, if you're making a case for one over the others, you argue all the points.

Handguns aren't rifles. Rifles hurl gelatin blocks off the stand unless they are tied down. Rifles do this to extra barriers on gel, if they aren't tied down. Handguns don't do this. Handguns are weak, use the best ammo in the biggest gun you can.

MY CHOICES

I select as much up-scale as I can. I select the biggest caliber I can. In that caliber I opt for the heaviest bullet I can, and if I have the option, I go for a bonded bullet where available. Why? I'm willing to pay the price in weight, bulk, recoil and capacity. I have worked in environments where inadvertent barriers might be a problem.

For instance, at the gun shop, we each thought about the most likely spots where we'd be, should a shooting occur. I would most likely have been off to one side of the shop, with displays of ammo, shelves, and other barriers in my path. My go-to gun was loaded with slugs. Yep, a 12 gauge shotgun was my first choice, and all the handguns were loaded with FMJs.

The building was a solid concrete shell, nothing was going to get out, so over-penetration wasn't my problem. Getting through the sheet metal shelving in front of me was.

If that's your problem, then your solution is going to be similar. If not, then it won't be. Make your choice depending on you, what you'll carry, and where you'll likely need it.

PROPER PRIOR PLANNING

If you are planning on, or even considering, using a firearm for self-defense, you need to take some steps. As mentioned before, the legal steps are prudent. Get a lawyer, before you need one. Make sure you know the law. But, there is also the matter of selecting your handgun and the ammunition to use in it.

A few decades ago, I had a really switched-on customer. Well, I had a bunch of them, but this one stood out. He was a private investigator, which was not, and probably still isn't, the exciting job you might think. It usually involved investigating insurance fraud.

His job, primarily, was following the people suspected of fraud, recording their days, and photographing or video-taping them while out of their houses. This meant lots of time sitting in cars, taking notes in notebooks, wrangling cameras (video and film, this was long before digital cameras or video) and occasionally taking a stroll to follow them.

He asked me, "What's the best ammo for my carry gun?" I told him at the time that all the current JHPs offered pretty much the same in performance, they were better than they'd been in the past (but not as good as they would become) and he should use whatever was reliable, that shot most-accurately in his gun. That's when he shoved the pistol case across the counter and said, "Do it."

Since this had the potential of becoming a legal issue, I documented everything. I logged the dates, time, mileage, ammunition tested and groups shot with the pistol, noted by serial number. Once I had the list narrowed down, I then put them in the Ransom rest and shot groups to save. I then wrote a report summarizing all this and presented him with the groups, the data, the report, a signed letter attesting to the work I had done, and a couple of boxes of that ammo. And a bill, of course.

I realize that task is now thirty years in the past, so the fact that I can't lay hands on my copy of all that probably isn't be an issue. He had it and, had he needed it, and most likely his attorney (or more likely, the company attorney) would have contacted me with time, date and location of the depositions to be held.

What does all this have to do with you? Simple: when asked the question "Why did you use the ammunition you used?" what will your answer be? If "it was cheap, on sale at the big-box store" is true, maybe they'll move on to the next question. If you selected what you used for some other reason, you'd best be able to articulate those reasons in the deposition.

So, how did you?

Did you select it from a magazine article? A book? Save a copy. Did you select it because of an advertisement? Save

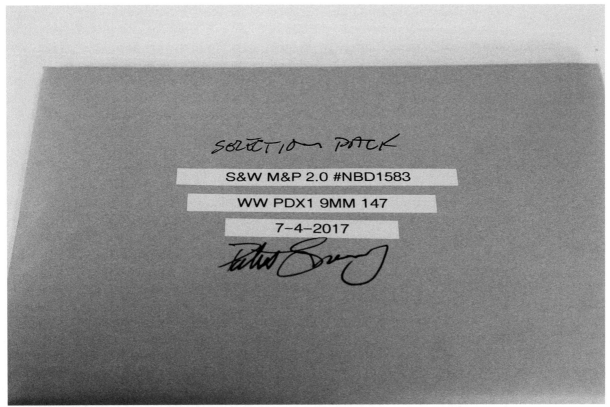
Here is a handgun and ammo combo selection and testing packet, ready to get stuffed into the safe.

Make sure it is sealed and dated, so there's no question when you did it.

CHAPTER 22: IN SUMMARY | **267**

a copy. Did you test ammunition, to see what shot most-accurately in your handgun? Save the targets. Better yet, save the targets and take time-and-date-stamped photos with your cell phone or camera. Save them on your computer. Print a copy and put it with the target.

Is it ammunition used by a law enforcement agency in the area, or one you know of? How do you know this? Make sure how you know is part of what you know. Any kind of PR handout, advertisement, visit to the police range on a Public Relations Day, document it. If the manufacturer has a PR campaign, and announces that this ammunition was adopted by this or that agency, save a copy.

Why are we doing all this? Simple, and it stems from something a friend of mine once said. A friend who spent his life in the law and law enforcement, while gently admonishing a subordinate about a minor predicament he was in, said, "If it wasn't written down, it didn't happen."

So, again, why did you pick that ammo? If you didn't make note of why, when it happened, and what happened since, then it didn't happen. "Oh, I don't know, it seemed like the best stuff." Just won't cut it. (Better to keep quiet, and let your lawyer do the talking.)

If you want to do it right, do what I did. Find the best ammunition, as reported by the industry, for your handgun. Or the best three. Test them in your handgun, and keep notes. Test for reliability, accuracy, point of impact, and save targets and data. Take photos, since modern digital cameras record time and date. Seal it all up in an envelope and date the envelope. Also put on it the handgun, and the load it involves.

This is a lot of work. But you will be secure in the knowledge that you have the information, and you also have the practice from the shooting. You may never need the information. If you don't, in thirty years you'll have a series of envelopes, each for a particular handgun that you have tested and carried through the years. If or when the time comes, you do not volunteer this information. You let your attorney know of it, and if it is needed he will use it.

This is your insurance. If the question comes up about why you used what you used (a question entirely different from what you did, or why you did it, or who you did it to) then you have solid answers.

"Your honor, the defendant used extra-lethal ammunition, high-velocity hollow points that explode viciously on impact."

"Your honor, my client used the exact same factory ammunition that the municipal police, the county deputies, and the state police use, because it tested as most safe and effective."

That's why you say nothing, your attorney knows when to play the trump card.

DO NOT REMOVE DOUBT

There is an old saying, along the lines of "It is better to keep one's mouth shut and be thought a fool, than open it and dispel all doubt."

You will find arguments about stopping power, bullet design, caliber and ammunition capacity everywhere you go. Well, everywhere there are people talking about guns, of course. Arguments rage. They will always rage, until we have replaced projectile weapons with directed-energy weapons. And even then, there will be arguments about the frequency that phasers should be built to, to have the "best" effect as stunners or vaporizers.

We've been using edged weapons for a long time. If you go back to the Neolithic, the "new stone" age, when knapped flint was the latest tool, we've been using edged weapons for something like ten thousand years. And still we argue over the best blade design.

So, when the question comes up, be careful. If you want to have an earnest discussion, have one. But have it with people who are also earnestly discussing it, and not trying to prove themselves right. And please don't wade in with "Sweeney says," because I might be wrong. Highly unlikely, really, but I might. Things change, and this book might be off the mark and need updating with new info by the time you get your hands on a copy.

And you might be wrong. I could have explained something badly. Or you read "X" as "Y" and then things get messy. Read, learn, understand, but don't pontificate. And if someone is clearly, demonstrably, wrong, resist the temptation to prove them so. If you have not lost a friendship because you just couldn't resist proving someone wrong, well, give it time.

The subject is one that is thoroughly plastered with urban myth, misinformation, and wrong-headed thinking, and some of that comes from official sources. You especially will not keep a friendship with a police officer by proving them wrong in public about something that is official doctrine in the department.

Think of this book as your personal, stopping power super-power. Promise to use it wisely, for good, and not for evil.

This is America, you have a choice. Use it.

APPENDIX: AMMUNITION PERFORMANCE CHARTS

RIMFIRES AND .25 ACP

BRAND, BULLET	VELOCITY	PENETRATION*	EXPANSION
.22LR			
Gemtech subsonic 42 gr	1017	14"	.222"
Winchester Expert 36 gr	1107	--	--
Remington GB 40 gr	1117	--	--
Aguila Super Extra 40 gr	895	--	--
Winchester Super Silhouette 42 gr	969	--	--
.22 Magnum			
Speer GDHP-SB 40 gr	1242	10"	.297"
Hornady FTX 45 gr	1024	11"	.312"
5.7x28			
SS195 LF 28 gr	1936	--	--
Training T194 28 gr	1871	--	--

American Eagle FMJ 40 gr	1638	--	--
SS 197 SR V-Max 40 gr	1686	--	--
.25 ACP			
Hornady XTP 35 gr	843	--	--
Winchester Xp-Pt 45 gr	776	--	--

*Bare gelatin for penetration and expansion, unless otherwise indicated

.32 & .380 AUTO

BRAND, BULLET	VELOCITY	PENETRATION*	EXPANSION
.32 ACP			
Winchester FMJ 72 gr	826	14"	.312"
Corbon 60 gr	1051	9"	.499"
Winchester Silvertip 60 gr	939	--	--
Remington UMC 71 gr FMJ	923	--	--
Hornady XTP 60 gr	930	8"	.349"
.380 Auto			
Black Hills X-PT 95 gr	831	--	--
CCI Blazer FMJ 95 gr	811	14"	.355"
Corbon DPX 80 gr	969	13"	.650"

Corbon DPX 80 gr**	980	15"	.450"
Federal HST 99 gr	884	--	--
Hornady FTX 90	908	--	--
Hornady Critical Defense 90 gr	969	10.5"	.521"
Hornady XTP 90 gr	1001	12"	.474"
Polycase ARX 56 gr	1199	15.5"	.355"
Remington Golden Saber 90 gr	911	10"	.579"
Sig V-Crown, 90 gr	897	8.2"	.545"
Speer GDHP 90 gr	1011	10"	.495"
Winchester Defend 95 gr	901	10.5"	.624"

*Bare gelatin expansion and penetration, unless otherwise indicated
**Windshield test

.32 REVOLVERS

BRAND, BULLET	VELOCITY	PENETRATION*	EXPANSION
.32 S&W			
Winchester LRN 85 gr	597	--	--
.32 S&W Long			
Magtech LRN 98 gr	532	--	--

.32 H&R Magnum

Black Hills FPL 90 gr	663		
Hornady FTX 80 gr	1079	12.5"	.365"
Hornady LFP 90 gr	687		

.327 Federal Magnum

Federal Hydra-Shok 85 gr	1342	13.5"	.405"
Am Eagle Softpoint 100 gr	1410	16.5"	.374"
Speer GDHP 115 gr	1316	14.5"	.417"
Buffalo Bore JHP 100 gr	1233	--	--
Buffalo Bore L-SWC 130 gr	1136	--	--

*Bare gelatin for penetration and expansion, unless otherwise indicated

9MM

BRAND, BULLET	VELOCITY	PENETRATION*	EXPANSION
Ruger Polycase ARX 80 gr	1461	16"	.355"
Barnes TAC-XPD 115 gr		14.1"	.692"	--
Black Hills TAC-XPD 115 gr	1163	14"	.693"
Black Hills Honey Badger 115 gr	1025	18.5'	.355"
Federal HST Micro 147 gr	1021	16.25"	.695"

Federal Guard Dog 105 gr	1254	13.5'	.602"
Black Hills XTP 124 gr	1146	17"	.547"
Hornady FTX 115 gr	1060	15"	.520
Hornady XTP, 124 gr	1150	13.5"	.611"
Hornady Critical Duty 135 gr	1121	14.5"	.575"
Remington HTP 147 gr	927	14.5"	.615"
Sig V-Crown, 115 gr	1149	14.75"	.501"
Sig V-Crown, 124 gr	1163	15"	.519"
Sig V-Crown, 147 gr	979	15.5"	.529"
Super Vel 90 gr	1463	--	--
Super Vel 115 gr	1352		
Winchester Ranger T 147 gr	16"	.711"	--
Winchester Ranger 127 +P+	1257	12"	.709"
Winchester Defend 124 gr +P	1196	12"	.626"
Winchester Defend 147 gr	995	14.25"	.591"
Winchester Nato 124 FMJ**	1180	26.5"	.355"
Winchester Forged 115 FMJ**	1105	27"	.355"
Winchester Kinetic 115 gr	1315	--	--

*Bare gelatin for penetration and expansion, unless otherwise indicated
**This is not unusual, FMJ is expected to penetrate fully, and then some. It is meant for military use.

.38 SPECIAL & .38 SPECIAL +P

BRAND, BULLET	VELOCITY	PENETRATION*	EXPANSION
Black Hills Honey Badger 100 gr	982	14.6"	.355"
Black Hills Sierra +P 110 gr	945	9.75"	.583"
Black Hills Sierra 125 gr +P	873	13.6"	.529"
Remington golden Saber 125 +P	767	--	--
Black Hills 148 gr WC	689	15.5"	.428"
Federal HST 130 gr	834	14"	.486"
Hornady FTX Lite 90 gr	1129	8.5"	.467"
Hornady FTX 110 gr	833	13"	.440"
Hornady FTX+P 110 gr	1031	12"	.501"
Hornady 125 gr XTP +P	807	16"	.437"
Polycase ARX 77 gr	1059	14.5"	.358"
Speer GDHP 135 gr	840	13'	.565"
Super Vel 90 gr	1278	11.5"	.574"
Winchester Defend 130 gr +P	939	11.5"	.617"
Winchester FBI 158 gr L-SWC+P	799	13"	.521"
Hornady XTP 158 gr	758	15"	.472"
Corbon FMJ 147 gr	773	27"	.357"

CCI Blaser LRN 158 gr	815	25"	.358"
Black Hills CNL 158 gr	725	--	--
Winchester FMJ RN 130 gr	765	28"	.358"
Remington HBWC 148 gr	655	30"	.358"
Oregon Trails 148 DEWC 2.7 gr Bullseye	657	36"	.358"

*Bare gelatin for expansion and penetration, unless otherwise indicated.

.357 SIG AND .357 MAGNUM

BRAND, BULLET	VELOCITY	PENETRATION*	EXPANSION
.357 Sig			
Sig V-Crown, 125 gr	1298	11.5"	.676"
Winchester Defend 125 gr	1311	12.75"	.581"
Fiocchi FMJTC 124 gr	1366	31"	.355"
Corbon JHP 125 gr	1470	13.5"	.614"
Georgia Arms FMJ 125 gr	1449	29"	.355"
Hornady FTX 115 gr	1199	14.5"	.568"
Hornady XTP 124 gr	1394	15"	.549"
Hornady XTP 147 gr	1241	16.5"	.504"
Hornady Critical Duty 135 gr	1206	14"	.605"

Speer Gold Dot 125 gr	1329	15.5"	.599"
Michigan Ammo FMJ 125 gr	1324	32"	.355"
Sig Sauer V-Crown 125 gr	1332	14"	.710"
.357 Magnum			
Super Vel 110 gr	1339	11.75"	.546"
Black Hills XTP 125 gr""	1083	16.75"	.525"
Black Hills XTP 125 gr***	1340	14"	.589"
Hornady FTX 125 gr	1257	13"	.575"
Sig V-Crown 125 gr	1394	--	--
Hornady Critical Duty 135 gr	1241	14.5"	.604"
Aguila JSP 158 gr	1183	--	--
Federal Premium 158 gr	1172	--	--
Hornady XTP 158 gr**	1199	18"	.567"
Black Hills XTP 158 gr***	1222	19.25"	.553"
Remington L-SWC 158 gr	1201	--	--

* Bare gelatin for penetration and expansion, unless otherwise indicated
** 4" barrel
*** 6" barrel

.40 S&W

BRAND, BULLET	VELOCITY	PENETRATION*	EXPANSION
Black Hills TAC-XP 140 gr	1131	12.75"	.763"
Corbon JHP 135	1390	--	--
Corbon DPX 140 gr	1163	--	--
Federal HST 155 gr	1171	14.5"	.637"
Federal HST 180 gr	--	14.5"	.777"
Federal Guard Dog 135 gr	1242	14.5"	.629"
Hornady XTP 155 gr	1123	13.2"	.649"
Hornady FTX 165 gr	1047	16"	.647"
Hornady Critical Duty 175 gr	1005	14"	.581"
Black Hills Nosler 180 gr	1005	12"	.739"
Black Hills Berry plates 180 gr	961	9.5"	.851"
Hornady XTP 180 gr	1037	14.5"	.697"
Polycase ARX 104 gr	1367	16.5'	.401"
Sig V-Crown, 180 gr	1011	14.75"	.625"
Speer GDHP short barrel 180 gr	907***	14.5"	.611"
	949****	14"	.633"
	1013*****	13.5"	.649"

Winchester Defend 180 gr	931	13.1"	.701"
Winchester JHP 180 gr**	1036	14.25"	.647"
Winchester PDX1 180 gr	1023	15.5"	.763"

*Bare gelatin for penetration and expansion, unless otherwise indicated
** Windshield test
*** 3" barrel
**** 4" barrel
***** 4.25" barrel

10MM

BRAND, BULLET	VELOCITY	PENETRATION*	EXPANSION
Hornady FTX 165 gr	1264	--	--
Hornady XTP 180 gr	1141	--	--
Hornady XTP 200 gr	1127	17.5"	.564"
Hornady Critical Duty 175 gr	1178	16.5"	.611"
Wilson Combat XTP 180 gr	1319	--	--
HPR JHP 180 gr	1226	--	--
ProGrade JHP 180 gr	1206	--	--
Doubletap Nosler JHP 200 gr	1198	--	--
CCI Blazer TMJ 200 gr	988	36"+**	.400"

Remington JHP 180 gr	1080	--	--
Federal Trophy Bonded 180 gr	1181	24"***	.601"
Civil Defense JHP 60 gr	2468	--	--

*Bare gelatin for penetration and expansion, unless otherwise indicated
**Exited the back of two blocks, not unusual for this or other big-bore cartridges.
*** This is a tough, hunting-focused bullet, for deer, not people.

.44s

BRAND, BULLET	VELOCITY	PENETRATION*	EXPANSION
.44 Magnum			
Hornady FTX 225 gr	1319	16.5"	.851"
.44 Special			
Black Hills LFN 210 gr	623	--	--
Black Hills JHP 200 gr	797	--	--
Hornady FTX 165 gr	817	10.5"	.617"
Hornady XTP 180 gr	798	--	--
Remington LRN 246 gr	623	--	--
Sig V-Crown 200 gr	699	--	--
Winchester Silvertip 200 gr	727	--	--

*Bare gelatin for penetration and expansion, unless otherwise indicated

.45s

BRAND, BULLET	VELOCITY	PENETRATION*	EXPANSION
.45 ACP			
Asym Bonded 230 gr	819	15.5"	.712"
Black Hills Honey Badger 135 gr	1311	18.25"	.452"
Black Hills TAC-XPD 185 gr	1012	12.1"	.819"
Federal HST 230 gr	866	15.5"	.699"
Federal Guard Dog 165 gr	1048	13.5'	.657"
Hornady XTP 185 gr**	998	16.5"	.565"
Hornady XTP 185 gr***	1057	15.25	.605"
Hornady XTP 185 gr****	1051	12"	.636"
Hornady FTX 185 gr**	846 fps	16"	.660"
Hornady FTX 185 gr***	933 fps	14.5"	.710"
Black Hills XTP+P 230 gr	895	13.75"	.737"
Black Hills Berry plated 230 gr	930	13.2"	.581"
Hornady XTP 230 gr**	786	13.8"	.700"
Hornady XTP 230 gr***	802	14.25"	.707"
Hornady Critical Duty 220 gr	946	14"	.708"
Polycase ARX 114 gr	1216	16"	.452"

APPENDIX: AMMUNITION PERFORMANCE CHARTS | 281

Remington HTP 230 gr	811	16"	.799"
Sig V-Crown 230 gr	874	14.5"	.695"
Speer GDHP 230 gr		14.2"	.719"
Winchester Defend 230 gr	899	13.5"	.812"
Winchester PDX1 230 gr	937	14"	.729"
.45 Colt			
Black Hills LFN 250 gr	803		
Hornady FTX 185 gr	871	12"	.689"
Hornady LFN 255 gr	723	--	--
Magtech FP 250 FP	610	18"	.462"
Winchester Silvertip 225 gr	752	13.5"	.598"
Winchester PDX1 225 gr	824	15"	.629"
Winchester LRN 255 gr	618	--	--
Corbon JHP 200	1123	14"	.671"

*Bare gelatin for penetration and expansion, unless otherwise indicated
** 4" barrel
*** 5" barrel
**** 5" barrel, windshield test

BIBLIOGRAPHY

Anderson, W. French, M.D. *Forensic Analysis of the April 11, 1986 FBI Firefight*, Paladin Press, 1996

Ayoob, Mas, *Deadly force: Understanding your right to self defense,* Gun digest Books, 2014

Bedsten, George B., *Handgun Bullet Stopping Power,* CCB Publishing, 2008

Cirillo, Jim, *Guns, Bullets, and Gunfights*, Paladin Press, 1996

Clede, Bill, *Police Handgun Manual*, Stackpole, 1985

DiMaio, Vincent J.M., *Gunshot Wounds*, Elsevier, 1985

Fackler, Martin L.; Malinowski, John A., *The Wound Profile: A visual method for quantifying gunshot wound components. The Journal of Trauma-Injury, Infection and Critical Care*, June 1985, Volume 25, Issue 6. pp 522-529.

Fairbairn, W.E., *Shanghai Municipal Police Pistol Manual*, Interservice Publishing, 1981

Fisher, Barry A. J., *Techniques of Crime Scene Investigation*, CRC, 1993, 5th Ed.

Frost, George E., *Ammunition Making*, NRA Publications, 1990

Garrison, Dean H., *Practical Shooting Scene Investigation*, Universal Publisher, 2003

Hall, John C. FBI-SA, *The FBI's 10mm Pistol,* FBI LE Bulletin, Vol 58, #11, 1989, pp 2-8

Heard, Brina J., *Handbook of Firearms and Ballistics,* Wiley, 1997

Hoyem, George A, *The History and Development of Small Arms Ammunition, Vol. 3,* Armory Publications, 1985

James, Frank W., *Effective Handgun Defense*, Krause, 2004

Jordan, Bill, *No Second Place Winner*, W.H. Jordan, 1975, 6th Printing

Keith, Elmer, *Keith's Rifles for Dangerous Game*, Standard Publications, 1946

Keith, Elmer, *Sixguns by Keith*, Bonanaza Books, 1955

Kleck, Gary, Gertz, Marc, *Armed resistance to crime: The prevalence and nature of self-defense with a gun*, 86 Journal of Criminal law and Criminology 1, 1995.

Kolbe, Geoffrey, *A Ballistic Handbook,* Pisces Press, 2000

LaGarde, Louis A., *Gunshot Injuries*, Lancer Militaria, 1991

LaGrange, Mike, *Ballistics in Perspective*, Professional Hunter Supplies Publishing Division, 2nd Ed 1990

Lowry, E. D., *Interior Ballistics*, Doubleday, 1968

MacPherson, Duncan, *Bullet Penetration*, Ballistic Publications, 1994

Marshall, Evan P., Sanow, Edwin J., *Handgun Stopping Power*, paladin Press, 1992

Marshall, Evan P., Sanow, Edwin J., *Street Stoppers*, Paladin Press, 1996

Massaro, Philip P., *Understanding Ballistics*, Gun Digest Books, 2015

Peter, H., *Mechanical Engineering Principles of Armament Design,* Trafford Publishing, 2004

Potocki, John, *The Colt Model 1905 Automatic Pistol,* Andrew Mowbray Publishers, 1998

Sharpe, Phil, *The Rifle in America*

Smith, Veral, *Jacketed Performance with Cast Bullets*, V. Smith, 1984, 3rd Ed.

Stone, William E. PhD, *Improvements in Handgun Ammunition*, FBI LE Bulletin, Vol 64, #1, 1995, pp 1-5

Suydam, Charles R., *U.S Cartridges and their Handguns*, Beinfield Publishing, 1979

Taylor, John, *African Rifle & Cartridges*, The Gun Room Press, 1948

Van Horne, *Left of Bang*, Black Irish Ent. 2014

Wood, Mike, *Newhall Shooting, a tactical analysis*, F+W media, 2013

Canadian Police Research Centre TR-01-95, *Comparative Performance of 9mm Parabellum, .38 Special and .40 S&W ammunition in ballistic gelatin*

Firearms Pressure Factors, Wolfe Publishing, 1990

NCJRS, *FBI Weapons Evaluation* August 1987, NCJRS #113821

NILECJ, *An Evaluation of Police Handgun Ammunition*, LESP-RPT-0101.01, 1975

NIJ, *Technology Assessment Program, Police Handgun Ammunition*, 100-83, 1983

NIJ, *Technology Assessment Program, Police Handgun Ammunition*, 101-83, 1983

NIJ, *FBI Wound Ballistic Workshop*, 1987

NIL, *Autoloading Pistols for Police Officers*, 0112.03 Rev A, 1999

Wound Ballistics Review, IWBA.

IT'S BACK!

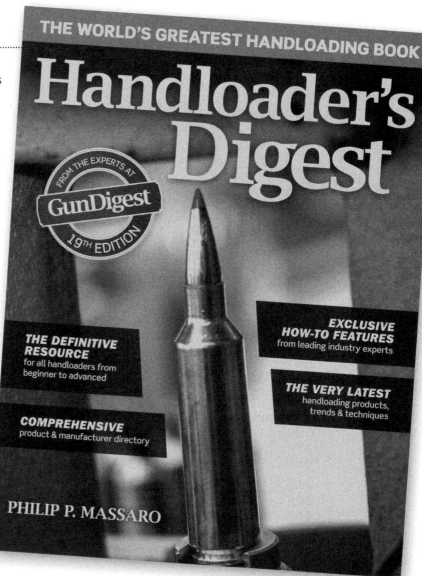

From the publisher of *Gun Digest*, the "World's Greatest Gun Book," returns the "World's Greatest Handloading Book." That's right – the *Handloader's Digest* 19th edition is back and it's better than ever with more in-depth features, industry resources and eye-catching photos. Whether it's information on this year's new ammunition reloading equipment or detailed articles on obscure wildcat cartridges, you're certain to find what you're looking for in this authoritative resource.

- Learn how to reload ammo
- Search for new techniques and equipment
- Expand your understanding of ammunition and ballistics

Visit **GunDigestStore.com**
or 855-840-5120

LETHAL FORCE LAW: Get the Facts

Massad Ayoob's first book on the use of deadly force by the private citizen in defense of self and others, *In the Gravest Extreme*, is considered the authoritative text in its field. *Deadly Force* is the follow-up to this groundbreaking guide, incorporating Ayoob's thirty extra years of experience, during which he's been an expert witness in weapons cases, chair of the Firearms Committee of the American Society of Law Enforcement Trainers, and much more.

This guide will help you understand any legal and ethical issues concerning the use of lethal force by private citizens. You'll also learn about the social and psychological issues surrounding the use of lethal force for self-defense or in defense of others. In addition to exploring these issues, Ayoob also discusses the steps a responsible armed citizen can and should take in order to properly prepare for or help mitigate a lethal force situation.

Retail: $21.99 • ISBN: 9781440240614

Get our *LOWEST* prices online at
GunDigestStore.com
or call **855.840.5120** (M-F 7am-6pm MT)

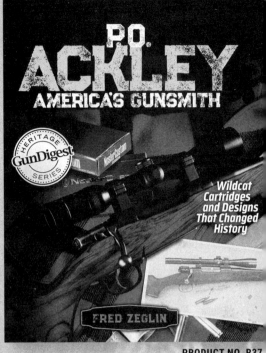

THE "ACKLEY IMPROVED"...
PLUS SO MUCH MORE!

P.O. Ackley, the eminent gunsmith, barrel maker and cartridge developer, imparted a remarkable and lasting influence on firearms and cartridge development. Ackley's ideas on reloading, rifle accuracy, safety, cartridge choice, and wildcat use are just as relevant for modern "gun cranks" as they were in Ackley's heyday.

Now, in *P.O. Ackley: America's Gunsmith*, author Fred Zeglin details Ackley's life and work while also sharing the most complete collection of accurate dimensions, loading data and history for the lifetime of cartridges created by Ackley, the most influential gunsmith in American history.

This hardcover, 256-page study of P.O. Ackley's work is the first in Gun Digest Media's Heritage Series celebrating the iconic guns, designers and manufacturers who shaped today's firearms landscape.

PRODUCT NO. R37

Featuring:

- Wildcat and standard cartridge history
- Accurate technical information
- Descriptions and reloading data for Ackley Improved cartridges
- Colorful Ackley quotes and entertaining "Ackleyisms"
- Bonus: Full-color photo section and an exclusive never-before-printed article by P.O. Ackley.

Get your copy today!

Exclusively at
GunDigestStore.com